THE MODERN LIBRARY WRITER'S WORKSHOP

STEPHEN KOCH

THE MODERN LIBRARY WRITER'S WORKSHOP

A GUIDE TO THE CRAFT OF FICTION

THE MODERN LIBRARY

NEW YORK

2003 Modern Library Paperback Edition

LIBRARY OF CONGRESS CATALOGING-IN-PUBLICATION DATA
Koch, Stephen.
The modern library writer's workshop : a guide to the craft of fiction /
Stephen Koch.
p.   cm.
Includes bibliographical references and index.
ISBN 0-375-75558-6
1. Fiction—Authorship. I. Title.
PN3355 .K59 2003
808.3—dc21   2002032593

Modern Library website address: www.modernlibrary.com

Printed in the United States of America

2   4   6   8   9   7   5   3   1

TO YOU:

students then, and now

ACKNOWLEDGMENTS

The acknowledgments appropriate to a couple of decades teaching the art of fiction cannot be confined to a page. Yes, of course, the students come first, and I dedicate this book to them. But I am also grateful to the programs that made me into a colleague of extraordinary people whom I might not otherwise even have known. When I taught at Princeton, I was fortunate to work with Joyce Carol Oates, Russell Banks, Robert Fagles, and ... but the list quickly gets too long. As for the list of those who worked with me at Columbia—that one is *really* long. Let me pause only to honor the memory of Robert Towers, the fiction critic of *The New York Review of Books,* the author of *The Summoning,* and the individual most responsible for making my time teaching the rich thing it was. American fiction had no better friend in his generation than Bob. And I had no better friend at Columbia.

On the editorial side, I remain grateful to a suggestion from Adam Bellow that set in motion the mental and practical events that produced this book. Two other distinguished editors had a hand in the earliest stages of the book's life: Deborah Futter and

Courtney Hodell. As for my longer-term editorial relationships with Timothy Farrell and David Ebershoff, I do not see how they could be bettered. And then there is my agent, Michael Carlisle, to whom I am indebted not only for firm practical guidance, but for the bright voice of sanity and cheer.

S.K.

CONTENTS

INTRODUCTION

Between 1977 and 1998—twenty-one years—I taught in one of the most noteworthy graduate writing programs in the United States, working term after term with aspiring young writers as they tried to get a grip on the elusive craft of fiction. For eight of those years, while simultaneously continuing to teach full-time, I served as the program's chair. For over two decades, then, without once missing even a single semester, I spent much of my energy thinking and talking about the craft of fiction in a perpetually renewed and perpetually changing dialogue with some of the most promising young writers of their several generations. I worked one-on-one with many hundreds of gifted people, and I have since had the quiet pleasure of seeing many among them emerge as the leading younger writers of our era. During those twenty-one years, I read thousands, maybe tens of thousands, of manuscripts in every stage of completion. I edited. I admired. I argued. I advised. I praised. I questioned. I doubted. I shut my mouth and hoped. I did my best to help people test their talent and find their way, struggling through what seemed to be every conceivable problem of literary technique. Though I cannot claim always to have found solutions, I did learn a whole lot about problems. As I tried again and again to help people with them, I saw failures of course, but I also saw, every week, gifted people inventing their way out, finding a path to transcendence on the page, discovering mastery in words, working their way toward clarity in steps that were sometimes small and uncertain, and sometimes sudden and giant. My long and thoroughly instructive immersion left me with a very highly developed sense of what can, and what cannot, be taught about writing narrative prose.

It also left me with an acute distaste for sending people off into deadly isolation to waste their time reinventing wheels. Except in journalism, writing is a necessarily solitary trade, the most chronically solitary of all the arts. Writing's inordinate quotient of solitude, and the need not only to tolerate that solitude but even to love it, is an immovable fact of the métier, and one of the most salient psychological facts you must grasp about it. Yet too often aspiring writers are condemned—as if in punishment for their wish to write—to feel their way to the most elementary methods of the craft entirely on their own, hit or miss, and without *any* help whatever. There is no need for this absurd waste. Every writer is fated to face things—and plenty of them—that will have to be mastered alone, in solitary struggle. These real problems will leave no time to waste fumbling for the obvious. Most writers tend to exaggerate the obstacles to getting good work done. Even a small technical problem—let's say, how to revise a draft—can leave them mired and hopeless. I've heard about entire projects, months and even years of work, lost over an issue that a few words of sound advice and ten minutes of straight talk might have solved.

Unfortunately, all too many perfectly intelligent people, generally of the writing-can't-be-taught school, really believe that writers are supposed to teach themselves everything, all alone, and by magic. They would never dream of asking a pianist or a painter or a composer—leave aside a record producer or a film director—to find out *everything* about the craft without help. In these areas at least, nobody would have the slightest difficulty grasping the necessary interplay between what must be taught and what must be picked up privately in the knack of any technique. Why not writing?

The Modern Library Writer's Workshop is an effort to assemble and integrate what I believe amounts to something like a consensus among writers about the basics of their craft. In these pages you will hear my voice—it's a prose variant on the voice I use in private conference with my students—along with many other voices, all of them talking about the craft. Most writers love to talk, and one of the things they love to talk about most is writing. In interviews and letters, in table talk and memoirs and manifestos, writers have always held forth in surprisingly full detail about how they do what they do. It adds up to a vast, largely untapped literature on technique. It is both ancient and modern, and it runs through literary history at every level of the culture, including the most exalted. Some of the most important figures of classical literature produced enduring *ars poetica*. Commentaries on oratory, poetry, drama, eloquence, and the sublime form an essential and large part of the classical anthology. No small part of the prophetic tradition in the Bible can be read as a meditation on inspired utterance, on what it is and how it is achieved. Inscribed within Shakespeare's work there can be found a great Renaissance treatise on the theater, poetry, and the workings of the dramatic imagination: Here is an *ars poetica* produced at the very summit. Listen carefully, and you can learn to hear the great novelists of the nineteenth century thinking about writing, about how to write, almost incessantly. The same is true of many major figures of the twentieth century. For example, a perfectly respectable—and surprisingly thick—manual on literary technique could be assembled from selected passages of Hemingway's novels alone. Not the interviews. The novels.

Moreover, the audience for this powerful substream of literature about technique reaches far beyond a small cluster of interested technicians, and it always has. Horace addressed a wider audience than just other poets. Shakespeare surely put interchanges on dramatic technique into his plays because he knew they would touch his larger audience. The craft of writing is bound to the experience of literacy and language itself. All of us are involved, consciously and unconsciously, in the way language is bound to all communication. All of us are involved, somehow, in how our thoughts and imaginings find focus. And while not everyone is a writer, every *reader* is a collaborator in the way any book is written, an active partner in a participatory event. Lots of people muse about writing even though they will never write a word. They are interested in what triggers the creative spirit; in how inspiration can be tapped and used; in how one gets hold of some nameless something in the mind and puts it out in the world as language, clear and knowable. That is the quiet drama that goes on every day at every writer's desk, and it is always a little fable, waiting to be told. Interest in it is expressed at every level of the culture, from Henry James's prefaces to the New York Edition of his novels to the talk show hostess asking her writer guests about how they do it.

I have tried to present here a loose intuitive consensus on the basics of the craft. Consensus of course incorporates, and sometimes masks, dissent. Some people—you may be one—may well disagree with some of the things said here. Maybe many things. Rest assured, there is some notable figure somewhere who could be found to take vocal and irritated exception to every single insight in this book. Yet on most of the big issues—the "invention" of a story, the development of characters, the honing of a style, the interior logic of "invention" itself—there seems to be more common ground among writers than even I expected to find when I started out.

But there are no rules. Please remember that. There are no rules. The moment some precept or other obstructs your path rather than opens it, you must stride right past it. The moment some opinion acts to stifle your work rather than help it onto the page, you must banish its power.

This is a writer's guide, not a reader's. In my "Postscript," I've added some thoughts about a number of the classic books on literary craft—but there is no reading list here. I have taken my illustrations mainly from familiar classics and from works such as *The Great Gatsby* or *The Catcher in the Rye*, stuff that I'm pretty confident almost every reader will already know. I cite them not because I think they are the last word, but because they are illustrative and ubiquitously known. In choosing the writers to comment on how to handle this or that technical issue, I have merrily disregarded every distinction between highbrow, middlebrow, and lowbrow taste. I see no reason not to mix Elmore Leonard with Henry James and J. K. Rowling with Proust. For one thing, surely any free reader's taste will embrace work at all these levels. More to the point, I have zero interest in propounding a manual of "good taste" or in adding even one more syllable to the interminable discussion of "the canon." I want this book to be useful, if possible, to *any* writer who happens to pick it up, whatever the real or imagined pitch of her or his "brow." I have been struck from the beginning by the wonderfully reckless way the issues of craft cut straight across the dreary distinctions of literary class, and frankly, that's fine with me. There seems to be something democratic in technique.

How you use the book will of course depend on you. My suggestion is that you breeze through once, noticing especially what excites you, what stirs you with the simple thought: *I could do that!* or what calls out *Hey! Use me!* Note what works and skip quickly through what perplexes you. Some things won't touch you—yet. Leave them for later. There's plenty of time. If you're a writer, you are going to be returning to these technical questions endlessly, for years to come. If you find this book useful once, you are likely to find it useful twice.

That's because all growth is a kind of superior beginning again. *The Modern Library Writer's Workshop* is clearly addressed to novice writers, but I hope its value does not exhaust itself at the beginner's level. I hope that colleagues at every stage of development will find something useful here. Writers' lives, most of them, move in phases, and each new phase of a creative life will necessarily entail a kind of a new start, and with it very possibly new craft, too. Beginning again is hard, and it can be frightening. We never begin again at the old starting point and rarely reach the old answers. To experience this uncertainty at any stage of life is troubling—but it is also a great and wonderful thing. We are speaking about the uncertainty of promise, the anxious tentative hope out of which everything of value must come. It may be that anyone experiencing that hope, at any stage of her or his working life, will find something useful in these few words to the wise.

THE MODERN
LIBRARY WRITER'S
WORKSHOP

1

BEGINNINGS

The only way to begin is to begin, and begin right now. If you like, begin the minute you finish reading this paragraph. For sure, begin before you finish reading this book. I have no doubt the day is coming when you will be wiser or better informed or more highly skilled than you are now, but you will never be more ready to begin writing than you are right this minute. The time has come. You already know, more or less, what a good story looks like. You've already got in mind some human situation that matters to you. You need nothing more. Begin with whatever gives you the impetus to begin: an image, a fantasy, a situation, a memory, a motion, a situation, a set of people—anything at all that arouses your imagination. The job is only to get some or all of this into words able to reach and touch an unknown, unseen somebody "out there" known as the Reader. You must plunge into it. And you must do it now.

It would be nice, I suppose, to begin at the perfect point in the story, in the perfect way, using the perfect voice to present exactly the desired scene. Unfortunately, you have no choice but to be wholly clueless about all of this. The rightness of things is generally revealed in retrospect, and you're unlikely to know in advance what is right and wrong in a story that has not yet been written. So instead of waiting until everything is perfect, begin anyhow, anywhere, and any way. The result probably will not be exactly right. It may not be even close. So what? You're going to persist until you *get* it right.

While I'm sure you can think of good reasons to procrastinate, I very much doubt there's much real merit in any of them. There is no need to wait for inspiration; no need to find your confidence; no need to know exactly why or what you're writing; no need read wise and thoughtful books about how to write; no need to know your story; no need to understand your characters; no need to be sure you're on the right track; no need even for your research to be complete. No need *now*. Later on, it will be very nice indeed to have some or all of these fine things. You will of course *eventually* want inspiration and confidence and self-knowledge and faith in your project and informed technique and a finished story with developed characters and completed competent research. But every single one of these things—even the research—comes to you only in the *process* of writing. They are the *result* of writing. If you let any one of them immobilize you *before* you write, I can guarantee that a year from now you will still be waiting to begin. The belief that you must have them to begin is the most common mistake of all, and it is fatal. Right here—on the jagged rocks of that false belief—is where most good ideas break up and sink without trace. Inspiration and confidence and conviction and craft and knowledge are not what make writing possible. It's exactly the other way around. *Writing makes **them** possible.*

"The common conception of how novels get written," says Martin Amis, "seems to me to be an exact description of writer's block. In the common view, the writer is at this stage so desperate that he's sitting around with a list of characters, a list of themes, and a framework for his plot, and ostensibly trying to mesh the three elements. In fact, it's never like that. What happens is what Nabokov described as a throb. A throb or a glimmer, an act of recognition on the writer's part. At this stage the writer thinks, *Here is something I can write a novel about.*"

Isak Dinesen used to say much the same: "I start with a tingle, a kind of feeling of the story I will write. Then come the characters, and they take over, they make the story. But all this ends by being a plot." Robert Penn Warren began the same way. "Any book I write starts with a flash. . . ." A "throb." A "tingle." A "flash." Pretty flimsy stuff. Most people have spent a lifetime shunting shimmers like that out of their minds. Now you must recognize them as a call to action, as a promise of what is to come.

And you must sit down and write. It doesn't even *really* matter if you feel like writing. As Tom Wolfe says, "Sometimes, if things are going badly, I will force myself to write a page in half an hour. I find that can be done. I find that what I write when I force myself is generally just as good as what I write when I'm feeling inspired. It's mainly a matter of forcing yourself to write. There's a marvelous essay that Sinclair Lewis wrote on how to write. He said that most writers don't understand that the process begins by actually sitting down." Joyce Carol Oates agrees: "One must be pitiless about this matter of 'mood.' In a sense, the writing will *create* the mood. . . . Generally I've found this to be true: I have forced myself to begin writing when I've been utterly exhausted, when I've felt my soul as thin as a playing card, when nothing has seemed worth enduring for another five minutes . . . and somehow the activity of writing changes everything."

This principle—*write it now*—applies not just to writers of fiction, but also to writers of all kinds. Interestingly enough, it is relevant even to scholars dependent on factual research. The great historian Samuel Eliot Morison used to tell his students: "First and foremost, *get writing*! Young scholars generally wish to secure the last fact before writing anything, like General

McClellan refusing to advance (as people said) until the last mule was shod. . . . In every research there comes a point, which you should recognize like a call of conscience, when you must get down to writing. And once you are writing, go on writing as long as you can; there will be plenty of time later to shove in the footnotes or return to the library for extra information."

"But"—you may say—"I don't even know my *story* yet." My answer is: "Of *course* you don't know your story yet." You are the very first person to tell this story ever, anywhere in the whole world, and *you cannot know a story until it has been told.* First you tell it; then you know it. It is not the other way around. That may sound illogical, but to the narrating mind, it is logic itself. Stories make themselves known, they reveal themselves—even to their tellers—*only* by being told. You may ask how on earth you can tell a story before you know it. You do that by letting the emerging story tell itself *through* you. As you tell it, you let the story give you your cues about where it is going to go next. At first, you must feel your way, letting it be your guide. You may eventually be able to plan the whole scope of the work down to its smallest details, as J. K. Rowling is said to have done with all her Harry Potter books. But in the very first phase of its creation, any story must be teased out from the shadows of your imagination and unconscious. As Isabel Allende says, the story is "hidden in a very somber and secret place where I don't have any access yet. It is something that I've been feeling but which has no shape, no name, no tone, no voice." It is waiting for you, untold, undefined, and latent. It will take shape only when you put it into words. So start putting it into words. As Allende concludes, "By the time I've finished the first draft, I know what the book is about. But not before."

Since you have no choice but to begin in uncertainty, you must learn to tolerate uncertainty and, if possible, to turn it into excitement. As Toni Morrison puts it: "I am profoundly excited by thinking up or having the idea in the first place . . . before I begin to write . . . it's a sustained thing I have to play with. I always start out with an idea, even a boring idea, that becomes a question I don't have any answers to."

Most writers start out uncertainly with a small thing called the "germ," or the "seed" of the story. That "germ," as E. L. Doctorow points out, can be anything. "It can be a voice, an image; it can be a deep moment of personal desperation. For instance, with *Ragtime* I was so desperate to write something, I was facing the wall of my study in my house in New Rochelle and so I started to write about the wall. That's the kind of day we sometimes have, as writers. Then I wrote about the house that was attached to the wall. It was built in 1906, you see, so I thought about the era and what Broadview Avenue looked like then: Trolley cars ran along the avenue down at the bottom of the hill; people wore white clothes in the summer to stay cool. Teddy Roosevelt was president. One thing led to another, and that's the way that book began, through desperation to those few images."

Writers use all kinds of metaphors to describe the way their imagination is originally aroused. Tom McGuane says it makes him feel like a hunting dog snapping alert, catching the scent. "When I start something it's like being a bird dog getting a smell; it's a matter of running it down in prose and then trying to figure out what the thing is that's out there." In the prefaces to the New York Edition of his novels, Henry James tells the many little tales of how each of his classic works began as some sudden impression, something "minute and windblown . . . the stray suggestion, the wandering word, the vague echo, at the touch of which the novelist's imagination winces as at the prick of some sharp point. . . ." Patricia Highsmith notes that story ideas "can be little or big, simple or complex, fragmentary or rather complete, still or moving. The important thing is to recognize them when they come. I recognize them by a certain excitement which they instantly bring, akin to the pleasure and excitement of a good poem or line in a poem." The "throb" can come to you as a whole story, but more often it will be a fragment. The job, once you've been aroused, is to expand your excitement: to let it grow, take on substance.

While you cannot force ideas into existence, you can coax them into view. When you first notice some exciting fragment, your impulse may be to brush it aside. It looks so . . . so small, so slight. Don't be deceived. What matters is not the idea's size but its resonance. Ray Bradbury has generated stories by simply writing down, in free association, image after image, looking for "a pattern in the list, in these words that I had simply flung forth on paper, trusting my subconscious to give bread, as it were, to the birds. . . . Where am I leading you? Well, if you are a writer, or would hope to be one, similar lists, dredged out of the lopside of your brain, might well help you discover *you,* even as I flopped around and finally found me. I began to run through those lists, pick a noun, and then sit down to write a long prose-poem-essay on it. Somewhere along about the middle of the page, or perhaps on the second page, the prose poem would turn into a story. Which is to say that a character suddenly appeared and said, 'That's *me!*' or, 'That's an idea I *like!*' And the character would then finish the tale for me."

But be careful. If you are like me, your first instinct will be to try to "take control" of a new idea, to assert yourself, to "turn this into something." Yet at this early stage, it may be a mistake to treat your idea too aggressively. The whole process of writing, from first to last, requires that you alternate steadily between a passive, open, daydreaming intuitiveness, followed by worked-out, thought-through, fully developed acts of judgment and control. You *must* have both, and you *must* get both to work not against each other but in concert. In the early stages, most developing ideas usually need lots of fertile, nurturing passivity. Something has moved you. You begin to write about it. You sketch. You jot down a chain of fantasies and associations. You dream the dream. You don't know what's coming; you're a vehicle for what's happening on your page, as was Flannery O'Connor when she wrote her great short story "Good Country People." "When I started writing that story, I didn't know there was going to be a Ph.D. with a wooden leg in it. I merely found myself one morning writing a description of two women I knew something about, and before I realized it, I had equipped one of them with a daughter with a wooden leg. I brought in the Bible salesman, but I had no idea what I was going to do with him. I didn't know he was going to steal that wooden leg until ten or twelve lines before he did it, and when I found out that this was what was going to happen, I realized it was inevitable."

We know the original fragmentary image that William Faulkner made into *The Sound and the Fury.* "[The book] began with a mental picture. I didn't realize at the time it was symbolical. The picture was of the muddy seat of a little girl's drawers in a pear tree, where she could see through a window where her grandmother's funeral was taking place and report what was happening to her brothers on the ground below. By the time I explained who they were and what they were doing and how her pants got muddy, I realized it would be impossible to get all of it into a short story and that it would have to be a book."

Writer after writer speaks of this fragmentary inspiration. William Trevor recalls a glimpse of two people on a train. "I remember being on a train, and I was perhaps walking down to the bar when I noticed a woman and a boy traveling together. He was in his school uniform, and she was clearly in charge of him. I can remember now the fatigue on her face. Afterwards—probably years afterwards—I wrote a story called 'Going Home.' " For John Hersey it was not a chance encounter but a world-historical cataclysm: "I think the first impulse comes from some deep emotion. It may be anger, it may be some sort of excitement. . . . To give you an example, the impulse to write *The Wall* came from seeing some camps in Eastern Europe when I was working as a correspondent in Moscow for *Time.* . . . This came at a time when the West had not yet known very much about the Holocaust; there had been some vague rumors of the camps, but we had no real pictures of them. To see these bodies, to hear from the people who survived, created a sense of horror and anger in me that made me want to write." For Eudora Welty, writing her unforgettable story "Powerhouse," the spur was music: "I wrote it in one night after I'd been to a concert and dance in Jackson where Fats Waller played. I tried to write my idea of the life of the traveling artist and performer—not Fats Waller himself, but any artist—in the alien world and tried to put it in the words and plot suggested by the music I'd been listening to. It was a daring attempt for a writer like me . . . I'm not qualified to write about music or performers. But trying it pleased me then, and it still does please me." For Grace Paley, stories can begin simply with one sentence sounding in her head. "It sounds dopey to say that, but it's true. Very often one sentence is absolutely resonant. A story can begin with someone speaking. 'I was popular in certain circles,' for example; an aunt of mine said that, and it hung around in my head for a long time. Eventually I wrote a story, 'Goodbye and Good Luck,' that began with that line, though it had nothing to do with my aunt."

So don't try to take control of your idea too early. Begin by letting *it* take control of *you.* You will be needing all your capacities for organization and judgment and mastery soon enough. For now, let whatever has stirred inside you gain strength. An image is glowing in your mind. A voice keeps nattering in your head. An incident on the street speaks to you. Like O'Connor and Faulkner, be a little passive in your nurturance. Let it become what it is going to be.

But do jot it all down. Use your notebook as a kind of seedbed. Once you've learned to recognize the seeds, you'll probably have more than you can use. With a little tending—sketching, adding, changing, seeing what moves you—some will sprout. Some will grow. Some will even make it to the harvest. How do you choose among them all? That's simple. Eventually, one idea, properly tended, becomes irresistible and fills the mind.

WRITING "WHAT YOU KNOW"

The most familiar of all advice on writing is the old classroom cliché "Write what you know." It is very much a cliché, and it is going to get rather rough treatment over the course of this book. Yet, like most clichés, it has the residual virtue of being a half-truth. Taken literally, it is nonsense. Applied unimaginatively, it would reduce us all to plodding autobiography. Yet once you have grasped the intimate and magical bond between what you "know" and what you imagine, the old saw does make some sense. Gabriel García Márquez, whom nobody is likely to accuse of undue literalism, says this: "If I had to give a young writer some advice, I would say to write about something that has happened to him; it's always easy to tell whether a writer is writing about something that has happened to him or something he has read or been told. . . . It always amuses me that the biggest praise for my work comes for the imagination, while the truth is that there's not a single line in all my work that does not have a basis in reality." Somerset Maugham said much the same thing: "I have never claimed to create anything out of nothing; I have always needed an incident or a character as a starting point, but I have exercised imagination, invention, and a sense of the dramatic to make it something of my own."

Yet "write what you know" misleads mainly because all of us "know" much more than we can easily say, and all of us can and do imagine more than we "know." As E. L. Doctorow says, "Writing teachers invariably tell students, Write about what you know. . . . [B]ut on the other hand, how do you know what you know until you've written it? Writing is knowing. What did Kafka know? The insurance business? So that kind of advice is foolish, because it presumes that you have to go out to a war to be able to do war. Well, some do and some don't."

Commenting on the need to "write from experience," Henry James said much the same thing, albeit in his very Henry Jamesian way. "What kind of experience is intended," James wondered, "and where does it begin and end? Experience is never limited, and it is never complete; it is an immense sensibility, a kind of huge spider-web of the finest silken threads suspended in the chamber of consciousness, and catching every air-borne particle in its tissue. It is the very atmosphere of the mind . . ."

Stephen King says much the same thing, except in *his* way. "I think you begin by interpreting 'write what you know' as broadly and inclusively as possible. If you're a plumber, you know plumbing, but that is far from the extent of your knowledge; the heart also knows things, and so does the imagination."

As a writer, you are using words to turn *your* unknown into what you "know." You are inventing, and reinventing, what you "know." Edith Wharton summed it up well: "As to experience, intellectual and moral, the creative imagination can make a little go a long way, provided it remains long enough in the mind and is sufficiently brooded upon. One good heartbreak will furnish the poet with many songs, and the novelist with a considerable number of novels. But they must have hearts that can break."

The key is to move on steadily from what you know, be it ever so little. Suppose you begin with a situation or character taken straight from real life. How do you turn that reality into fiction? This is a big subject, and we are going to explore it carefully in chapter 6. For the moment, John Irving has some sound advice. Starting from real material, Irving begins by keeping what he calls a "diary" of that experience. "I begin by telling the truth, by remembering real people, relatives, and friends. The landscape detail is pretty good, but the people aren't quite interesting enough—they don't have quite enough to do with one another; of course, what unsettles me and bores me is the absence of plot. . . . And so I find a little something that I exaggerate, a little; gradually, I have an autobiography on its way to becoming a lie. The lie, of course, is more interesting. I become more interested in the part of the story I'm making up, in the 'relative' I never had. And then I begin to think of a novel; that's the end of the diary. I promise I'll start another one as soon as I finish the novel. Then the same thing happens; the lies become much more interesting—always."

WHERE TO FIND YOUR STORY

When you're in doubt about where to find a story, try childhood. If you have a strong imagination, you'll soon move beyond your own experience of it, but it's a good place to begin. Childhood is, in every sense, the cradle of narrative. If you're uncertain about a beginning, here is Anne Lamott's advice: "Plug your nose and jump in, and write down all your memories as truthfully as you can. Flannery O'Connor said that anyone who survived childhood has enough material to write for the rest of his or her life." Richard Price, a very different writer, offers the same advice. "As I always told my students, 'We all grow up with ten great stories about our families, our childhoods . . . they probably have nothing to do with the truth of things, but they're yours. You know them. And you love them. So use them.' And that's what I did. That's what I reached for, to become a writer."

INVENTING YOUR STORY

Many novices simply freeze, terrified, at the thought of "making up" a story. We'll discuss that freeze-up at length in chapter 3, but let's get one basic thought into play right now. *You can **make up** a story only by **finding** it, and you can **find** a story only by **making it*** *up.* The Latin root of the word *invent* means "to find." And since you cannot know what you have to say until you have said it, writers of both fiction and nonfiction "invent" *through* "finding." They *find* their voices, *find* their characters, *find* their own persona. Another way to put this is that there are many ways of knowing things. Yes, you "know" what you can easily articulate right now. But you also "know" what you only obscurely sense, what you have not yet articulated; you "know" what you intuit prior to language; you "know" what you can only vaguely and distantly feel, what is out of your grasp, what you must dig to reach or even touch. This is where you will find your story. The germ is only the visible tip of something big buried inside you, your first glimpse of what is to be. The whole will emerge feeling as though it were already inside you, already present to your imagination.

Stephen King compares stories to fossils and thinks stories need to be as much *dug* up as *made* up. "Stories aren't souvenir T-shirts or GameBoys. Stories are relics, part of an undiscovered preexisting world." They are dug up in the shadow region between fabrication and discovery.

Here are some of the most essential tools for digging.

PROVIDE MOTIVATION. Every story *is* what its characters *do.* Therefore, you have to show us only secondarily what your characters are like, or what they *look* like, or what they *feel* like. You must show us what they do.

They will not act without a motivation. As Kurt Vonnegut shrewdly points out, motivation is *the* point of entry into every story. "When I used to teach creative writing, I would tell the students to make their characters want something right away— even if it's only a glass of water. Characters paralyzed by the meaninglessness of modern life still have to drink water from time to time." Motivation leads to conflict, and conflict is the key to drama. Vonnegut goes on: "When you exclude plot, when you exclude anyone's wanting anything, you exclude the reader, which is a mean-spirited thing to do. You can also exclude the reader by not telling him immediately where the story is taking place, and who the people are [and what they want]. And you can put him to sleep by never having characters confront each other. Students like to say that they stage no confrontations because people avoid confrontations in modern life. 'Modern life is so lonely,' they say. This is laziness. It's the writer's job to stage confrontations, so the characters will say surprising and revealing things, and educate and entertain us all. If a writer can't or won't do that, he should withdraw from the trade."

Ray Bradbury also calls motivation the key to story. "My characters write my stories for me. They tell me what they want, and I tell them to go get it, and I follow as they run, working at my typing as they rush to their destiny. Montag, in [*Fahrenheit 451*], wanted to stop burning books. Go stop it! I said. He ran to do just that. I followed, typing. Ahab, in *Moby Dick*, wanted to chase and kill a whale. He rushed raving off to do so. Melville followed, writing the novel with a harpoon on the flesh of the damned whale!"

There's a story inside every motive, because wanting something invariably has a result, some kind of outcome. That result may be nothing more than pure frustration—but then the frustration will have some outcome. In any case, the wish will lead to a result, and therein lies, always, some sort of tale, a path to narrative, and a route to the end.

The *kind* of motive and the nature of its outcome are entirely up to the writer. That's what gives the art its metaphysics and magic. It can be comic or tragic, silly or sublime, cataclysmic or microscopic, and depicting it is how the artist experiences and finds her or his style and identity.

LOOK FOR A BEGINNING—OR AN END. Better yet, both. A story—any story—recounts a sequence of events. Those events happen in time. You do not *have* to begin at the literal beginning of the sequence. The ancients advised beginning in medias res, in the middle of things. But you must begin somewhere. Once you've begun, you must proceed to some end. Some strong sense of where to begin, accompanied sooner or later by a strong sense of where to end, has to play a very large role shaping whatever you write. Even writers who begin their stories with nothing more than a phrase sense that it is a *beginning* phrase, a phrase that impels them to what *follows*.

Intuition counts for everything here. Obviously, you cannot be *logically* certain that a given moment begins or ends a story before you yourself know exactly what the story is. You've got to feel the rightness of the thing. You won't be able to prove that sense of "rightness" until you are done and the tale told. But do trust it. Stick with it. Let it be your navigating star.

The search for that feeling can be hard work. As Philip Roth explains, "Beginning a book is unpleasant. I'm entirely uncertain about the character and the predicament, and a character in his predicament is what I have to begin with. Worse than not knowing your subject is not knowing how to treat it, because that's finally everything. I type out beginnings and they're awful, more of an unconscious parody of my previous book than the breakaway from it that I want. I need something driving down the center of a book, a magnet to draw everything to it—that's what I look for during the first months of writing something new. I often have to write a hundred pages or more before there's a paragraph that's alive. Okay, I say to myself, that's your beginning, start there; that's the first paragraph of the book. I'll go over the first six months of work and underline in red a paragraph, a sentence, sometimes no more than a phrase, that has some life in it, and then I'll type all these out on one page."

It is almost the same with endings. Sometimes an ending will occur to you before the beginning. Good. Once you have a last scene or last line glowing in your mind, you can start writing toward it. There are many short-story writers who don't start work until they have their end. Katherine Anne Porter was one: "If I didn't know the ending of a story, I wouldn't begin. I always write my last lines, my last paragraph, my last page first, and then I go back and work towards it. I know where I'm going. I know what my goal is. And how I get there is God's grace."

YOU AND YOUR NOTEBOOKS

You prepare in your notebook, both before and while you do the main work. You should be "preparing" all the time, and "preparing" for more than one project. A writer should always be writing. At any given moment in your writing life, some main project should be on the front burner. But other possibilities should also be brewing on that back burner of the literary life, your notebook.

"A writer," as Paul Johnson says, "should not see his craft solely in terms of particular books or projects. The input must be continuous. All is grist to the mill. A writer must train himself to observe and to record. It is essential he keep notebooks, and always have one in his pocket. The rule must be: Write it down instantly. Never trust your memory. Get it on paper. If you see something in a newspaper or magazine, clip it, not tomorrow but now. . . ."

Opinion among writers is somewhat divided about notebooks and their usefulness. "At one time," Truman Capote claimed, "I used to keep notebooks with outlines for stories. But I found doing this somehow deadened the idea in my imagination. If the notion is good enough, if it truly belongs to *you*, then you can't forget it—it will haunt you till it's written." Dorothy Parker, a blocked writer, could never make up her mind whether to keep a notebook or not. Frank McCourt, a once-blocked writer who came spectacularly unblocked with *Angela's Ashes*, warns eloquently against the danger of using notebooks as a substitute for the work itself. "I retired from teaching in 1987. By then I was fifty-seven, and I was still poking at this book, still trying to write it—I had notebooks, notebooks, notebooks—and not knowing what ailed me. The paradox is that I used to tell my students . . . 'Forget about writing. Just scribble, scribble, scribble. scribble. Put down *anything.* Write honestly. Write from your own point of view and your own voice, and it eventually takes form. There's no such thing as writer's block.' So why didn't I go home and do it myself? Why didn't I just tell my story naturally? With all these notebooks piling up, and the tremendous desire to write this book, and knowing that if I hadn't written it I would have died an unhappy man?"

These are wise words of warning. Writers love to procrastinate, and notebooks are among their favorite places to do it. Scribbling in a notebook feels so much like real writing. Once you grasp that a notebook is most useful *after* you've begun the main text, the danger diminishes a little. Yet you will need your notebooks. The fantasy that you will remember whatever is important enough without notes is just that: a fantasy. Anne Lamott explains, "I used to think that if something was important enough, I'd remember it until I got home, where I could simply write it down in my notebook. . . .

"But then I wouldn't.

"I'd get home. . . . And I'd stand there trying to see it, the way you try to remember a dream, where you squint and it's right there on the tip of your psychic tongue but you can't get it back. The image is gone." Tom Wolfe adds: "If it's a situation in which it's impossible or very awkward to take notes, I try to write down everything I can remember before going to sleep. I find that memory decay is very rapid. Even going to sleep and waking up the next day, there's an awful lot that simply doesn't come back."

Meanwhile, a notebook can be invaluable in helping to get you going when you're stuck. Never try to *think* your way out of a problem, unaided by the written word. *Write* your way out—in the notebook. If you freeze up over a scene or character, slip into the sweet anonymity of the notebook and talk out the problem. Get loose again in that privacy. Sue Grafton keeps a journal *as she writes* for every one of her novels. She writes in both every working day. "Some of the freest writing I do is in the journal because psychologically that feels like playtime. Once I get into the chapter itself it starts feeling too earnest. I think, this is a solemn piece of writing here and I had better not make a mistake, and so I start getting tense. In the journal I can just write down exactly what I'm thinking. Often it's quite lovely writing. . . ."

"I have never been blocked," says Lorrie Moore, "never lost faith (or never lost it for longer than necessary, shall we say), never not had ideas and scraps sitting around in notebooks or on Post-its adhered to the desk edge. . . ." Whenever a story idea flickers through your mind, jot it down. Not later. Now. Once it's jotted down, don't forget it. Schedule time for your notebooks. Some ideas will keep their vitality, and some will die on the vine. But the only place they can germinate and grow is on the page.

Your notes may at first seem almost random—too random for use. But if you're alert, these traces of your excitement will sooner or later begin to form a mosaic that reveals your enduring preconscious interests. Nabokov once remarked that most of his novels emerged from seeing the pattern in a cluster of seemingly unrelated images. The editor and agent Betsy Lerner says: "If you are struggling with what you should be writing, look at your scraps. Encoded there are the times and subjects that you should be grappling with as a writer."

Once you see that an idea is persistent enough to be really important for you, start a separate notebook for it. If you work only on the computer, start a separate folder. Put into it every idea, every insight, every scrap of research, and every meandering random phrase that forms itself in your mind. If you use a paper notebook, make it not loose-leaf but bound: You are not going to throw out *anything*. Even if something looks like a foolish mistake now, cross it out with a couple of thin lines. You may change your mind. If you find you have started shaping real sentences in your head, be sure to get them down, too. You may find you're writing the story even *before* you begin. It's wonderful what can suddenly emerge from a random jotting. "Never throw away a story with a good story line, even in synopsis," Patricia Highsmith advised. "Novelists—most of them—have a lot of ideas that are brief and minor, that cannot or should not be made into books. They may make good or spectacularly good short stories." She adds, "Write down all those slender ideas. It is surprising how often one sentence, jotted in a notebook, leads immediately to a second sentence. A plot can develop as you write notes. Close the notebook and think about it for a few days—and then presto! You're ready to write a short story."

SHORT STORY OR NOVEL?

If you are a novice, you will probably begin by writing short stories, assuming that once you have mastered the short story form, you'll graduate to writing a novel. This is a perfectly natural thought. It is also a little misleading. The short story has a close and obvious kinship to the novel, but a transition from one form to the other is neither obligatory nor inevitable. Not every novelist has a gift for the short form, and there are many short story writers who are not natural novelists. Raymond Carver moved from short stories not to the novel but to lyric poetry. Anton Chekhov himself, often seen as the greatest among the founders of the modern short story, made the transition not to novels but to plays.

In fact, the short story and the novel are very different forms. Both are, to be sure, narrative prose, but they often narrate very different kinds of things. Every novel must provide some account of a sequence of events. Movement and change are its essence. A short story, like a lyric poem, may be comparatively static. It may use its narrative as much to establish and fortify an image as to follow the tale to its dramatic outcome.

Let me illustrate with Robert Frost's poem "Stopping by Woods on a Snowy Evening." Let's try to reconceive that great lyric as a short story. The poem *could* be a short story. It has everything a short story needs. It has a setting: those freezing, voluptuously enticing woods. It has its moment: "the darkest evening of the year." Though the poem is a meditation on solitude, it has a number of characters. There's the man stopping by the woods. There's his horse. There's the owner of the woods—the one whose house is in the village. And there is some person or persons to whom the traveler has made some promises that must be kept. The traveler also has a destination. It is miles away but near enough to reach tonight. Above all, there's a conflict. The traveler wants to stay where he is, rapt in all that is "lovely, dark and deep." Yet he feels pulled away by his obligations. The poem has all the elements of a story collapsed within a single murmuring image.

Transformed into a story, all this could easily begin and end with that image, exactly as the poem does. The traveler stops to look and then resolves, reluctantly, to go ahead. The essential structure could remain: first, stopping; then silent rapture; then conflict—those promises—followed by an outcome: the decision to proceed. But it would all be more amply shown. We'd learn more about how the traveler is so touched by the freezing, all-but-silent nocturnal vision; we'd be given more about his promises and the person or persons to whom they were made. We'd get information, living information, about how hard it is to break away from the cold, uninhabited depths of the woods and start covering the miles ahead. In short, we would know more about everything, and especially more about the conflict. But structurally, the poem and the story might look very much alike.

A *novel* based on this poem would tell us a great deal more, and it would give us a sequence of events that would not be contained within the embrace of a single image. In a novel, the poem's one long moment, the stop by the woods, would be a single scene. It might be a great scene. It could be the first scene in the novel—but it wouldn't *have* to be. It might appear in the middle, or be the final scene. Each different placement would make a very different book. Meanwhile, as the novel progressed, we would learn a lot more about the traveler, and a whole lot more about his promises. We would be drawn, through drama, into his troubled resolve to keep them. Moreover, the conflict's center of gravity would shift, probably quite emphatically, away from the traveler's purely internal debate. We would see the whole problem between him and those to whom he owes whatever he owes. The conflict would slip loose from the confines of a single image. The characters on both sides would be vivid and alive: We would see and hear them, like or dislike them, and feel that we know them, clearly grasping what they want, and why. We would be pulled into their problems, maybe even tempted to choose sides. We would certainly be asked to care about the outcome in a way that the poem does not ask us to care about the outcome—and which even a short story might easily shrug off as beside the point.

RULES FOR THE FIRST DRAFT

- **Do** it. Hemingway said that the only thing that really matters about a first draft is getting it done. You are looking for the sound and shape of a story, and this is the only place you can hope to find them. So get to it
- Do it **quickly**. Eloquence, according to Cicero, resides in "an uninterrupted movement of the mind," a *motus animi continuus.* Stephen King, admittedly a wildly prolific writer, claims that writing the first draft of a novel should never absorb more than a single season; three, maybe four, months. If you are writing a short story, write the entire first draft, if possible, in a single

sitting. If something has to take up lots of time, let it be the second draft, and then proceed to a finishing draft in a single sustained push, following the rhythm Eudora Welty used to recommend: "My ideal way to write a short story is to write the whole first draft through in one sitting, then work as long as it takes on revisions, and then write the final version all in one, so that in the end the whole thing amounts to one long sustained effort."

You don't have time? *Make* that time. This is essential. Only you can make and defend the time you need for your work. Nobody is going to give it to you. I know, I know, it's horribly hard. Writing is outrageously time consuming. Of course, if you have an equally time-consuming job or heavy personal responsibilities, you'll be slowed down. But you must make the time or you will not write at all. Simple as that. And be warned: For every writer, at every level of fame and productivity, making and defending writing time is a lifelong battle. It's not just hard now. It will *always* be hard.

And for the moment, don't even think about perfection. Right now, perfection is your enemy, simply because it is the enemy of getting it down and done. You are going to have to tolerate imperfection, and lots of it. As Anne Lamott says: "Get it all down. Let it pour out of you onto the page. Write an incredibly shitty, self-indulgent, whiny, mewling first draft. Then take out as many of the excesses as you can." You are looking for movement, energy, and a preliminary sense of completion. "Write freely and as rapidly as possible," John Steinbeck advised, "and throw the whole thing on paper. Never correct or rewrite until the whole thing is down. Rewrite in process is usually found to be an excuse for not going on. It also interferes with the flow and rhythm which can only come from a kind of unconscious association with the material."

Let nothing stop you. If you get stuck, write *through* the problem, as Christopher Isherwood used to do: "If I get into some nonsense or digressions, I write it through to the end and come out on the other side. I'm not at all perfectionist at first. I do all the polishing in the final draft." Or follow Steinbeck's procedure and simply skip over it altogether. "If a scene or a section gets the better of you and you still think you want it—bypass it and go on. When you have finished the whole, you can come back to it and then you may find that the reason it gave trouble is because it didn't belong there." Or switch to the notebook and write your way back into the main text as quickly as possible.

In your first draft, simple speed may be the force behind that wholeness and eloquence about which Cicero spoke. But it has other advantages. Honesty is one. Ray Bradbury asks, "What can we writers learn from lizards, lift from birds? In quickness is truth. The faster you blurt, the more swiftly you write, the more honest you are. In hesitation is thought. In delay comes the effort for a style, instead of leaping upon truth which is the *only* style worth deadfalling or tiger-trapping."

Speed can also help get you past a writer's block. Tom Wolfe remembers freezing up over writing a magazine piece for *Esquire* under its then editor, Byron Dobell. But in the process, he made a breakthrough into his famous style. The piece was to be called "Kustom Kar Kommandoes." "I suddenly realized I'd never written a magazine article before and I just felt I couldn't do it. Well, Dobell somehow shamed me into writing down the notes that I had taken in my reporting on the car customizers so that some competent writer could convert them into a magazine piece. I sat down one night and started writing a memorandum to him as fast as I could, just to get the ordeal over with. It became very much like a letter that you write to a friend in which you're not thinking about style, you're just pouring it all out, and I churned it out all night long, forty typewritten, triple-spaced pages. I turned it in in the morning to Byron at *Esquire,* and then I went home to sleep. About four that afternoon I got a call from him telling me, 'Well, we're knocking the "Dear Byron" off the top of your memo, and we're running the piece.' That was a tremendous release for me."

Russell Banks sees yet another advantage: "From the beginning I've found that I have to sneak past the internal censor who basically wants me to shut up and be silent, and the best way for me to get something said has been to move real fast. The faster I can write, the more likely I'll get something worth saving down . . ."

Fast or slow, once your first draft is done, be ready for it to be bad. Some parts may give you a pleasant surprise over how good they are, and the whole may not turn out to be quite as horrible as you feared during your very worst moments. Even so, it's going to be bad. Do not let that badness bother you. *Use* the badness. I once heard Philip Roth tell a crowded roomful of writing students that, when it came to sheer stinking lousiness, he would match his first drafts against those of any writer in the place. Your own first draft will probably be ragged, inarticulate, blundering, dull, and full of gaping holes and blank spots—a mortifying mess. Use every mistake. The inarticulate parts point to where you must make the words say exactly what you mean. The ragged parts point to what you must polish. The gaping holes tell you what has to be filled. The dull parts tell you unfailingly what must be cut. The blank spots show exactly what you must go out and find. These are infallible guides, and though they talk tough, they are your friends.

TRANSGRESSION AND PERMISSION, IMITATION AND ORIGINALITY

A beginner's chief enemy, on the other hand, is usually lack of confidence, and almost all writers suffer from that lack, over and over, most of their lives. Some books on writing—Anne Lamott's *Bird by Bird,* for example, or Dorothea Brande's dated but excellent *Becoming a Writer*—face this psychological issue head-on and in depth, and they offer many useful ways of dealing with it. I recommend both. Remember that you are not alone: Every writer—well, *almost* every writer—has suffered from problems of confidence, and some of the greatest have endured nothing short of agony. If it is any reassurance, I can tell you that with experience and time, the problem does get a little better. Yet it never goes away. It can be handled, but not banished. The get-down truth is that to write, you have to develop a tolerance for anxiety. Steel yourself. Be brave. "Courage, first," says Maya Angelou, ". . . the most important of all the virtues. Without that virtue you can't practice any other virtue with consistency." Katherine Anne Porter would have agreed: "One of the marks of a gift is to have the courage of it. If they haven't got the courage, it's just too bad. They'll fail, just as people with lack of courage in other vocations and walks of life fail. Courage is the first essential."

Of course, courage *is* a gift, and some people have more of it than others. Yet, like talent itself, courage can be recognized, developed, and *en*couraged. How? Most writers feel a baffling, seemingly contradictory mix of petulant, almost blind self-will swimming in a pool of yearning need for permission. In truth, you will be needing both: *both* go-it-alone brashness *and* the consent of peers. Writers need *both* some kind of permission to go ahead, *and* the will to go forge ahead even without that permission. As Toni Morrison says, "When I read women's biographies and autobiographies, even accounts of how they got started writing, almost every one of them had a little anecdote which told about the moment someone gave them permission to do it. A mother, a husband, a teacher . . . somebody said, 'Okay, go ahead—you can do it.' Which is not to say that men have never needed that; frequently when they are very young, a mentor says, 'You're good,' and they take off."

Well, men and women writers both need some credible sign of consent and permission to produce. Both badly need to hear just that simple statement of faith: "Go ahead—you can do it." Getting and meriting that basic support—and avoiding situations that undermine it—should play no small role in how you arrange your life. You will need to find and trust people—teachers, mentors, friends, spouses, partners, and lovers—who are unequivocally on your side. Not stupidly on your side, not uncritically. Unequivocally. Blind or uncritical support can only damage you. But you must have support, and it must be unfeigned.

You will need mentors, and you will need to find them both in your daily life and in books. Hemingway pointed out that he had spent his youth learning from everyone he could, living or dead. Listen to how Gabriel García Márquez began: "One night [at college] a friend lent me a book of short stories by Franz Kafka. I went back to the pension where I was staying and began to read *The Metamorphosis.* The first line almost knocked me off the bed, I was so surprised. The first line reads, 'As Gregor Samsa awoke that morning from uneasy dreams, he found himself transformed in his bed into a gigantic insect. . . .' When I read the line I thought to myself that I didn't know that anyone was allowed to write things like that. If I had known, I would have started writing a long time ago."

Note García Márquez's exact words: "I didn't *know* that anyone was *allowed* to write things like that [emphasis mine]." I cannot tell you how many people have sat in my office astonished to discover that they were *allowed* to write the way *they* wanted to write. That it was okay to say what *they* had seen and thought and imagined. That it was okay to say it *their* way.

But even as you look for permission, you are unlikely to succeed as a writer unless you learn to cherish and exploit whatever in you is nervy and defiant—the rather transgressive you who insists that no matter what other people want, no matter what other people say you should think, you are going to say what *you* want to say, in *your* way or not at all. There are sure to be plenty of forces—some but not all of them internal—pushing you to do it *their* way. As Joyce Carol Oates says: "I believe that any form of art is a species of exploration and transgression. (I never saw a 'No Trespassing' sign that wasn't a summons to my rebellious blood. Such signs, dutifully posted on tress and fence railings, might as well cry, 'Come Right In!').

"To write is to invade another's space, if only to memorialize it. To write is to invite angry censure. . . . Art by its nature is a transgressive act. . . ."

It is only a seeming paradox that a search for the nerve to say it your way can be *served* by a parallel search for guidance. You find your way through others. When he encountered Kafka, García Márquez experienced what Melville said he encountered when he read his mentor, Nathaniel Hawthorne: *"the shock of recognition."* It knocked him out of bed. This "shock of recognition" usually hits when it is least expected, and the jolt it delivers is a signal event in the life of any artist. Whenever it strikes, it is invariably telling you something vital about yourself. Do not confuse it with mere liking for another writer's work, or even with respect or reverence. The shock of recognition is a moment of excitement that shakes the soul. It may be hard to describe, but like other forms of love, you will know it when you feel it. Whenever and wherever you experience it, something important has occurred in your artistic life. Of course, not every mentor or teacher will affect you in anything like such a profound way. Most will merely teach and help. But they *must* do that. They *must* make your work more possible. And if they fail in that obligation, you must turn your back on them.

Do not fear imitation. Nobody sensible pursues an imitative style as a long-term goal, but all accomplished writers know that the notion of pure originality is a childish fantasy. Up to a point, imitation is the path to discovery and essential to growth. After discovering Kafka, "I immediately started writing short stories," García Márquez recalls. "They are totally intellectual short stories because I was writing them on the basis of my literary experience and had not yet found the link between literature and life." The wish to appear original is a form of vanity, and as treacherous a form of vanity as any other: It has wrecked many a talent. García Márquez's first stories were frankly derivative of Kafka, yet they set their author on a path that made him one of the most strikingly original stylists of his era. The youthful Anton Chekhov taught himself by rewriting, in his own terms, whole stories by Tolstoy and Turgenev—transposing them, as it were, into his own language. Numerous writers—Somerset Maugham and Joan Didion come to mind—recall copying long passages *verbatim* from favorite writers, learning with every line. The result may be forthrightly aimed at the wastebasket, yet this kind of close encounter offers a wonderful intimacy with the prose.

Finally, let's admit that this ambition of yours *ought* to make you a little anxious. Paul Johnson may exaggerate, but not by much: "Writing is a painful trade with a high casualty rate. Most writers end in partial or total failure. They must fight despair in youth, fear in maturity, and the cumulative evidence of declining powers in age." Who wouldn't be a little scared? So be daring. You are going to need all the daring you've got. You'll need daring to lead a writer's risky life. You'll need daring to avoid the formulaic and the safe. You'll need daring to keep your freshness and force, and you'll need daring to say things your way and make yourself heard. Don't let the butterflies and fears stop you. You are not alone: Whatever their gifts or level of success, most writers spend much of their lives managing the inner drama of confidence. Your business is spinning the dusty straw of your uncertainty and fear into the pure gold of clarity and conviction. It is the task of a lifetime.

2

THE WRITING LIFE

YOUR TALENT AND YOUR CALLING

You've got to start with a certain amount of talent, the sine qua non. Very occasionally, a literary gift shows up that is vast, awe-inspiring, as it was in Tolstoy, Proust, or Dickens, compared to whom even big talents seem small. Yet many fine, even famous, careers have been built on making the most of relatively ordinary gifts. Be it modest or magnificent, you've got to have some talent. It may be latent; it may be undeveloped; it may be neglected. But it must be there.

What is literary talent? A nimble fluency. A way with words. An imagination that's easily aroused, quick to see, to hear, and to feel. An ear for the music of the language and a tendency to become absorbed in the mysterious movements of its significance and sound. A sense of audience. Skill at organizing verbal concepts solidly, effectively, and fairly swiftly. An aptitude for catching the elusive forms and figures of a vivid imagination and a knack for pinning them down on a page.

IT IS NOT ENOUGH. "Talent is insignificant," James Baldwin said. "I know a lot of talented ruins. Beyond talent lie all the usual words: discipline, love, luck, but most of all, endurance." Graham Greene said much the same, albeit less bluntly: "Talent, even of a very high order, cannot sustain an achievement, whereas a ruling passion gives to a shelf of novels the unity of a system." Your talent will go to waste unless it is sustained and strengthened by the nagging, jagged, elusive thing called obsession, that stone in the shoe of your being known as a calling, a vocation. Call it dumb persistence. Call it passion. Call it a fire in the belly or the madness of the art. It is less the ability to write than the *insistence* upon writing. It made Anne Frank write in that attic. It made Edith Wharton, on the morning she opened her first acceptance letters (there were three in one delivery), charge up and down the staircase of her house in New York "senselessly and incessantly," just to calm down. It made Proust decide he'd rather write his novel than live. These were driven people. And in your own way, you must be driven, too.

A vocation is obsessive. Many writers—nice people, some of them—go so far as to use the word *ruthless.* A literary vocation is not as easy to define as talent, but it's much harder to miss. "I started out," Katherine Anne Porter said, "with nothing in the world but a kind of passion, a driving desire. I don't know where it came from, and I do not know why—or why I have been so stubborn about it that nothing could deflect me. But this thing between me and my writing is the strongest bond I have ever had—stronger than any bond or any engagement with any human being or with any other work I've ever done." John Irving describes it as a physical need: "I am compulsive about writing, I need to do it the way I need sleep and exercise and food and sex; I can go without it for a while, but then I need it." We are not talking here about "will power" or "discipline." We're talking about what you can't stop yourself from doing. As Betsy Lerner observes, "I assure you, you will never *make* yourself write. When writers say they have no choice, what they mean is: *Everything in the world conspired to make me quit, but I kept going....* If the voices keep calling, if the itch remains, no matter how punishing the work or inhospitable the world, then you must take a long hard look at all the writing you've been attempting to do all your life and commit to it."

Most literary callings announce themselves early. John Dos Passos did not discover his calling to write until after graduate school, but the obsession hit Truman Capote around age eleven; William Styron at thirteen. Susan Sontag was nine. Even though she did not publish her first book until she was forty-two, P. D. James always knew she wanted to write. "I think I was born knowing it.... I think writing was what I wanted to do, almost as soon as I knew what a book was."

"I was solitary," says Robert Stone. "Radio fashioned my imagination. Radio narrative always has to embody a full account of both action and scene. I began to do that myself. When I was seven or eight, I'd walk through Central Park like Sam Spade, describing what I was doing, becoming both the actor and the writer setting him into the scene. That was where I developed an inner ear." P. D. James likewise recalls changing her young life into mental prose: "I did something which other writers have told me they did as children: I described myself inwardly in the third person. 'She brushed her hair and washed her face, then she put on her nightdress . . .' as if I were standing outside myself and observing myself." In his *Autobiography*, Anthony Trollope speaks of how, as a lonely kid—his mother was herself a remarkable writer—he spent weeks and months in fantasy, casting himself as a hero and "obeying certain laws," inventing his own adventures. The small Trollope guarded the space of his daydreams and kept them secret. Yet he learned in his dream land. "I learned in this way to maintain an interest in a fictitious story, to dwell on a work created by my own imagination, and to live in a world altogether outside the world of my own material life."

The surest sign of a literary vocation is its durability. I've often run into former students who have a guilty secret to confide. They have faced the real world. They went to law school. They went to business school. They're married now. They have kids, they have responsibilities. People need them. Some fascinating job came their way, and it is just eating them alive. And just as I am about to congratulate them on the decent and fulfilled life they seem to be living, they break the "bad" news. "I . . . I—uh . . . I don't do much writing anymore. I mean, I tried for a while, but with all the other pressures . . . ." Then they look at the floor. They blush. There's a little stammer of shame.

Shame? Why *shame?* For a person to discover that she or he does *not* have a calling to write can be good news, too. Okay, some old romantic dreams may have to be shelved, but consider the opposite: Consider committing your life and struggling for years in an impossibly difficult, underpaid profession that is not right for you. Ethan Canin went to medical school, and Scott Turow did law school, and their vocations as writers remained intact and thriving through anatomy, organic chemistry, and residency; undeterred by wills, torts, and passing the bar. Meanwhile, three seats away in the lecture hall sat maybe another literary hopeful, astonished to discover herself, or himself, utterly engrossed in medicine or the law and forgetful of old fantasies. That can be finding yourself, too.

Lorrie Moore begins her famous short story "How to Become a Writer" with this blunt recommendation: "First try to be something, anything, else." Though vocations, like talent, can be damaged, they are rather hard to destroy. "I still think," Moore says, "you should become a writer only if you have no choice. Writing has to be an obsession—it's only for those who say, 'I'm not going to do anything else.' "

YOUR TRAINING AS A WRITER

The four prime disciplines of any writer are: *Imagining, Observing, Reading,* and *Writing.* Since these happen to be four things that everyone else also does, you may suppose that you can approach them in the way everyone else does. That would be a mistake.

IMAGINING. It may seem paradoxical to apply the word *discipline* to the imagination, but unlike most people, a writer must learn to hover over the passive experience of imagining, poised for action, waiting to pounce. You start like everybody does, with a daydream: strolling down the street, driving a particularly dull stretch of freeway, taking a shower. Your mind has leaned back with a sigh and is taking a break. Nothing fancy. Pictures appear, tunes, words, scenes come to you unbidden. They come out, they appear, almost unnoticed. Like the evening star, they shine in the dusk of passive permission.

And if you leave them in that dusky passivity, they will drift away and die. "Writing a novel is gathering smoke," says Walter Mosley. "It's an excursion into the ether of ideas." Most people dismiss most of their imaginative life with amused indifference, and maybe even a little contempt. That is where you must part company with most people. Your fantasies are a resource, and the place where they change and mingle in your mind is the place where ideas are conceived. You must catch them, hold them, and exploit them. They will flicker around the edges of your thoughts like moths, and your likely impulse will be to brush them aside. Use that flick of your hand to catch your fluttering thought instead. "There's no time to waste," Mosley says. "You must work with that idea as well as you can, jotting down notes and dialogue. You have to get it down." Some ideas will unfold slowly; and some will dash out ahead of you. Be ready, your notebook at your side. "Sit quietly and think," says John

Braine, "and think at every opportunity. There must be no panic and no hurry. There is no deadline, and you're not dependent upon writing for your daily bread. Put all generalizations out of your head. Don't think in the abstract. See your characters as real people and visualize how they'll meet the reader. Don't think about the plot of the novel; think about specific situations. Aim at making pictures, not notes. Relax and let your mind go free."

The goal is to connect to your excitement and follow the images it generates to something that feels like an end. "Do not think," says Richard Bausch. "Dream." Avoid intellectualizing. Imagining is less a matter of explaining things than seeing them. "Dream the story up, make it up, be fanciful, follow what occurs to you to say, and try not to worry about whether or not it's smart. . . . Just dream it up and let the thing play itself out as it seems to want to, and then write it again, and still again, dreaming it through, and *then* try to be terribly smart about it."

The intellect can *understand* a story—but only the imagination can *tell* it. Always prefer the concrete to the abstract. At this stage it is better to *see* the story, to *hear* and to *feel* it, than to think it. As Walter Mosley says, "These ideas have no physical form. They are smoky concepts liable to disappear at the slightest disturbance. An alarm clock or a ringing telephone will dispel a new character; answering the call will erase a chapter from the world."

REMEMBERING. Remembering is a variety of imagining, and imagining is really a kind of creative remembering. Neither happens without the other. Memory will be essential to your writing even if you never touch the form of memoir. This is because, in prose, memory—and memory alone—bestows concreteness. Memory is your sole path to recovering *exactly* what things look like, feel like, and taste like. Fiction writers, no less than poets, must be what Marianne Moore called "literalists of the imagination" who make "imaginary gardens with real toads in them."

Remembering and imagining are ballast for each other, and every writer's individual balance between the two, her or his private mix, tends to be a defining attribute of his or her style. "What's taken directly from life," says Philip Roth, "helps to place and fix a book's level of reality; it provides something against which to measure what you make up. . . ." Roth's remark is as true for great fantasists like Gabriel García Márquez and Lewis Carroll as it is for committed realists like Theodore Dreiser or Tom Wolfe or (sometimes) Philip Roth himself. The memory of García Márquez's real past in Colombia defined what García Márquez "knew" when he was creating the fantastic village of Macondo. A remembered, real little girl named Alice Liddell led Lewis Carroll straight down the rabbit hole.

"The dreaming self," as Russell Banks points out, "has a more powerful memory than the conscious self." It's in the shadowy regions of latent memory that the files of genuine vividness are stored. Let's suppose you're writing a story in which somebody slaps somebody. You have read about a thousand slaps and seen ten thousand on the screen. Yet unless your life has been an exceptionally gentle one, there is almost certainly at least one real live slap buried somewhere in your memory. That authentic whack—maybe even more than one?—is worth all the images of slaps you have witnessed at an aesthetic distance. It is part of your equipment as a writer, and your task is to retrieve it.

Retrieving memories involves a oddly concentrated kind of passive work. Hemingway had a cot—not unlike a psychoanalyst's couch—where he would lie and reach into the half-remembered past, getting it exactly right. Eileen Simpson did much the same thing writing her memoir "Poets in Their Youth." "I would lie on the couch and try to think my way back to 1947. I would wait and see what came up on the memory screen. . . . It was like waiting under water for a certain species of fish to swim by.

"The effort of trying to recall the past was hard work—every bit as hard as writing. Sometimes an hour would pass and nothing would come. . . . Finally, one day, I remembered with great clarity a Sunday when the Lowells and I went to church together. I saw the inverted funnel of the hat Jean was wearing. I saw 'Cal' Lowell's untied shoelaces. I saw Cal taking me to the cemetery after mass—the cemetery that would later appear in his poem 'The Mills of the Kavanaughs.' "

The process of recovery may reveal all sorts of surprises. The structure of memory is not narrative in form but associative. One memory leads to another not in linear sequence but in clusters. When seen together, these clusters of images can reveal multiple unseen meanings and form a unity. As Vladimir Nabokov wrote, "I witness with pleasure the supreme achievement of memory, which is the masterly use it makes of innate harmonies when gathering to its fold the suspended and wandering tonalities of the past." After summoning up one of the lost and distant places of his own past—his boyhood schoolroom—Nabokov paused in *Speak, Memory* to reflect on the vividness he had recovered. "That robust reality makes a ghost of the present. The mirror brims with brightness; a bumblebee has entered the room and bumps against the ceiling. Everything is as it should be, nothing will ever change, nobody will ever die."

OBSERVING. Most of us, most of the time, shunt most of what we notice into the same recycling bin where we dump what we imagine. Luckily for writers, at least a little of what we dump there can be retrieved and recycled. Once you are at work, most of the memories that serve you will be pulled from your vast back file of the half-noticed and half-forgotten. As a writer you must observe the unobserved. The details that give life and vividness are seen mostly out of the corner of your eye. Hemingway spoke of training himself to do precisely this: "Searching for the unnoticed things that made emotions, such as the way an outfielder tossed his glove without looking back to where it fell, the squeak of resin on canvas under a fighter's flat-soled gym shoes, the gray color of Jack Blackburn's skin when he had just come out of stir, and other things I noted as a painter sketches."

"*Noted* as a painter sketches." Organizing and retaining some useful part of what you observe will take some focused remembering and creative note taking. Chekhov's breakthrough as an artist came with his first great novella, *The Steppe: The History of a Journey.* One of Chekhov's biographers, David Magarshack, says that in *The Steppe,* Chekhov began consciously to build his work on material taken directly from life. In 1887, Chekhov decided to revisit the wretched little town on the Black Sea, a place called Taganrog, where he'd spent the first part of his unhappy childhood. Before departing, Chekhov made a deal with his sister Marya. Every day, he would write her one long letter retelling the details of that day's travel. Because he and Marya had shared that unhappy childhood, she was an ideal recipient: Marya gave Chekhov just the focus he needed. Because they were letters, his "notes" could not be mere jottings. They had to be *written,* made coherent, for somebody else. When he got home, Marya handed him that thick packet of observations, and with his letters arrayed before him, Chekhov wrote *The Steppe.*

You are looking for what you can put into words. If you are a screenwriter, you want to make what you see into scenes and dialogue. If you're a critic, you're trying to turn what you've noticed into evocations and insight. If you are a reporter, you are transforming it into news. But if you are a fiction writer, you are looking for a *narrative.* All kinds of people will observe the world just as well—often better—than you do, if only because they are trained in some discipline. Think of how a doctor is trained to observe, or a lawyer, or a cop in a cruiser, or a lifeguard or a cat burglar or a kindergarten teacher. Each has her or his own kind of expert eye. You must observe as a *writer.* You are noticing what imparts vividness, feeling, and meaning. You are, like Hemingway, isolating "the unnoticed things that make emotions." But above all, you are looking for *prose.*

Once your unconscious mind has really begun to focus on a given project, it is likely that your powers of observation will focus with it and seem to be suddenly transformed. Things that fit your project seem to pop up everywhere you look. The project becomes a kind of lens that gives the mind an uncanny ability to organize randomness with an inner focus that will make what matters jump out at you from every side. Suddenly, the world seems to overflow with what you need. "When I'm writing," says Edmund White, "I find that my brain begins to store information in a different way than it usually does. That is, I'm out looking for things that I need, and I will grab them anywhere. And there's a magic which any writer can tell you about: The world provides you with just the information you need, it seems, just when you need it."

Consider Anthony Trollope's jovial wisdom: "Unless it be given to him to listen and to observe,—so to carry away, as it were, the manners of people in his memory, as to be able to say to himself with assurance that these words might have been said in a given position, and those other words could not have been said,—I do not think that in these days he can succeed as a novelist."

Or as Hemingway put it, "If a writer stops observing, he is finished."

READING. Asked whether she had always wanted to be a writer, Toni Morrison replied, "I wanted to be a reader.... I only wrote the first book because I thought it wasn't there...."

Frankly, there is something suspect—even bewildering—in the nonreader who claims she or he wants to write. Do you really want to play baseball if you hate watching the game? "If I had a nickel," says Stephen King, "for every person who told me he/she wanted to become a writer but 'didn't have time to read,' I could buy myself a pretty good steak dinner. Can I be blunt on this subject? If you don't have time to read, you don't have the time (or the tools) to write. Simple as that. Reading is the creative center of a writer's life."

Reading and writing are, in fact, so intimate that they almost merge. "I read fiction," says Philip Roth, "to be freed from my own suffocatingly narrow perspective on life and to be lured into imaginative sympathy with a fully developed narrative point of view not my own. It's the same reason that I write." Eudora Welty carried this intimacy one step further: "Indeed, learning to write may be part of learning to read." Stravinsky remarked that all art is a collaboration between the artist and the audience. Writing is accomplished not for but *through* the reader. As Percy Lubbock noted, "The reader must... become, for his part, a novelist, never permitting himself to suppose that the creation of the book is solely the affair of the author. The difference between them is immense of course. . . . But in one quarter their work coincides; both of them make the novel." To be sure, the reader follows the writer's lead; but only the reader's imagination, collaborating with the writer's, can make anything happen on any page. It's the reader who visualizes the characters, the reader who feels and finds the forward movement of the story, the reader who catches and is caught in the swirls of suspense, rides the flow of meaning, and unfolds the whole kaleidoscope of perception. Reading is as close to writing as singing is to all other music. Whether we do or don't literally hum along, whenever we are *really* hearing, we are also, somehow, singing in our minds.

And please, don't sink into this woeful nonsense about not having time to read. Find it. Make it. How much time each day do you give to TV? To the daily paper? The crossword? The real culprit here is almost never your schedule. It is your *boredom*—your boredom with the books you think you are *supposed* to read. Find a book you want, a book that gives you real trembling excitement, a book that is hot in your hands, and you'll have time galore. All serious education necessarily involves a certain amount of obligatory reading. That is how it has to be and exactly as it ought to be. Yet this essential aspect of growth does have a dangerous downside: It can darken all reading under the dull shadow of obligation. At a certain moment in your life as a writer, you should resolve to read only what really matters to you. Not what people *say* should matter. What *does*. You should seek that out relentlessly, find it, and then you should read and read and read.

That is your only hope of ever developing a decent individual style. To begin, reading alone trains you for correct usage, getting the words right. This is no minor matter: The lack of correctness is the lack of communication. If you misuse the language, people will not understand you. You must know exactly what words mean and exactly how to use them. *Fowler's Modern English Usage* (in the Burchfield revision) should never be more than two feet from your desk, nestled beside an absolutely first-rate dictionary. But you are also reading to hear the whole music of the language, be it high or low. For low style, listen in the streets and to whatever captures their music. As for the rest, opt for the classics, beginning but never ending with Shakespeare and the Bible.

Include a steady diet of poetry. "Read poetry," says Ray Bradbury, "every day of your life. Poetry is good because it flexes muscles that you don't use often enough. Poetry expands the senses and keeps them in prime condition. . . . Ideas lie everywhere through the poetry books, yet how rarely have I heard short story teachers recommending them for browsing."

Above all, read to chase down your real interests and expand what you "know." As a writer, you *are* your interests. They must be fed and developed even when you don't know where they are going to lead. Whenever a new interest digs into his mind with enough tenacity, Michael Crichton opens a file and starts reading. The books beside his bed pile up. Where will it lead? Maybe nowhere, or maybe a novel, three books down the road. "I think of it as farming," says Crichton. "I have these seeds planted and eventually, after many years usually, there's a crop I can harvest. The subjective experience is: I start to think more and more about a particular subject, and I can't let go."

Read to mark and to learn; read also to forget. The preconscious mind is a great editor. It has its own mysterious way of adding to what you know and eliminating what does not matter. This is what Gabriel García Márquez has in mind as he describes the process he went through preparing himself for *The Autumn of the Patriarch*. "I read everything I could find about Latin American dictators of the last century, and the beginning of this one. I also talked to a lot of people who had lived under dictatorships. I did that for at least ten years. And when I had a clear idea of what the character was going to be like, I made an effort to forget everything that I had read and heard, so that I could invent, without using any situation that had occurred in real life."

Read for love. Every writer ought to fall in love with some new writer or work with fair regularity, and the passion should hit with a fervor that makes each new book a hot date and every stolen fifteen minutes of browsing an intoxicated rendezvous. Only love can join another writer to your own being. Love makes you *reread*, and it is in rereading that the really deep events take place. In time, of course, these ecstasies can and should fade. After passion you become . . . just good friends. Or maybe not such good friends. But "being swept away," says Stephen King, "by a combination of great story and great writing—of being flattened, in fact—is part of every writer's necessary formation. You cannot hope to sweep someone else away by the force of your writing until it has been done to you."

This love can't be faked, not inside your own soul. Yet among those who are merely trying to impress, it is of course faked all the time. At my university, we foolishly used to ask applicants for a list of the writers and books that had "influenced" them. This is not an entirely fair question to ask any writer, but for a board of academics to spring it on a bunch of young, inexperienced, aspiring writers was madness. Of *course* the answers we got were mainly intended to impress. The question became the single most insincere item in the entire application—bypassing the mendaciousness even of professorial letters of recommendation. The lists we got were almost always very grand, academically impeccable, and exactly the same: that year's higher-than-highbrow list of what every applicant assumed a bunch of professors wanted to see. We should have been ashamed. We were doing people damage by inducing them to lie about their real tastes and their real identities, leading them into a form of self-betrayal that at worst can be a symptom of self-contempt. Dishonesty about what *really* pleases your imagination is outright dangerous to you as a writer.

WRITING. A writer writes. Constantly. Obsessively. Every chance she or he gets. "Write, write, write—till your fingers break," Chekhov advised one aspirant. "Write on all sorts of subjects, funny and tearful, good and bad.... Write a story at one go...." To another he wrote: "You are a 'beginner'... and you must not forget that every line you write now constitutes your capital of the future. If you do not train your mind and your hand to discipline and forced marches now, you will find that in three or four years it will be too late.... You must force yourself to work for hours every day. You work too little."

Productivity is the *only* path to confidence. The young William Kennedy studied writing with the young Saul Bellow. "Bellow," Kennedy recalls, "also talked about being prodigal. He said that a writer shouldn't be parsimonious with his work, but 'prodigal, like nature.'" Curiously, Chekhov once remarked that his brother Aleksandr had "written himself out" by producing not too much but too *little*. This is not an empty paradox. Since writing is what generates inspiration—and not the reverse—abundant writing produces abundant inspiration. The two most dangerous enemies of a young writer's productivity are his or her mismanagement of time and an undue vulnerability to self-doubt and self-criticism. Both must be dealt with firmly. Paul Johnson is right: "A bad novel is better than an unwritten novel, because a bad novel can be improved; an unwritten novel is defeat without a battle. A writer as long as he lives faces the difficulty of striking a balance between an overcritical view of his work and complacency. In my view, a young writer should err on the side of complacency while he is writing, then sit in judgment afterwards. He must keep the typewriter going, and watch the pile of blank pages on his right gradually diminish and filled pages on his left rise. Thereby he acquires confidence, and in writing, as in all art, confidence is the beginning of skill."

In the first chapter, I pushed you to begin. Here I am going to push you to finish. Cultivate whatever serves your persistence. Sometimes—many times—the muse appears wearing the mask of a deadline: It is a pity that more fiction writers are not subject to them. In my twenty years of teaching, I saw students miss a workshop deadline—that is, just not show up or show up with nothing—four, maybe five times. Maximum. Almost always, when we all gathered, waiting, in that classroom, there was *something* on the table. It wasn't always wonderful, and it wasn't always new. But it was there.

The next best thing to an enforceable deadline is a daily word count. All kinds of mentors recommend it—even insist upon it. John Braine suggested 350. Stephen King thinks 1,000 is starting slow, "and because I'm feeling magnanimous," he says, "I'll also suggest that you take one day a week off, at least to begin with. No more; you'll lose the urgency and immediacy of your story if you do." Tom Wolfe does around 1,800. "I set myself a quota," Wolfe says. "Ten pages a day, triple-spaced, which means about eighteen hundred words. If I can finish that in three hours, then I'm through for the day. I just close up the lunch box and go home—that's the way I think of it anyway. If it takes me twelve hours, that's too bad, I've got to do it. To me the idea 'I'm going to work for six hours' is of no use. I can waste time as handily at the desk as I can window-shopping, which is one of my favorite diversions."

A daily word quota, religiously observed, may not be for everybody, but it can move mountains. Anthony Trollope, perhaps the most productive English novelist of his era, explained his own simple method in his *Autobiography*. Whenever he began a book, Trollope set himself an absolutely *realistic* deadline for finishing it, based on two things most writers don't come close to having: an exact estimate of his own ability to produce and an exact estimate of the length of the book. The resulting deadline was one he never—*never*—failed to meet. He would create a diary and mark off the days "so that if at any time I have slipped into idleness for a day or two, the record of that idleness has been there, staring me in the face. . . . an insufficient number of pages has been a blister to my eye, and a month so disgraced would have been a sorrow to my heart.

"Nothing surely," Trollope concluded, "is so potent as a law that may not be disobeyed. It has the force of the waterdrop that hollows the stone. A small daily task, if it be really daily, will beat the labours of a spasmodic Hercules. It is the tortoise which always catches the hare."

A WRITER'S TIME

Seneca said it first: *Ars longa; vita brevis.* Art is long and life is short. Except for the miraculous times when it doesn't, EVERY-THING YOU WRITE WILL TAKE LONGER THAN YOU THINK IT SHOULD. What's more, not one of your readers will ever give a damn if you wrote your story in half an hour or half a year. Are you Trollope? Can you *reliably* produce a daily word quota and *reliably* estimate the length of your project? If not, the schedule for any project you undertake should probably be expanded by 50 percent over what you think is right. Mentor after mentor raises the same cry: "There isn't a moment to lose!" As Hemingway put it, "The time to work is shorter all the time, and if you waste it you feel you have committed a sin for which there is no forgiveness."

You must learn to mark off, manage, and defend your work

time. "Find the time to write," says Ann Beattie. "Protect the time to write. Be inventive: get gorgons. Forget e-mail. Whatever it takes. Because you'll still need more time than there is, and also it's important to leave enough time to waste."

If you are still kidding yourself about the glamour of this business, a serious work schedule will fix you. "It's work," says Philip Roth, "just endless work. There isn't time for any bullshit. I just have to work all the time, very hard, and cut everything else out. . . . I write from about ten till six every day, with a hour out for lunch and the newspaper. In the evenings I usually read. That's pretty much it." Legend has it that Balzac chained himself to his coffee urn, and it's rumored that John Cheever sometimes tied himself to his chair. "I'm always reluctant to start work," says Gore Vidal, "and reluctant to stop." Don't stand around, sticking your toe into the pool all day. The water may be frigid, but dive in now. You'll get used to it finally, and with any luck time will melt away. "The most interesting thing about writing," says Vidal, "is the way that it obliterates time. Three hours seem like three minutes." And schedule your work time when your mind is fittest and most free. "To give the best of the day to your work," says John le Carré, "is most important." Recalling the years when he still had his day job with British Intelligence, le Carré adds: "I was always very careful to give my country second-best."

WRITE EVERY DAY? Many writers will tell you, as Chekhov told novices, to work every day. I would tell you the same thing if I didn't know about so many excellent and even quite productive writers who do not write every day. I still think every day is best. Thomas Mann worked every day without exception, weekends, Christmas, holidays, and vacations included. Does this sound dreary? One of the most glamorous writer-actors of the twentieth century, Noël Coward, sat at his typewriter in a solitary room working from 8:00 A.M. to 1:00 P.M. Monday to Saturday, every week of his working life. Then, at the stroke of 1:00, he would step out of the monkish cell of his creative solitude and turn into Noël Coward, star.

"If you want to be a writer," says Walter Mosley, "you have to write every day. The consistency, the monotony, the certainty, all vagaries and passions are covered by this daily recurrence. You don't go to a well once but daily. You don't skip a child's breakfast or forget to wake up in the morning. Sleep comes to you every day, and so does the muse."

Yet there *are* exceptions. If you have a day job and kids, there are going to be many days in which you cannot find even half an hour. "I am not able to write regularly," Toni Morrison explains. "I have never been able to do that—mostly because I have always had a nine-to-five job. I had to write either in between those hours, hurriedly, or spend a lot of weekend and predawn time. [Writing after work] was difficult. I've tried to overcome not having orderly spaces by substituting compulsion for discipline, so that when something is urgently there, urgently seen or understood, or the metaphor was powerful enough, then I would move everything aside and write for sustained periods of time."

Neither does Susan Sontag work every day, though Sontag's reasons are different from Morrison's. "I write in spurts. I write when I have to because the pressure builds up and I feel enough confidence that something has matured in my head and I can write it down. But once something is really under way, I don't want to do anything else. I don't go out, much of the time I forget to eat, I sleep very little. It's a very undisciplined way of working and makes me not very prolific. But I'm too interested in many other things. . . . Writing requires huge amounts of solitude. What I've done to soften the harshness of that choice is that I don't write all the time. I like to go out—which includes traveling; I can't write when I travel."

Edmund White is outright impatient with the write-every-day rule: "Writers say . . . things that strike me as nonsense. One is that you must follow an absolute schedule every day. If you're not writing well, why continue it? I just don't think this grinding away is useful."

I've known productive teacher-novelists (teacher-scholars too) who do not even *try* to write while classes are running. While others bask in all those delicious "vacations" of American academic life, they become galley slaves. And when do they take their own vacations?

They don't.

Whatever it is, find your rhythm, learn to work anywhere, and brush aside all obstacles. "You can write any time people will leave you alone and not interrupt you," Hemingway remarked. "Or rather you can if you will be ruthless enough about it." Richard Bausch advises that you "teach yourself to work in busy places, under the barrage of noises the world makes—work in rooms where children are playing, with music on, even with the television on." Watch out for e-mail and that telephone. Like many people in this chronically solitary trade, you are quite possibly a gregarious soul. Almost every writer I know loves to talk. "You lead a dangerously interesting life," Joyce Carol Oates once remarked to a talented but unproductive colleague. For all its inner excitement, the writer's life is ascetic and solitary. You are going to be spending almost all your working life alone in a bare little cell. True, the day job that you will almost certainly need may relieve the solitude. But it will increase the pressure. You will have to carve writing time from the corners of exhaustion and self-denial, and defend it from competing claims that will flow unendingly from family and friends, from your own enthusiasms and—not least—from your own impulse to escape.

Most people won't get it and won't help. One of Thomas Mann's more censorious biographers, noting that the German master's children used to stare, silent and awestruck, at the closed door of their father's study, invokes that closed door as a symbol of Mann's self-absorbed and narcissistic mind. This is unfair. Only writers, it seems, are expected to beg forgiveness for having a time-consuming job. "Ask a doctor to be a doctor two hours a day," John Irving snaps. "Your friends and family," says David Bradley, "may honestly want you to do what you want to do, but they also want you to do what they want you to do. They want you to do things for them. Worse, they want you to do things *with* them—go to lunch, go for a drink, go to the movies. They may accept it if you say you don't have time for a while, but they'll want to know how long it's going to be. They will probably not accept the answer a writer *has* to give: It may be quite a while. In fact, it may be forever."

The painful truth is that to function as a writer you must choose what to sacrifice. Of course, those you love will have priority. Nadine Gordimer draws a sharp distinction between the demands of family life and social life. "I think writers, artists, are very ruthless, and they have to be. It's unpleasant for other people, but I don't know how else we can manage. Because the world will never make a place for you. My own family came to understand and respect this. . . . What I have also sacrificed, and it hasn't been a sacrifice for me, is a social life. . . . A writer doesn't only need the time when he's actually writing—he or she has got to have time to think and time just to let things work out. Nothing is worse for this than society. Nothing is worse for this than the abrasive, if enjoyable, effect of other people."

"There is no known excuse for not working," adds Richard Bausch, "*when you are supposed to be working. Remember that it is* an absurdity to put writing *before* the life you have to lead—and I'm not talking about leisure. I'm talking about the responsibility you have to the people you love, and who love you back—no arduousness in the craft or art should ever occupy one second of the time you are supposed to be spending with your family."

Meanwhile the nature of your workday will change at varying stages of any project. At every stage, it is essential to maintain momentum. When you are moving through a draft, the pause of even a few days, not to mention a week or more, can be decimating. Hemingway kept the rhythm steady by stopping, always, at a moment when he was sure what would come next. Somerset Maugham invariably left the desk in midsentence. So did Andre Dubus: "I learned from Hemingway to stop each day's work in midsentence, while it is still going well, then to exercise the body, and not to think about the story till you go to your desk the next day." The project's continuity must be kept at a level that is refreshed daily, even hourly. "I have formed the habit," says Nadine Gordimer, "... of spending half an hour or so reading over what I'd written during the day just before I go to bed at night. Then, of course, you get tempted to fix it up, fuss with it, at night. But I find that's good."

Never stray very far from the task. *"Be open for business,"* says Richard Bausch, "all the time."

HAVING TWO JOBS. Face it: Even if you are quite successful, it will be hard to maintain a decent income strictly through your work. So make your peace with the need to make your living elsewhere—and make the most of it. The most famous physician-writer of them all, Chekhov, said, "I feel more confident and more satisfied when I reflect that I have two professions and not one. Medicine is my faithful wife, and literature is my mistress. When I get tired of one, I spend the night with the other. Though it is disorderly it's not so dull, and besides, neither really loses anything through my infidelity." A simple list of distinguished and productive writers who had another job while writing would fill not only this page but also many pages after it, all in fine print. Moreover, much in your job is likely to serve your writing, too. Please understand; I do not mean this advice to sound complacent. Of *course*, dividing your time and resources between two things is hard. Of *course*, it would be wonderful not to feel necessity's sharp pinch. You will undoubtedly many times bitterly resent the all-but-impossible claims each job will make against the other. "One luxury of making enough money to support myself as a writer," says John Irving, "is that I can afford to have those eight-, nine-, and twelve-hour days. I resented having to teach and coach, not because I disliked teaching and coaching or wrestling but because I had no time to write."

Yet it is a fatal error to permit your writing and your day job to become enemies. Must the young writer see law school as a defeat? Only if she or he sees it that way. Lawyer-writers like Scott Turow, Louis Auchincloss, Louis Begley, and John Mortimer all admit to the crucial influence of their profession on their work as artists. When Turow went to law school after leaving the writing program at Stanford, he did not abandon his calling as a writer. He found it. "Engaging the jury was indispensable," Turow says of his early training before the bar, "and again and again I received the same advice about how to do it: Tell them a good story. There were plenty of good stories told in the courtroom, vivid accounts of crimes witnessed or conspiracies joined. The jury hung in primal fascination, waiting to find out what happened next. And so did I." John Mortimer speaks of precisely the same experience: "You have to tell the story to the jury or to the judge *very*, very simply. . . . You may have to assemble the facts of some very, very complicated cases and narrate them in a way that will *arrest* [the jury]. So that's good training for a writer." Even politics, that most gregarious of all professions, can sometimes merge with the most solitary. Benjamin Disraeli was a working novelist who became prime minister of England. James Webb, whose novel *Fields of Fire* Tom Wolfe calls "to my mind, the best of the Vietnam novels," was Ronald Reagan's secretary of the navy. As his memoir *'Tis* makes clear, Frank McCourt could never have written *Angela's Ashes* until he had opened up and grown up, standing in front of his students in New York City high school classrooms. "I taught at Stuyvesant for eighteen years. That's where I learned to drop the mask." Jon Scieszka, once he got his MFA, was in debt and unpublished. He got himself a job teaching second grade. And it was there—not in grown-up school—talking day after day to a roomful of seven-year-olds, that Scieszka found himself as a writer, emerging as one of the most successful authors of children's books in his generation.

Your other job can serve you only if it does not consume you. One of my strongest students of the early '90s put himself through our too-expensive MFA in a much-envied job as a personal assistant and scriptwriter for one of the most famous broadcast news personalities in the country. Here was an MFA writing student who was also in the dead center of every major breaking story; being swept around the world from hot spot to hot spot; meeting some of the most well-known people in the world, and on twenty-four-hour call that came all too often. His glamour job ate him alive. Glamour jobs have a way of doing that. "I finally took a look at my roommates, guys who'd made it a *point* to get nothing jobs—sub-sub-boring stuff. Their fiction was surging ahead while I was heading straight toward burnout."

This leads us to journalism. It's a weakness of most MFA writing programs in America to disdain journalism and leave their students clueless and incompetent before journalism's special opportunities and demands. The notion that journalism and "serious writing" are antithetical is an absurd, unhistorical, academic myth. The two realms have always overlapped, and they will continue to do so. Virginia Woolf worked as a literary journalist, often anonymously, all her professional life. So did Henry James. "I've always been convinced," says Gabriel García Márquez, "that my true profession is that of a journalist. What I didn't like about journalism before were the working conditions. Besides, I had to condition my thoughts and ideas to the interests of the newspaper. Now, after having worked as a novelist, and having achieved financial independence as a novelist, I can really choose the themes that interest me and correspond to my ideas. In any case, I always very much enjoy the chance of doing a great piece of journalism." García Márquez rejects the notion that there is an essential difference between journalism and "serious writing." "I don't think there is any difference. The sources are the same, the resources and the language are the same. *Journal of the Plague Year* is a great novel, and *Hiroshima* is a great work of journalism." Tom Wolfe took part in a transformation of the journalistic profession and has repeatedly skewered snobbish "literary" disdain for the journalism that taught him his artistic method. Does journalism feel beneath you? Listen to Martin Amis: "I think you have a duty to contribute, to go on contributing to what Gore Vidal calls 'book chat.' . . . I have no admiration for writers who think they can wash their hands of book chat. You should be part of the ongoing debate."

HOW HARD IT IS

A writer's life is hard. Everybody says so, and everybody is right. All the fabled difficulties of the trade are the reason you'll be needing your vocation, needing its oxlike persistence, its wily ingenuity, its irrational refusal to accept no. Yet let's not accentuate the negative *too* much. If you are lucky, writing will be and will remain your greatest pleasure; intense, surprising, a kind of lifelong love story.

Early in my teaching career, my sometimes-lugubrious sense of moral obligation convinced me that I should devote one session of every workshop term to laying out all the hard truths of the writer's life. It seemed to me that I had to level with the students. Tell them about the numbing, humiliating rejections; the poor or nonexistent money; the probability of failure; that knife with the special twist: partial success. I never *liked* delivering these dreary little monologues, but I thought I owed them to the students. Gosh, unless I tell them the truth, won't they be, well . . . *deluded? Misled?*

So once a term I would plow into how hard it was going to be.

"Even if your book is finally accepted, you'll have a new set of difficulties. . . ." And as I spoke, something terrible would be happening all around me. All the trust, all the rapport, all the carefully nurtured buoyancy that had been built up over the term would simply drain out of the room. I noticed the change, of course, but I was determined to do my duty. I droned on; I expanded on the ravages of rejection and fear. Bill X, always so attentive, had started to loudly chomp on some gum and was rolling his eyes toward the ceiling. Marisol B., the smoldering dark horse in the room, was, inch by inch, sinking down in her seat, crunching into a nauseated sulk. Irrepressible Dave, the babbling class wit, always so much fun, had drawn up one knee and was resting his chin on it, staring out the window, stolid, firm-jawed, and insolent. No matter: I was telling them *the truth*.

At last one nervy student fixed me. We were in a private conference. "Professor Koch, there's something you don't seem to *understand*. I know you mean well and everything, but all this stuff about how we'll never get anywhere, how we'll never make a dime, how nobody will ever give a damn—you think you're bringing us some sort of *news*? Handing us something we haven't *heard*? Every single one of us has an uncle out there who has been telling us those exact same things *all our lives*. Yeah, maybe you know more and say it better, but basically you are saying just exactly what those uncles always said. We've been hearing it nonstop from the minute we read that book that blew us away and made us want to be writers. Every one of us has always had somebody telling us and telling us and *telling* us, 'Forget it, it can't work, you'll fail.' You're wondering who's going tell us how hard it is? Who's going to warn us about failure? *Everybody*, that's who. What we need is somebody, just *one* person—like maybe *you*—who for *once* isn't telling us that, who for *once* says it's hard, but it's possible. Who says go ahead. Who says it's a great thing to do, the best, nothing better, so be brave and do it. Who's not looking at us like a bunch of unrealistic self-indulgent brats who should all just throw in the towel and turn into good little boys and girls and go off to law school and grow up. You're scared we're deluded? Okay, right. We're deluded. But do us a favor. Leave us deluded. Because we're going ahead."

It was the best lesson I ever had from a student, and it cured me. I have ever since left the dreary duty of telling writers how hard and miserable their life is going to be to somebody—excuse me, to *everybody*—else.

3

SHAPING THE STORY

Beginning writers of fiction are beset by every imaginable kind of anxiety, but in my experience the single most damaging fear they are likely to feel is a fear of storytelling itself. I've watched that fear attack and undermine young writers' confidence a hundred times, even—sometimes especially—when they are unusually talented. Again and again, young writers, who when I saw them last were flying high on a new idea—excited, inspired, working hard—would come into my office looking pale. They would close the door firmly behind them and sit down, steeled to confess their dark secret. That dark secret was that something was missing from the package of their literary gift: *They just could not make up a story.* The mere word *story* immobilized them as headlights immobilize the deer. The dreaded monosyllable *plot* worked on them like Kryptonite: Flash it before them, and they would slump down helpless. Sometimes this confession seemed covered in shame. Weren't they deluding themselves as writers? A fiction writer who can't invent a narrative is ridiculous: like a swimmer who can't dive, a musician who can't carry a tune. Other times, I was pretty sure I caught a glimmer of pride in the confessor's eyes. Okay, maybe they *were* having trouble with their plot. So what? Isn't there something low-class about storytelling anyway? Doesn't "plot-driven" prose have a reputation for being a little—uh—commercial? Maybe their deficiency in storytelling was actually proof of their good taste. After all, hadn't Henry James himself several times called plots "vulgar"? Maybe it didn't really *matter* that they just could not turn their project into a story.

I was still in the early years of teaching when, after witnessing the rush of this self-destructive fear and its rationalization maybe fifty or sixty times, I began to grasp that the problem might be less about some hypothetical "defect" in all these talented young people and more about some larger problem they shared, some elusive mystery of the art itself. Here was a set of very different yet gifted young people, all seemingly afflicted with exactly the same problem. And I simply did not believe that they all somehow were suffering from some innate incapacity as storytellers, even though they all kept saying, over and over, "I can't do plots!" This was, I suspected, nothing but a self-fulfilling prophecy. Yet clearly things were going badly. They kept circling around some situation, or character, or image, or obsession. It suggested a story to them, but try as they might, they could not get at it. It was smoke. When they reached for it, it was gone. And it was driving them to distraction.

All too many of these novices believed that *real* writers—the happy few—concocted stories through some magic process denied to lesser mortals like themselves. Stories came to "real writers"—that mystery elite—complete, perfect, and intricate from the moment of inspiration onward. *Real* writers had only to wish for a story and that "real" gift of theirs would fly on wings of uncanny wit straight to some wonderful fiction. *They* would never end up in somebody's office, clutching a pile of pages without a story, some mess that proved only that they were not "real" writers at all. My students felt cheated. They were *almost* "real" writers. They were close—but no deal. This one fateful gift had somehow got left out of their genome. They lacked the one thing they needed most.

This was almost always simple nonsense. These writers were not suffering from any defect in their talent. They weren't even suffering from the absence of a story. They were suffering from the tantalizing, maddening *presence* of a story that they could not reach or get within their grasp. They were being tortured by the *nearness* of narrative they couldn't yet get into words or even define except in the vaguest kind of way. They were suffering from *almost* possessing a story to which they had no access. *Yet.*

And they had started out so well. Some character or situation or image or place had aroused their imagination and made them feel there "might be a story in it." They had plunged in. Good things had happened. Characters appeared, pages piled up. Sometimes the prose was really pretty nice. There were strong moments, good lines. But there wasn't much of a story yet. Each day's work began without much story, and each day ended, a little glumly, without much more. When they had been through enough days like that, inspiration began to falter, then to flicker into fear. They'd told their friends that they were writing something, and their friends had naturally asked what it was about. And they hadn't known quite . . . what to say. "Well, it's a story about . . . about . . ." They would fumble. Some lame excuse would rise to their lips. They would stare into puzzled faces. It was mortifying. They did not know their own story. They couldn't even produce a good line about it. And it was making them feel just plain nuts, and making their precious inspiration look like just plain nonsense.

Story panic! Story despair!

Which made them come to see me.

In chapter 1, we pointed out that the Latin root of the word *invent* means "to discover." Writers do not make up stories. They *find* them. They *un*cover them; they *dis*cover them. Sometimes they find them in the real world. Sometimes they find them in the depths of their imaginations. In either case, they invent stories *by* finding them and, conversely, they find those very same stories *by* inventing them. Which comes first? That's the elusive part—the interplay between making it up and digging it up. Your imagination will not always know the difference.

The people in my office had failed either to grasp or to remember this. In their panic, they had forgotten that making up their story was a search. Instead, they were trying to "make it up" out of more or less thin air. But there wasn't any story waiting for them in thin air. Since they were not looking for it in the right place, they were naturally not finding anything at all.

The search for a story is a matter of slowly, calmly, carefully, tentatively coaxing a hidden set of somethings into visibility: Those somethings may be characters, places, situations, scenes, hopes, fears—the unseen possibilities of drama that are lurking under what we know. Once your imagination has been aroused, you usually know or sense the presence of these elements clustering around what you intuitively recognize in some obscure, preverbal, wordless way. Each of them needs to be slowly, carefully brought out into the open and put into language. It is a process of discovery, and it rarely happens easily or quickly. Most of the time it is the longest, slowest, most delicate part of the entire process of writing. My panicky students didn't know that "real" writers are likely to be still searching for the basic elements of a shadowy and elusive story until a very late stage, often finding themselves adding crucial touches and even major turns up until the very last moments of work. Very verbal people have a hard time tolerating being speechless over something that excites them, and the people sitting in my office were mainly verbal people who were speechless over a story they could not put into words. *Yet.* They did not know that storytelling—all storytelling—begins in precisely this speechlessness.

GETTING ACCESS TO YOUR STORY

The way—the only way—to "find" your story is to tell it. Nobody in the whole world has ever before told the story you are about to tell. You yourself have never told it to anyone, not even to yourself. You may have lots of intuitions about what the story is going to be, and you may even have a sort of summary overview of it. These are good and useful things to have; they are fine places to start. They are not enough. Until you actually tell the story, the *whole* story, it will be nothing but smoke. Moreover, you probably will not tell the story exactly right the first time you try. You'll make wrong turns, use the wrong key, or use the right key in the wrong door. After all, you have nobody to guide you. If you are like most people, you will have to tell this story more than once—maybe even several times—before you really get it down.

Be prepared for this process of trial and error to take a while. In the earliest phases, working with the germ of the story, you probably won't know much of anything about what is to come. All kinds of hints and hopes and possibilities will be flying around your imagination. But no story. That's fine. No journalist beginning to investigate a news event would apologize for not knowing the story *yet*. Is your situation really so different? True, you are digging up your story from different ground, using a different kind of research. Some of it comes from the world. Some comes from your imagination. But it all takes digging. Like some Woodward and Bernstein of the imagination, at the beginning all you see is perhaps one small corner of something big.

But how do you "know" what you are looking for? What's so hard to grasp at first is that you can intuitively "know" your story long before you are in any position to *tell* it. The imaginative arousal that makes you begin working in the first place—that "throb"—is likely to reveal no more than a cryptic corner, a fragment of the story to come. You sense its importance, but you could no more give us its whole buried narrative shape than a dreamer can predict tonight's dream, or a singer hum a tune she has never heard. The story, like the dream, is somewhere waiting to happen, but it's nothing you can talk about. *Yet.*

You must learn to tolerate this admittedly uncomfortable but preliminary, inarticulate state of mind. You'll be flying at first on a wing and a prayer. The wing is your excitement; the prayer is your faith—faith that your imagination has been aroused by something significant enough to become a story. You can't see it yet. Once aroused, your imagination will be on a search. You need to believe that it has been aroused by something real, and that that something is bigger, maybe much bigger, than the perplexing fragment you can see now; that the fragment is only part of something *already in your imagination,* waiting to be found and dug out, like the thigh bone of a dinosaur. "The writer's job," says Stephen King, " is to . . . get as much of each one out of the ground intact as possible. Sometimes the fossil you uncover is small: a seashell. Sometimes it's enormous, a *Tyrannosaurus Rex* with all those gigantic ribs and grinning teeth. Either way, short story or thousand-page whopper of a novel, the techniques of excavation remain basically the same."

Robertson Davies began his novel *Fifth Business* with nothing but the mental image of some boys on a street in a cold Canadian village having a snowball fight. "I hesitate to talk about this," Davies explained, "because it sounds mystical and perhaps rather absurd, but I assure you it is not: The minute I recognized that the picture meant something I should pay attention to, the whole thing began to come to life, and I knew who the boys were, and I knew what the situation was, and I quickly became aware of what lay behind it. Some of it had to be invented, some of it had to be fetched up and rejected—a great deal is rejected in the course of such work—but it was all there as soon as I began to work."

Davies was speaking of how it is possible to "know" and *not* "know" your story *at the same time*. It may indeed sound a little mystical, but leaving aside the vexed question of the literal pre-existence of your story (in what sense does a dream preexist its dreaming?), I can assure you it is exactly what the process often *feels* like. And it is not the result of some bizarre psychic visitation, but a quite ordinary mental process.

Let me illustrate just how ordinary it is. If you're like most people, you already "know," more or less vaguely, the story of your mother and father's courtship. It's a personal tale, a chapter from the family romance, and though you may never have told it *to* anyone, even to yourself, you do "know" it—sort of.

That story has various aspects, and you can only "know" them in various ways. For example, you've doubtless heard your parents' official version a thousand times. You may accept this account as accurate and complete—or you may have your doubts. There may be certain details, or even important parts of the story, that hover in the shadows and are not part of that account. Yet you know they happened. You learned about them from somebody else, or Mom or Dad let them slip in a moment of less-than-official intimacy. About other things, Mom may say one thing, and Dad another. There may be other twists in the story that you *think* happened without being sure. You infer them. Or you have them on shaky evidence. Then there may be gaps in your knowledge, things you don't know but could maybe find out. Finally, you may have embellished certain things in your own imagination, and then maybe even have "forgotten" what is fact and what fiction. Or you may be pretty sure that certain things are *not* true. Not really. Not literally. They would come as news to Mom and Dad. Yet they too are in your head, because they are . . . revealing, or romantic, or exciting, or plausible, or they make a better story, or something.

All these parts of the mosaic—even ones you know are fiction—are aspects of a single story. You "know" each, each with a different kind of "knowing." All lie buried inside you. To tell the whole story, you would somehow have to integrate all these different *kinds* of "knowledge" and make them one. But until you tell the story, you will both "know" the story of your parents' courtship and "*not* know" it *at the same time.*

This mix of knowing and not knowing is where all storytellers begin, and it lights up the process of finding the story in a curious paradox. What you find feels like what you always knew. And what you always knew comes as revelation.

The process can start slowly. John Irving is a demon worker. When he gets near the finish line of a book, he often puts in ten- or twelve-hour workdays. And yet—"When I'm beginning a book, I can't work more than two or three hours a day." Why so few? "I don't *know* [emphasis mine] more than two or three hours a day about a new novel." Virginia Woolf's diaries show that her process of digging up the story of *Mrs. Dalloway,* getting to know what was there, took something like two years. Woolf started searching for *Mrs. Dalloway* very slowly, looking for the story, speaking in an early 1922 diary entry of "dredging my mind for Mrs. Dalloway bringing up light buckets," adding that "I don't like the feeling I'm writing too quickly." Later in 1922, Woolf was still unclear about even the leading theme of *Mrs. Dalloway*—that is, insanity: Septimus's insanity. Once that much came clear (and it hadn't been during the many months before) Woolf worked another full year before she managed to see how the novel's several stories would fit together—how to link what she called the "caves" of story she had "[dug] out" "behind" each of her characters. She was trying to find the links between them so they could all, as she said, "[come] to daylight at the present moment": that is, in the culminating moment of Clarissa Dalloway's dinner. Even once she more or less had those connections, Woolf worked yet another ten months before she could see the whole book clearly enough to say, "I am writing, writing, & see my way clear to the end now, & so shall gallop to it, somehow or other." Three months after that—and almost exactly two years after fearing "going too fast"—Woolf noted that she was racing so fast to the end that she couldn't stop.

The search for your story may be slow—though it does accelerate. It is slow for many writers, even the accomplished and the great.

But do not delude yourself. *You must get to that story.* Even if you don't begin with a story, you *must* end with one, and it must be a real story, one that fascinates and excites readers *and* is fully satisfactory to you. That's the job. Your search for the story begins with your first notebook jotting and ends with the final printout of the last page, and that search will dominate everything else you do. It is the one arena in which you must not fail. You won't be done until *it* is done. Do not let the siren song of "plotlessness" or the sudden panic cry *"I can't do plots!"* or some tired academic fantasy about replacing a story with style or character or ideas let you settle for anything else. That would be surrender. That would be defeat.

FICTION IS A NARRATIVE ART FORM. Writing fiction means telling stories. That's how the art is *defined.* If you don't like telling stories, if you feel that telling stories is beneath you, or bogus, or trivial, I fear you are in the wrong business. At first glance, this statement may seem either dogmatic or banal. I'd call it true rather than dogmatic, and it is far too controversial to be banal. It makes many people nervous and many others angry. Lots of people would call it wrong, and not a few would even call it immoral. But fiction *is* narrative. It is possible, of course, to write more or less storyless novels, and if you want to try, by all means do. Sadly, the result will probably be unreadable. The tiny list of *interesting* novels that are *genuinely* storyless is made up mainly of exceptions that prove the rule. Almost always, novels without stories turn out to be loose concatenations of half-told, digressive mini-stories and near-stories held in the loose embrace of one large, loose, lumbering tale. *Tristram Shandy* is the classic example.

STORY, STRUCTURE, AND PLOT

As you feel your way to your story, it may prove useful to draw a distinction between "story" and "plot." The words are often used as near synonyms, and they obviously are intimately linked. But for our purposes, let's focus on what distinguishes them.

A *story* is an account of any real or fictitious sequence of linked events. As such, a story can be collapsed into a sentence or it can be told at length in its full complexity. That complexity can be configured in many different ways and still remain more or less the same story. Its shape, its movement from beginning to end, can be suggested rapidly and felt intuitively. In other words, it is subject to paraphrase.

Yet in order to be fully told, every story must also have a *plot*. That plot will consist of whatever makes the story move: It is made up of the twists and turns that give focus to the precise way the reader is induced to participate imaginatively in whatever is supposed to be happening; it organizes and gives focus to the reader's curiosity and comprehension; it determines when and how the reader will be engaged emotionally or intellectually, and through what kind of suspense—all in order to propel her or him from the story's beginning through its middle and into its outcome. Since any plot will consist of the storytelling methods that organize narrative energy and drive it forward, plot is often described with metaphors of machinery: We speak of plot "mechanisms." They are nothing if not concrete.

Let me illustrate. At this very moment, you are probably pretty sure that you "know" the story of *Hamlet,* and you doubtless could tell that story, in loose summary, in under a minute. The only reliable way to test that knowledge, of course, would be to go ahead, take that minute, and summarize *Hamlet.* In the process, you might fumble or misremember some twist or turn in the events, but you would not be wrong in your original claim:

You *do* "know" the story of *Hamlet*. If you were to see the play tonight, it would "all come back."

The *plot* of *Hamlet*, on the other hand, consists of all the causes and effects, recognitions and reversals, incentives and accidents, intrigues and counterintrigues that Shakespeare uses to drive Hamlet's story forward as a dramatic experience on the stage, starting at that first moment, late at night, when sentinels guarding the chilly parapets of Elsinore speak of having seen on the late watch a seeming apparition of the recently dead king and ending when Hamlet's lacerated and poisoned corpse is solemnly lifted up and Fortinbras says, "Go, bid the soldiers shoot." These are quite complex. To remember them all, you would probably have to check the text. They are filled with concreteness and energy. They lift the story out of the audience's vague and shifting summary awareness and into the detailed, vital, visualized, energized forward movement of a complete narrative, the play itself, as it works on the stage and screen.

So you "know" the *story* of Hamlet in a quite different way than you "know" its *plot*. They feel almost like two different kinds of knowledge, and in fact they work a little like the author's own two ways of "knowing" the story. One is highly intuitive, and the other is carefully calculated. One is quite vague and summary; the other is precise and concrete. Both will be at work in any story you ever tell. You must have a feeling for both and, above all, for how they work together.

Plot and story naturally reinforce each other at every stage of their development, but the rule of thumb has to be that, generally speaking, just as intuition tends to precede calculation, so *story precedes plot*. YOU CANNOT "PLOT" A STORY THAT YOU DO NOT KNOW. That would be like trying to sing that tune you've never heard or tell the dream you've not yet dreamed. Yet at the beginning, no aspect of writing is more highly intuitive than story formation. Your story is likely to present itself first in an obscure intuited shape, with only this or that fragment of the whole—the end, maybe, or the beginning, or a character—clear in your mind. Like that dream, your story has to be unearthed in the depths of your imagination. You may uncover it bit by bit, or you may glimpse it suddenly in a flash, as Truman Capote described it: "a long sustained streak of lightning that darkens the tangible, so-called real world, and leaves illuminated only this suddenly seen pseudo-imaginary landscape, a terrain alive with figures, voices, rooms, atmospheres, weather." But whether the story first hits you complete or in fragments, it will probably take a form at first so intuitive that it will be located on the extreme outer edge of what can be put into words. Plotting becomes possible when—and only when—this intuitive knowledge has emerged with enough clarity for you to identify its details. Once that has happened, the two processes—*feeling* the story, followed by *figuring* the story—can start working together in a dynamic reciprocity from which the real shape of the story can emerge in an alternating shimmer of certainty and surprise.

Capote describes the difference between these two kinds of "knowing." "I invariably have the illusion that the whole play of a story, its start and middle and finish, occur in my mind simultaneously—that I am seeing it in one flash. But in the working-out, the writing-out, infinite surprises happen. Thank God, because the surprise, the twist, the phrase that comes at the right moment out of nowhere, is the unexpected dividend, that joyful little push that keeps a writer going."

So *story precedes plot*. Always. Story precedes plot even in "formula fiction"—although most people miss that fact, because in formula fiction, the story starts out as a given, a cliché so familiar that the writer knows it before she or he even begins. The story is a formula so familiar that the writer doesn't "invent" it at all—prefabricated, standard-issue stuff. All its principal characters, along with its beginning, middle, and end, are known by rote before the writer even starts. Writing such a formula is really a variety of *re*writing: You tilt the story a little this way or that; you change names and places and a certain number of details, and you use the same weary "plot mechanisms" to generate the same weary tale for the ten thousandth time. At best, the reader gets a "new twist" here or there—not too many, though!

From this machine, pulp pours out. Pulp fiction is often denounced for putting "story" before "character." It does nothing of the kind. Pitting "story" against "character" is a contradiction in terms, and speaking of it is an intellectual bad habit that has done incalculable damage to the art of fiction. Formula fiction does not invent its own story at all, but uses mechanisms of the plot to repeat a preexisting story *ad nauseam,* changing only details, usually trivial ones. There are publishers of pulp romances who send aspiring writers work sheets explaining exactly on which *pages* of the manuscript each and every stock character must appear and precisely what those stock characters must do, when, and why.

This is not writing. This is typing.

So when Stephen King tells us that for the fiction writer the story is always "the boss," and then turns around to call "plot" the "good writer's last resort and the dullard's first choice," is he contradicting himself? Not once you grasp that a story and its plot are two different albeit intimately connected things. The "dullard's first choice" is the cookie-cutter formula that stamps out a preexisting story yet again, or that uses a plot formula to generate movement in a story that is otherwise inert. "Plot" in this sense—a formula forcing a story—is what everyone from Henry James to Stephen King disdains. "Plot," says King, "is . . . the writer's jackhammer. You can liberate a fossil from hard ground with a jackhammer, no argument there, but you know as well as I do that the jackhammer is going to break almost as much stuff as it liberates. It's clumsy, mechanical, anticreative." Yes, Henry James did indeed repeatedly refer to "plot" as "vulgar." Yet *The Turn of the Screw* and *The Wings of the Dove* tell carefully plotted stories, and I assure you that James did not view them as "vulgar." *Every story,* once written, has to be plotted. It will not move otherwise. What James found "vulgar" was a mechanical formula substituted for the integrity of an authentically invented and discovered tale. And so does Stephen King.

And yet—isn't there something formulaic in every story? Aren't the very concepts of comedy and tragedy, in some real sense, "formulas"? If you follow Richard Rhodes's advice and hone your sense of narrative by reading Northrop Frye's great study *Anatomy of Criticism,* you may conclude that all fiction, always and everywhere, is in some measure "formula fiction." You may even deepen that view by wondering if both life itself and our vision of it are likewise formulaic, but that the "formula," so far from being debased, is the most exalted thing that we can ever hope to know.

Any time you create drama, you will use devices that can be derogated as "formulas." Don't let the issue be whether there is or is not some "formula" in your story. What matters is the kind of imaginative authenticity you find for that story, formula or no. That authenticity must be the work of your hands. You must find it—"invent" it—in your imagination and on the page, again and again and again. The very parables of the Bible are shaped *in order* to be in a state of continuous development. The truth of fiction is imaginative truth partly to remind us that authenticity is a changing stream; that every new generation, and every group and individual within every generation, must rediscover it. We never reach the Last Word.

STRUCTURE

When it comes to shaping a narrative, structure joins story and plot as the third force that must be at work. In order to be told, a story has to have a plot. And in order for that plot to be coherent, it must have some structure.

Structure consists in the large units that organize the movements of your story and supply them with their overall shape. The broad outlines of a given structure are not necessarily specific to their stories. In fact, the basic, universal, and invariable structural sequence of *every* story, as Aristotle noted in his dry, definitive way, consists of a beginning, a middle, and an end. This is a truism; it is also profound. The structure of *Hamlet* consists of five acts, each composed of a number of scenes. That structure is not unique to *Hamlet:* It is the structure of all of Shakespeare's tragedies. Every one of Mozart's piano concertos, for all their sublime inventiveness and intricacy, operates within the same structure: three distinct movements that go, every single time, *fast-slow-fast*. Most modern plays—and most screenplays and novels—consist of three acts. It is the simplest of all structures: introduction, complication to crisis, and resolution. And that simple structure can be used to tell an infinite number of stories, some of them very, very complicated.

This means that any story you're likely to tell will have a "natural" end and a "natural" beginning, and that what makes that end and beginning "natural" is a middle, which will usually (not always) take the shape of an arc, at the apex of which will likely come some crisis or climax. This sounds prescriptive: It is actually wonderfully loose. A feeling for a story's structure can offer you a shape vaguely envisioned long before you have a firm grasp on the plot, and even before you have much of a grasp on the story itself.

Structure is likely to give you your first dim glimpse of your story's *wholeness.* Russell Banks describes the role of structure in his process with exceptional clarity: "Usually, with a novel, I have a pretty good idea of the arc of the narrative and its breaking points. I know if it's going to be a five-act or a three-act novel, or to drive right through to one place or require a reversal, come this way for a while, then reverse and go that way. I do work that out. I also have a short-term outline that covers the next fifty or sixty pages, which I keep rewriting as I work. Of course, it's all tentative; I can change it at will as new ideas, plot turns, characters appear and develop. The trick, I suppose, is to find the point between control and freedom that allows you to do your work. . . .

"With a short story, I never know where I'm going until I get there. I just know where I entered. That is what comes to me: the opening, a sentence or phrase, even. But with a novel, it's like entering a huge mansion: It doesn't matter where you come in, as long as you get in. I usually imagine the ending, not literally and not in detail, but I do have a clear idea whether it's going to end with a funeral or wedding. Or if I am going to burn the mansion down or throw a dinner party at the end. The important question—the reason you write the novel—is to discover how you get from here to there."

The interplay between structure, story, and plot is incessant and largely intuitive, and so long as you understand that you must give your story a plot and that any plot must have a structure, I advise you to keep it that way. You are going to need to focus on the separate elements more concretely when you get into trouble. The prime test of a good structure will make your story more tellable, and usually more *completely* tellable. Good structure clarifies.

Structure may or may not be complicated. A complicated structure—let's say an episodic structure—will be all wrong for telling a simple love story. On the other hand, suppose you want to tell the story of a big fractious family over several generations. If you think you can keep all those feuds and romances within the structure of one uncomplicated beginning, middle, and end, you are in for trouble.

There's a lot to think about here. Some of the greatest literary criticism of the last hundred years has focused on structure. If you are curious, Northrop Frye's *Anatomy of Criticism* is a good place to start: It will wonderfully enrich your understanding of the *kinds* of fiction, the genres of the art. A next step might be to read the great Russian critic Mikhail Bakhtin—a very penetrating and useful analyst of novelistic structure. Yet criticism never can replace the feeling for structure that comes from reading lots and lots of the fiction you love, fiction like what you want to write, and taking away from it a developed feel for its possibilities.

Let's take a look at just one variety of narrative structure, the kind we just called "episodic." An episodic structure often looks very complex because it consists of many tight, punchy, intense, and rather short stories—the episodes—each with its own beginning, middle, and near-end, and all held in the embrace of one slow-moving, rather loose, very long story. The most familiar episodic form in the West right now is the weekly television series: Almost all television series and all soap operas without exception are episodic by definition.

But episodic structure is also a thoroughly classical form. Most of Dickens's novels, for example, are highly episodic, and most, like a television series, first appeared in serial form. If you were to string together the weekly episodes of a continuing television series, as John Mortimer points out, the effect would be very much like the Victorian novels for which Dickens is the paradigm. "If you asked anybody what the plot to *Bleak House* was, they would never really be able to tell you, but they *would* be able to tell you all about the funny little things that happened along the way. But if *Bleak House* didn't have a central plot, they wouldn't have gone on reading it and discovered those things along the way."

From the Pentateuch to *The Sopranos,* the great episodic genre is the saga—the chronicle of a family. Tolstoy's *War and Peace,* Mario Puzo's *Godfather* novels, and Gabriel García Márquez's *One Hundred Years of Solitude* are all sagas. And if you want to talk about *really* influential literature, the saga also gives structure to much of the Old Testament, including everything from both books of Samuel through both books of Chronicles, buttressed by long passages from Genesis and Exodus.

Some structural ideas are not, strictly speaking, narrative at all. They are musical. Music is by far the most powerful way human beings have discovered to endow time with structure. Narrative has to be influenced by such a force. That should come as no surprise in an age of instant access, where the very air around us numbs the mind with unheard melodies in every cab and elevator and telephone call on hold. Hemingway once remarked that his writing had been influenced by Mozart and added, "I should think that what one learns from composers and the study of harmony and counterpoint would be obvious." There is nothing avant-garde in fiction's structural bond to music: It is as old as the art. The earliest great narratives in the Western tradition—Homeric epics, for example—were sung. Writers from Edmund White to Mary Gordon speak of writing against a counterpoint of music. Being able to listen to music hour after hour while working at one's desk is something that came only with the second half of the twentieth century, but many earlier classics are still fully indebted to music. Stendhal's *The Charterhouse of Parma* is unimaginable without Mozart's operas. Among the great modernists, Thomas Mann filled his works with echoes of Wagner, and James Joyce's lyrical ironies are steeped in Italian opera. In fact, literary modernism's focus on the guiding lyricism of "the voice" in fiction derives in the twentieth century from Joyce's genius, and in the nineteenth from Whitman's, and it has clear analogies to the bravura of sung arias grounded in recitative that were so addictively important to both those writers. The tendency is obvious in all the great American lyricists of the "voice," from Faulkner to Welty: Consider only Welty's classic short story, the all-but-sung showstopper "Powerhouse." Or consider Susan Sontag's novel *The Volcano Lover:* "I had the story in some sense, and the span of the book. And what was most helpful, I had a very strong idea of a structure. I took it from a piece of music, Hindemith's *The Four Temperaments*—a work I know very well, since it's the music of one of Balanchine's most sublime ballets, which I've seen countless times. The Hindemith starts with a triple prologue, three very short pieces. Then come four movements: melancholic, sanguinic, phlegmatic, choleric. In that order. I knew I was going to have a triple prologue and then four sections or parts corresponding to the four temperaments. . . . I knew all of that, plus the novel's last sentence: 'Damn them all.' Of course, I didn't know who was going to utter it. In a sense, the whole work of writing the novel consisted of making something that would justify that sentence."

CONFLICT: THE KEY TO ACCESS

The entryway into every story is conflict. This is because conflict—that is, some contested issue between people that must be resolved—is the thing, the only thing, that makes us ask: *What happens?* The reader who does not care about this question will not care, period. Without some conflict keeping *what happens?* somewhere in the reader's mind, your story will fall inert, doomed to rest stagnant and unread. The need to know what happens—to learn the outcome of a conflict—is not the *only* source of psychological power in fiction, but it is the one without which all the others fall slack. Readers turn pages *only* when they can be induced to join you in this search. Style alone, character alone, situation alone—none of these, no matter how superbly rendered, will turn the trick unassisted. " 'The cat sat on the mat,' " as le Carré points out, "is not the beginning of a story, but 'The cat sat on the *dog's* mat' *is.*"

All this means that suspense—suspense in *some* form—muses and broods over the whole art of fiction in all its kinds. Now don't misunderstand. I am not (not necessarily) talking about knuckle-whitening, page-turning, whodunit suspense. The range of thoughts and feelings aroused through imaginative involvement in the search for an outcome is much richer and broader than that. But your readers' engagement in your search for an outcome is what makes them *care*. They will not care without it. Once you have determined exactly how a character or situation is gripped by conflict, you are halfway home.

In the early stages, the way you define a character's conflict should probably be rather loose. You're searching, you're experimenting. The conflict may deepen and change—maybe several times—before you're done. Don't force a definition too early. Leave things loose—loose, but not vague in the emotional sense. However you define it, the conflict must make you—through your characters, of course—care. You must feel the conflict gripping their gut because it grips your gut, and you must feel it from the start. Does the conflict with which you begin seem too simple, at first? Even crude? Let it. Better crude than weak or phony. As you go, the story will give it nuance and dimension. "You're looking, as you begin," says Philip Roth, "for what's going to resist you. You're looking for trouble." We rub our eyes in disbelief to learn that Dostoyevsky began the book that became *Crime and Punishment* supposing he was writing an attack on alcoholism in Saint Petersburg. (*Dostoyevsky? Writing "father, dear father, come home with me now?"*) Yet Dostoyevsky cared passionately about the damage he saw alcohol doing to the Russian family, and he let that feeling flow into the conflict between the noble Sonya and her vodka-blasted father. Modern readers may smile at these scenes: They seem scraps from some antiquated barroom melodrama. Yet it was from just these roots in conventional melodrama that Dostoyevsky produced his incomparably original masterpiece of psychological terror.

But conflict also defines the literary form of your work, and how you determine what is relevant to it. Every story—like every human situation—swims in a vast shoreless sea of possible information and detail. Almost all that information is totally uninteresting. Some small—very small—part of it is revelatory. What separates details that matter from those that don't is the force field of conflict. It is conflict that pulls scattered information into an articulated shape, extracting relevant detail from the detritus of the irrelevant. The effect is a little like those scattered iron filings in the familiar classroom demonstration of magnetism's field of force: A mess on a piece of paper is suddenly pulled by unseen energy into lovely concentric arcs.

And, of course, conflict also shapes character, more even than the more amorphous thing called "personality." Since conflict alone tells us who cares about what in the story, conflict is the real force that assigns characters their roles. The specific "personality" of the character named Juliet is defined by the fact she is going to love, and die with, a character named Romeo. Juliet has a "personality," of course, but her personality is made dramatic only by her destiny. In a similar way, the situation of every character on your page will be defined by her or his place in the larger conflict of the story, and the character's personality must be part of that.

Lastly, conflict determines genre. Is this story going to end with a funeral, or a wedding, or a party, or a soulful stare at a brick wall? Is it going to make us laugh, or cry, or cringe, or get mad, or feel awe, or pity, or gentle sadness, or excitement, or what? The answers you find to questions like these determine your story's genre. By *genre,* incidentally, I do *not* mean merely the "genre" fiction you see on the drugstore rack—horror, romance, Westerns, spy thrillers, and science fiction—all the "popular" fiction that is so monotonously and misleadingly opposed to the "literary" fiction in our time. I mean nothing more or less than what Aristotle meant when he spoke of the "types" or "kinds" of stories. Like comedy and tragedy, most "kinds" of story (perhaps not quite all) are determined by the feelings they arouse, the emotional affect that the story aims to induce the reader to feel. And these, in turn, determine the story's outcome, its end.

The truth is that writers imitate genres as much as they imitate life. This is what John Gardner means when he says that "the artist's primary unit of thought—his primary conscious or unconscious basis for selecting and organizing the details of his work—is *genre,*" adding, in a dismissal of our old friend "write what you know," "The writer ... is presenting not so much what he knows about life as what he knows about a particular literary genre. A better answer, though still not an ideal one, might have been 'Write the kind of story you know and like best—a ghost story, a science-fiction piece, a realistic story about your childhood, or whatever.'"

NARRATIVE THINKING. You are looking for a story. So ask questions that have to be answered with a story. Rather than ask what something means, ask what its outcome is going to be, and ask how that outcome will be reached. Ask what I call "narrative questions." "What happens?" is the narrative question par excellence. (It has many variants: *What happens if? What happens when? What happens after?*) It can be answered only with what people do—not merely what people think or feel, but what they do.

In contrast, the antinarrative question par excellence is *What does this mean?* Now of course there is nothing wrong with *What does this mean?* It is almost the definition of a reasonable question. It's just that its answer cannot take you where you need to go.

You need questions that lead to a story—and most questions that lead to a story pivot on questions of motivation. When you are looking at a new character, ask what Vonnegut and Bradbury ask: *What does the character want?* Short term, long term: Walking down the street or embracing their destiny, people act through desire. When you know what a character wants, you can ask, *Is he or she going to get it?* And then finally: *If yes, how, and if no, why?* This trio of interlocking questions is a potent and dependable engine for narrative. Ask them right, and they will *invariably* produce some sort of tale.

It's possible to interrogate a setting in just the same way. The ultimate nonnarrative question about a setting is: *What does this place look like?* That's a perfectly okay question, and you'll doubtless want to answer it, but unless you're writing a travel book, it will never get you where you need to go. Suppose, on the other hand, you ask: *Who lives here? Who wants to come here? Who wants to leave here? Why?* Now you can tell us what the place looks like in the context of people and their desires. Now your setting has life, and now you can ask: *What do these people want? Are they going to get it? If yes, how? If no, why?* And you will be in business.

STORY AND CHARACTER

Once the germ of a story starts to grow in your mind, it may suddenly leap into raucous and unruly disorganization. You think you have nothing, until—*shazam!* You've got way, way too much: a clamoring crowd of potential stories; new characters popping up everywhere; brand-new story lines, and sudden new slants twisting and turning all around you. You began with nothing, and now you're overwhelmed.

What to do?

FOCUS ON CHARACTER. When a story starts multiplying and spreading in all directions, one natural response might be to try regaining control by cramming the twisting, turbulent mess into some orderly preordained "plot." This is a mistake. It seeks to limit the story, not organize it. Remember: What organizes fiction is conflict—and only characters experience conflicts. So when your story becomes disorganized, don't focus on plot but on your characters. Get back to the dominating human conflict in your situation and find what is motivating the people who are making it happen. Above all, find the conflict and the motivation of the main mystery figure in your dramatis personae: your *protagonist.*

The word *protagonist* may smell a bit of the classroom, but let's ignore that little whiff of chalk dust in the air and agree that *pro-*

tagonist is a good word: a lot less argumentative than *hero* and a lot more precise than *main character.* Many of your characters will have some sort of conflict, and many of those conflicts will lead to some sort of outcome. Figures may fall in love or die or go mad or become murderers or inspiring heroines. All kinds of characters can play important roles. That does not necessarily make them the protagonist—the figure whose problem is the story's prime focus and whose fate decides the story's meaning.

There is usually only one protagonist in a given story. Sometimes there are two: Consider *Romeo and Juliet.* On rare, rare occasions there may be more. More often the protagonist will face a clear antagonist: the character that most significantly embodies the other side of the conflict your protagonist undergoes. The identity of your protagonist (and maybe an antagonist, too) may be laughably obvious from the first moment the story hits you. Or her or his identity may remain elusive for a long time. The protagonist doesn't have to be the figure to which the most pages are devoted. Nor does the protagonist have to be the character from whose point of view the story is told. The protagonist is *the character whose fate matters most to the story.* And that, in turn, is the character whose fate matters most to you.

You have got to find that character, because in that character lies your whole focus. Her or his destiny may seem vague at first. Let it be vague. Just like your view of her or his conflict, the more dense and nuanced view of your protagonist's fate will come with your search for the outcome that will resolve and settle them both.

And so the warning sign of a story that is growing disorganized is likely to be too many characters, and the solution to that problem is likely to be the discovery of the one character—your protagonist—whose fate matters most. Chekhov warned against the proliferation of characters: "Don't have too many characters. The center of gravity should be two: he and she." Edith Wharton also warned against "unemployed characters." (Mrs. Wharton had her serious reservations about the "unemployed.") "Neither novelist nor playwright should ever venture on creating a character without first following it out to the end of the projected tale and being sure that the latter will be the poorer for its absence."

True, when you begin work, a proliferating cast of characters may seem a welcome sign of life. Each will seem a candidate for some big role. But once you have found your protagonist, once you are sure about the unmistakable center of your story, some of these intruders will start to fall away. What endows your story with unity? More than any other element—more than style, more than point of view, more than plot—that unifying force is the singularity of your protagonist and her or his conflict. Everything else forms around this center. Every other role is found in relation to that role, and any character without a significant connection to the protagonist is going to wander through your pages a clumsy intruder, lost and in the way.

DRAMA AND IMPROBABILITY

Two final points: *Embrace drama.*

Just as important: *Embrace improbability.*

Above all, don't *fear* either one of them. Verve in fiction almost always means a readiness to seize upon—and love—either drama or improbability or both. Drama rests on improbability, and taken together, these two are our prime means for uncovering—for "inventing"—the unseen significance of things. On their forking path can be found those "exceptional happenings" that Truman Capote called the writer's business. They are your levers for lifting the carapace of banality to reveal meaning. *All* drama is based upon unlikely events surging up into ordinary life and changing it. *All* narrative is engaged, at some level, with the improbable. Part of your job, of course, is to make the improbable credible. Then, once you have made it credible, you proceed to make it inevitable. And then you may have art.

It is disheartening to consider how many aspiring novelists become paralyzed at the very first sign of something intensely dramatic, and therefore unlikely. They panic. They are sure something has gone wrong. Yet improbability is the *basis* of drama, if for no other reason than that drama is based upon the exceptional. When they pop up in your story it is not bad news. It is often—not always, but often—a gift from the muse.

Do not greet this gift with dismay, as if it were a sign of failure. It is your one hope of making things realer than real. I cannot count the times when, sitting with the writer of a beautifully crafted but inert, and therefore boring, piece of prose, I would suggest a dramatic possibility, only to be greeted with a shocked—even horrified—"Oh, but I wouldn't want to be *melodramatic*."

Now hold it right there. *Drama* is not *melodrama*. Quite aside from the fact that melodrama is an artistic mode with a rich and respectable history—opera, for example, wouldn't exist without it—the inability to distinguish melodrama from its plainer cousin is simply disabling to a writer. Incredibly, there are people—smart people—who think a prim disdain for drama is somehow a sign of "good taste." It is more often the reverse: a lamentable insensitivity to the essence of the art, a failure to "get it" on the most essential level. It is more often a sign not of good taste but of artistic insecurity. Not knowing how far to go, the writer goes nowhere. Lifelessness is not a form of elegance you should pursue.

If drama scares you, the really delicious challenge of improbability will likely leave you petrified. Yet improbability is a necessary concomitant of any and all drama. Improbability pounds like a heartbeat through the greatest classics of the West, from *Oedipus the King* to *Hamlet* or *Othello* to *The Brothers Karamazov*. Balzac's *Cousin Bette* keeps its reader every minute on the very edge of her or his seat by being every minute on the very edge of startled disbelief. Consider the climax of *The Great Gatsby*—the road accident that kills Myrtle Wilson and leads to Gatsby's murder at the hands of her deranged husband. A thoroughly improbable highway accident, precipitated and followed by "melodramatic" hysteria occasioned by—get this!—a case of mistaken identity. Fitzgerald walks into that preposterous improbability with the confidence of genius and lifts it into an unforgettable tragic vision.

John Braine spoke with classic British reserve about what he calls the "point of improbability." "However appropriate the actions of your characters are, however solid their background, you're telling a story. You're planting the hooks to pull the reader on; you're directing the narrative to its culmination. You're presenting real human beings. But the story is still an artificial creation. Nothing in real life is ever neat and ordered, there are no real endings, the threads are left untied. . . . something will happen which couldn't possibly happen in real life. Get rid of it, substitute a credible happening, and the Point of Improbability will pop up somewhere else.

"There isn't any way of getting rid of it; to attempt to sneak quietly past it by means of a brief summary makes the incredible even more incredible. The best way of dealing with it is with the maximum of brio; make sure that no one misses it."

THE SENSE OF RIGHTNESS

All of these elements, from the most intuitive to the most carefully calculated, must work together in a kind of synchrony that not only begins in intuition but ends in it, too. And how do you make your way from beginning to end? You can be guided at every step by only one intuition: *your own sense of rightness.* But the sense of rightness can come only after you have been guided away from ten thousand wrong turns by your sense for what is *wrong.* The sense of rightness and the sense of what is wrong have no independent existence: Each is the other's reverse side. Most good stories die before they are born simply because their authors fail to understand this. That little voice inside says to them, "This is *wrong,* all *wrong,*" and they panic, they think they have failed, and they quit. They think that inner voice—*wrong; this is wrong*—is a reason for stopping. In fact, it is your art's best friend, the other voice of rightness. You must listen to them both, trusting that your intellect is capable of responding to their cues and discerning at least many of their mute meanings. They will be in play every hour you spend at your desk, and they alone can guide you on your path from perplexity, complexity, and conflict to the inevitable. That movement from the improbable to the inevitable is the truest course of a story, and it defines your path.

"Finding the right form for your story," Truman Capote said, "is simply to realize the most *natural* way of telling the story. The test of whether or not a writer has divined the natural shape of his story is just this: After reading it, can you image it differently, or does it silence your imagination and seem to you absolute and final? As an orange is final. As an orange is something nature has made just right."

4

Making Characters Live

By far the best way to develop a character is to tell that character's story. And by far the best way to develop a story is to tell us what its characters do. In the end, stories *are* what their characters do, and characters *are* what they do in stories. Unlike human beings, characters do not have any life at all outside their life on the page. As a result, their life consists almost exclusively of action. Now don't misunderstand: By "action" I do not mean merely street fights, car chases, and passionate love scenes. By "action," I mean any thought, word, or deed that engages your character with some *other* character, and thereby becomes an event. Action in fiction consists of human interchange. For that reason the place—the *only* place—to find your characters and their stories is in the arena of exchange. You can of course depict characters who are alone or isolated, but watch out for mere empty solitude. Even Molly Bloom's soliloquy, which is as narcissistic a passage as modern literature has to offer, consists of Molly obsessing compulsively about her relationships to others. You'll create action on the page only when your character has an encounter with another character that matters, somehow, to at least one of them. Dramatic exchange is the thing—it is the *only* thing—that makes characters visible, even to their authors. Like a hunter peering into the leafy dusk, your imagination will never spot its quarry until it *moves.*

And beware of depicting too much mere empty "behavior." Here I must draw a distinction between "behavior" and true "action." I define *behavior* as the busywork of life, the stuff your character does pretty much the way everybody else does it, from brushing his teeth to driving her car. "Behavior" has its place in any kind of characterization; you will need to ground a character in whatever is significantly typical about her or him. A few deft lines showing a guy brushing his teeth will help him join the human race. But overdone, mere behavior will smother the character in banality and suffocate the story. Do show the typical, but remember that a little of the typical—precisely because it *is* typical—goes a very long way. The task that matters most is showing what is special about your character, and that means being vivid and clear about her or his role: what she or he is doing with others to transact the story's "exceptional happenings."

You will find your characters in the same place you find your story, in that nameless region between finding and making to which we keep returning: the shadow realm of "invention"—"invention" in our sense. It doesn't really matter much whether your characters are modeled on yourself, on somebody else, or on nobody at all. You are going to "invent" every single one of them in exactly the same way you "invent" the story. Sometimes you will start out with a vivid situation populated by a skeleton crew of characters made up of blurs or stick figures. Other times you may begin with a character who feels realer than real, even though you're clueless about her or his narrative destiny. To have one—situation or character—is to become acutely aware that you lack the other. Don't let that insight become a disability. The truth is that either situation or character is a perfectly okay starting point. You can begin only by playing the hand your imagination has dealt you. After all, it is nothing more than a starting point. So start.

Story *is* character. Character *is* story. You are going to hear many voices trying to persuade you that this ancient verity is no longer valid. I urge you to ignore them. Many will try to pit "character-driven" fiction against "story-driven" fiction. This imaginary opposition is a critical cliché, and it can only damage your work. The notion that you can get clarity about either character or story by slighting one in favor of the other is just plain wrong. Your characters are defined by their stories, and your story consists in nothing other than the action of its characters. To pit "character" *against* "story" is like trying to walk on one leg. Of course, any little stroll *starts out* on one leg. Your first step may be a clear situation without clear characters. Or the reverse. But after the first step, you are going to take a second, and then a third. It's on both legs that you walk.

If you begin with a character, Ray Bradbury advises that you "find a character like yourself, who will want something or not want something, with all his heart. Give him running orders. Shoot him off. Then follow as fast as you can go. The character, in his great love, or hate, will rush you through to the end of the story." Shelby Foote also starts out with a character, and he takes a tough line on those who don't. "Character comes first. I separate the mass of novels into good and bad. A good book could be described as one about a man who, in a situation, does such and such. A bad book is about a *situation* in which a man does such and such. In other words, plot ought to grow out of character."

"Character comes first." That is Shelby Foote's position, and many agree. But not everyone agrees. "The situation comes first," Stephen King says of his own work. "The characters—always flat and unfeatured, to begin with—come next. Once these things are fixed in my mind, I begin to narrate." He adds: "My books tend to be based more on situation rather than story. Some of the ideas which have produced those books are more complex than others, but the majority start out with the stark simplicity of a department store window display or a waxworks tableau. I want to put a group of characters (perhaps a pair; perhaps even just one) in some sort of predicament and then watch them try to work themselves free. My job isn't to *help* them work their way free, or manipulate them to safety—those are jobs which require the noisy jackhammer of plot—but to watch what happens and then write it down."

Edith Wharton probably would have sided with Shelby Foote in this argument, though perhaps not in quite his judgmental way. Wharton drew a distinction between "novels of situation" as opposed to "novels of character and manners." "In the first, the persons imagined by the author almost always spring out of a vision of the situation, and are inevitably conditioned by it, whatever the genius of their creator; whereas in the larger freer form, that of character and manners (or either of the two), the author's characters are first born, and then mysteriously proceed to work out their own destinies."

Wharton is right. While certain works do indeed turn out to be stronger on character than on story—or the reverse—situations *inevitably* "spring out of" characters, and characters *inevitably* "spring out of" situations. Although story and character are invariably united, each particular work will unite them in a relation that is its own. Yet some generalizations are possible. Most episodic narratives, from *Don Quixote* to *I Love Lucy*, pull together their long sequence of short little adventures through some exceptionally vivid main character. In a road story or picaresque—Dean Moriarty blazing across America or Holden Caulfield making his flight toward home—a single vivid voyager holds a large loose story together. On the other hand, in a story that's long on intrigue—let's say *The Great Gatsby* or *In Cold Blood*—the situation dominates a variety of characters, sets them in array, and locates their position in the play of events. That is, it finds their role.

You may even start out without *either* a character or a situation. You may be inspired by some general idea about society, or politics, or human life in general, as Chinua Achebe usually is. "I think I can say that the general idea is the first, followed almost immediately by the major characters. We live in a sea of general ideas, so that's not a novel. . . . But the moment a particular idea is linked to a character, it's like an engine moves it. Then you have a novel under way. This is particularly so with novels which have distinct and overbearing characters. . . . with characters who are not commanding personalities, there I think the general idea plays a stronger part at the initial stage. But once you get past that initial state, there's really no difference between the general idea and the character; each has to work."

POINT OF VIEW

Many teachers of writing will tell you that the way to unify your story and integrate it with its characters is through something called the narrative "point of view." There are even certain purists who will insist that an "integrated point of view" is the *only* way a narrative can achieve unity. Their argument typically runs roughly like this: To be a story, a narrative has to be told. To be told, it must be told by somebody. Even when it is told in the third person, its coherence depends upon being told through the perspective of a given character. As Edith Wharton noted, "The same experience never happens to any two people, and . . . the storyteller's first care, after the choice of a subject, is to decide to which of his characters the episode in question happened, since it could not have happened in that particular way to more than one." Therefore, the writer's first job is to find the personage in the story whose perceptions can serve as both its substance and as its source of unity and artistic power. Therefore, the writer must begin with someone's point of view.

This argument sounds perfectly plausible, and it is sometimes rehearsed in English classes and writers' workshops as if it were infallible doctrine and established fact—a linchpin in the drive shaft of advanced literary opinion. John Gardner, on the other hand, dismissed it as a classroom platitude, part of the litany that teaches students "that one should always write about what one knows, that the most important thing in fiction is point of view, perhaps even that plot and character are the marks of antiquated fiction. To a wise and secure innocent all this would seem very odd, but students in a college classroom are defenseless, and the rewards offered for giving in are many, the chief one being the seductive sweetness of literary elitism."

I happen to be on John Gardner's side here. The academic emphasis on "point of view" in fiction is precisely that—academic. The notion that "the most important thing in fiction is point of view" is a beguiling but vacuous theory that bears only a marginal relation to real practice. And it causes vast amounts of misunderstanding.

To begin, most works of fiction—whatever their quality, whether they are modern or not, and whether they are written in the first person or in the third—regularly and without apology tell their stories by depicting the responses and perceptions of more than one character. In addition, they achieve artistic unity through means that may or may not have much to do with the isolated consciousness of some privileged witness. Even in the touchstone masterpieces of first-person narration, the teller of the tale is not necessarily the protagonist: The narrator of *Gatsby* is Nick Carraway, while its protagonist is of course Gatsby himself, and the story's unity derives from the events around Gatsby, not Nick's perception of them. Catherine Earnshaw is the protagonist of *Wuthering Heights*, but her story is told from the point of view of two seemingly incidental characters. On the other hand, the protagonist of *Jane Eyre* is Jane, and though every single perception in the book belongs to her, the unity of her story derives from the outcome of her tumultuous relationship with Rochester.

The fact is that unity may or may not be supplied by some singular point of view. As Aristotle pointed out in *The Poetics:* "A story does not achieve unity, as some people think, merely by being about one person. Many things, indeed an infinite number of things, happen to the same individual, some of which have no unity at all."

Of course, a consistent point of view can indeed be a guide to unity, and of course, you will want your prose to have a coherent texture. But it is a mistake to assume that point of view itself necessarily endows any story with either unity or coherence. Too often, this rather fussy doctrine pointlessly constricts writers' options and narrows their range. As for the claim that the reader can't *follow* multiple or shifting points of view, it is simply false on its face. The whole history of the novel is testimony to the contrary, from Jane Austen to Thomas Pynchon. In masterpiece after masterpiece, the narrative point of view readily changes from page to page, or even from sentence to sentence, and only delights as it does so. In fact, one of prose fiction's grandest strengths, which it exercises for once in effortless superiority over all other narrative media, including the movies, is its ability to dart in and out of any character's mind at will. To forgo this splendid artistic advantage in the name of some pallid academic theory is really madness.

So what does supply unity, if not point of view? Aristotle's answer is simple and strong. Coherence comes from "unity of action." That is, coherence comes from finding the dramatic conflict of some true protagonist, putting it into play, and pursuing it to its outcome. This is what *really* endows a narrative sequence with wholeness. That "unity of action" may be enhanced and developed wonderfully by all kinds of other elements: a voice, a style, an obsession, a set of images, and—yes, indeed—a coherent point of view. But they cannot replace it.

Meanwhile, classroom overemphasis on "point of view" often leaves writers blind to one incomparably rich perspective that is usually left out of this discussion. I'm speaking of the voice, the mind, and the "sensibility" of the novel itself. In any decent piece of fiction, there will be certain perceptions and thoughts that cannot be ascribed to *any* of the characters. They are the thoughts and the perceptions of *the work*. The work sees, comprehends, and conveys all kinds of meaning that are quite inaccessible to any given character. They belong to the work alone. It is the mind not just of Jane Austen but of *Pride and Prejudice* that tells us that "It is a truth universally acknowledged, that a single man in possession of a good fortune, must be in want of a wife." The certainty, the severity, and the ironic smile of that sentence are an exchange between the reader and the work. The voice of the novel belongs to everyone and no one. It can be in the third person or the first, and, incidentally, it has nothing whatever to do with "omniscience" in any philosophic sense. "Omniscience" is always raised in these discussions, and it is a red herring, a waste of time. The voice of the novel is grounded in the narrative intelligence of the prose. This intelligence will always have some set of limitations or another, but variants on its voice can be heard speaking throughout the greatest fiction ever written.

Inflating point of view, often at the expense of such a voice, is really a hobbyhorse of the modernist movement in its middle, most tepid, academic, and now exhausted phase. The endlessly reiterated claim that only one sensibility can perceive and give substance to any pure, well-wrought story is little more than a rather priggish critical fantasy, launched mainly on the strength of Percy Lubbock's idolatrous relation to Henry James's late fiction (where, I agree, it does have a certain arguable plausibility), and popularized by E. M. Forster in his immensely influential *Aspects of the Novel,* a book that has kept the notion firmly fixed on the American academic map for many generations. It is not eternal truth. It is not even an accurate insight into how most novels work. Forster himself knew perfectly well that Lubbock simply did not make sense on this subject. Speaking of the seemingly anarchic point of view in *War and Peace*, Forster says: "We are bounced up and down—omniscient, semi-omniscient, dramatized here or there as the moment dictates—and at the end we have accepted it all. Mr. Lubbock does not, it is true: Great as he finds the book, he would find it greater if it had a viewpoint; he feels Tolstoy has not pulled his full weight. I feel that the rules of the game of writing are not like this. A novelist can shift his viewpoint if it comes off, and it came off with Dickens and Tolstoy. Indeed, this power to expand and contract perception (of which the shifting viewpoint is a symptom) . . . [is] one of the great advantages of the novel-form, and it has a parallel in our perception of life."

CHARACTERS AND ROLES; TYPES AND INDIVIDUALS

The real way that character and story are usually fused is through the character's role. Let's say some figure flickers out of the murk of your imagination asking for visibility. Your question must be, "Visibility as what? Visibility in what role?" With the drama still emerging, you may not be in a position to assign anyone a clear role quite yet. We've already spoken about the moment when your imagination leaps from having too little to work with to having too much; when your notebook is suddenly crowded with characters angling for prime time. We've said the thing to do is to focus not on plot but on character, and above all to focus on a search for your protagonist. Find the character in the conflict whose fate matters to you most. Once you know whose role is in that top spot, you can begin to determine the roles of all the other characters. But not until—because the identity of the protagonist defines all other roles.

That all sounds very neat. Unfortunately, sorting out who truly owns your story may turn out to be the most confusing part of the job, especially if your story is about an event that is bound together by the intrigue of many networked characters. It may take time for any one character to assert herself or himself as preeminent. When it comes to deciding whose conflict and fate matters most to you, you may have to live with the story awhile. Among a range of active characters, you may hesitate. Your doubts may feel insoluble. You can't shape the story without a protagonist, and without a shaped story you can't find your protagonist. Are you trapped? The only way out of this chicken-egg dilemma is to feel your way to the outcome, watching as you work, and waiting—waiting with the absorbed attention of a predatory beast. You are waiting for the flash of excitement that sparks certainty. It may be subtle, but it should feel like subtle certainty, and it should last and grow stronger, until you can't believe you were ever in any doubt. It is true but not obvious—it takes some time and thought to see it—that the protagonist of *In Cold Blood* is Perry Smith. Harper Lee was with Truman Capote in his first trips to Kansas. She remembers when the young murderer was brought in handcuffs into a courtroom and feeling a jolt go through Capote beside her when the author spotted how, when Smith sat, his short legs, like Capote's own, did not touch the floor. That was the moment, she said, when she knew there would be a book. You may know your protagonist on the first day of work, or it may take a while. You must persist. Without discovering the identity of this key character, you will not have a story. You will wander lost. And how will you recognize her or him? You will recognize her or him by the way you *care*.

TYPES AND STEREOTYPES. Certain novices feel so painfully afraid of letting any hint of a "stereotype" creep into their work that they stumble over one of the most basic truths of the art. Fiction and drama—all fiction, all drama—see and recognize individuals *only* through the prism of types. There is no individuality in fiction without the typical. A character's type is the doorway through which she or he enters the reader's imagination. If you are afraid to show how a character is typical, you will never be able to show anything special about her or him either. We are none of us sui generis. We are all typical of something; in fact, we are typical of many things. At the same time, we are all also absolute individuals: uniquely ourselves, facing our fate in the universe alone. In art as in life, we can face that fate only while occupying some definable place in the world, and our individualism can articulate itself *only* through the lingua franca that comes with our role.

THE FLAT AND THE ROUND. The drawing of characters in fiction is a process subtly bound to the depiction of exaggerated traits—the great and much misunderstood art of caricature. No writer can characterize anyone without *some* exaggeration, if only because selecting any trait over any other distorts things a little. There is nothing wrong with this: The timid fear of exaggeration, like the fear of types, and the fear of drama and improbability, has sunk many a young talent in banality. The real question is not, Whether exaggeration? It is, What kind?

Perhaps the best-known modern discussion of caricature appears in E. M. Forster's *Aspects of the Novel.* It is most remembered for its famous distinction between "flat" and "round" characters. Here is Forster defining "flatness." "Flat characters were called 'humours' in the seventeenth century, and are sometimes called types, and sometimes caricatures. In their purest form, they are constructed round a single idea or quality: When there is more than one factor in them, we get the beginning of the curve toward the round. The really flat character can be compressed in one sentence such as 'I never will desert Mr. Micawber.' There is Mrs. Micawber—she says she won't desert Mr. Micawber, she doesn't, and there she is."

Flat characters, then, are built on some singular trait that defines them unchangeably, come what may. That trait marks their every move. It makes them memorable, predictable, and pure. Flat characters are not necessarily *minor* characters: Many very important characters in Shakespeare are quite flat. Iago, for instance. His single trait: *I hate the Moor*. And though George Santayana pointed out that the streets of mid-Victorian London were overrun with real people who were dead ringers for the caricatures in Dickens's novels, in truth no real person in real life is ever "flat." Flatness is an attribute of the page. Or, mutatis mutandis, the stage. Television sitcoms are riddled with flat characters, not because their flatness makes them simple but because it makes them comic. Occasionally, flatness reaches beyond comedy and into the bizarre: Miss Havisham, in Dickens's *Great Expectations,* manifests flatness as madness—not a long step, when you come to think of it. Comedy and melodrama are built upon the ground of flatness. The whole art of parody, which burlesque and American radio and television humor have made such a tremendous force for laughter, is based upon simply taking a manifestly round character and making her or him flat. Since they are incapable of change, flat characters can go on and on and on, having an endless sequence of adventures. That makes for long runs. Mary McCarthy spoke of the flat quality of comic characters with her typical startling directness. "I have this belief that all comic characters are immortal. They're eternal. I believe this is Bergson's theory too. He has something, I'm told, about comic characters being *figé*. Like Mr. and Mrs. Micawber: They all have to go on forever and be invulnerable. Almost all Dickens's characters have this peculiar existence of eternity, except the heroes, except Pip, or Nicholas Nickleby, or David Copperfield. . . . I would say that it is a law that applies to all novels: that the comic characters are *figé*, are immortal, and that the hero or heroine exists in time, because the hero or heroine is always in some sense equipped with purpose."

Round characters, then, are round because they come "equipped with purpose." Something they want or need that makes them capable of change. They can succeed. They can fail. They will be different afterward. They can leave the past behind. They fall from hope to defeat, or rise up in the reverse. They are not locked into the comedy of some frozen, interminably repetitious destiny. As Christopher Tilghman puts it: "Any story has major and minor characters. And for me, whether they're major or minor has little to do with how much they're on stage. It has to do with whether they develop and change over the course of the story."

Tragedy depends on roundness, while comedy favors the flat: Flatness makes you funny. Yet flatness is not an exclusively comic property. Much villainy, like much heroism, feeds on flatness. Sykes in *Oliver Twist,* like Iago with his "motiveless malignity," is flat. Such villains are evil in essence; it is silly to wring one's humanistic hands and say that they must have something good about them deep down inside. Not in this story, they don't. Iago is a major character and flat as a pancake. Iago's wife Emelia—an intensely moving but minor character—becomes round when the story transforms her gossipy servility into truth telling and courage. There is even something flat about Desdemona, since she dies exactly as she lives: loving and pure. And Othello? Othello is as round as the whole wide world.

YOUR CHARACTERS AND YOU. I keep saying that you must find your characters in your imagination. But then, everything in your imagination was first found somewhere else, wasn't it? Characters are always some elusive combination of yourself and others. Even if you're flying on pure fantasy, *something* in that fantasy is sure to touch on *someone* you've really known. Occasionally a writer will claim she or he never uses models of any sort. "I never use anyone I know," Toni Morrison insists. "I really am very conscientious about that. It's never based on anyone.... Making a little life for oneself by scavenging other people's lives is a big question, and it does have moral and ethical implications." But Morrison is in the minority. J. K. Rowling is more typical: "Mostly, real people inspire a character, but once they are inside your head they start turning into something quite different. Professor Snape and Gilderoy Lockhart both started as exaggerated versions of people I've met, but became rather different once I got them on the page. Hermione is a bit like me when I was eleven, though much cleverer."

Whatever their source, your characters must stand before your mind's eye with the vividness of another being. You must see them, feel them, and care for them as beings apart, distinct from you. This is true even—maybe even especially—of the ones who are based primarily on you. Of the flawed autobiographical fiction I have read, by far the most frequent fault is the failed depiction of the central character. Most novice short stories have some character more or less modeled on their author. Many if not most first novels are at least partly autobiographical. And most such efforts fail simply because the depiction of that prime character is ineffective and dull. It can happen that the peripheral figures are not bad at all; the minor characters, antagonists, foils, and walk-ons may be quite bright and alive. Too bad: They cannot save the day when the autobiographical protagonist is a boring blur. You can't depict what your imagination doesn't see and hear, and most of us see and hear ourselves rather poorly.

We'll be taking a long look at this problem in chapter 6. For the moment, let's leave it with the observation that most autobiographical fiction fails because the author has not been able to "invent"—"invent" in our sense—a workable persona. You must see yourself as a character; you must endow the "yourself" on paper with a vivid separateness from the real "you." To accomplish that, it's best to overlook the familiar distinction (we all make it) between "yourself" and "other people." Replace it, if you can, with another distinction: a distinction between you the imaginer and all that you imagine, including "yourself."

"You" contain multitudes. Tolstoy's biographer Henri Troyat

notes that while the principal characters of *War and Peace* were mainly modeled on real people who can be easily identified in the life of their creator, Tolstoy also endowed most of them with aspects of his own complicated and conflicted personality. "Absorbed in the fate of his heroes," Troyat writes, "Tolstoy became less concerned with himself. By distributing his contradictory emotions among a cast of imaginary characters, he forged his own unity and thereby his balance. Significantly, as soon as he began work on the book, toward the end of 1863, the entries in his diary became shorter and less frequent." Or consider Chekhov's great play *The Seagull:* Every male character in that masterpiece is clearly based on some facet of Chekhov's own personality—and his unseen link to the women, while perhaps not quite so direct, is likewise profound. Here is Ingmar Bergman describing how he broke himself into the pieces that became the characters in his 1969 film *The Ritual:* "I divided myself into three characters. . . . Sebastian Fischer is irresponsible, lecherous, unpredictable, infantile . . . epicurean, lazy, amiable, soft, and brutal. Hans Winkelmann, on the other hand, is orderly, strictly disciplined with a deep sense of responsibility, socially aware, good-humored, and patient. The woman, Thea . . . is unbearably sensitive—cannot even stand to wear clothes at times."

THE DISTINCTNESS OF CHARACTERS. The novelist, Trollope wrote, "desires to make his readers so intimately acquainted with his characters that the creatures of his brain should be to them speaking, moving, living, human creatures. This he can never do unless he knows those fictitious personages himself, and he can never know them unless he can live with them in the full reality of established intimacy. They must be with him as he lies down to sleep, and as he wakes from his dreams. He must learn to hate them and to love them. He must argue with them, quarrel with them, forgive them, and even submit to them."

Writer after writer speaks about this living otherness, about the way the character seems to stand apart from her or his creator, even in the imagination. "The writer's characters," John Gardner wrote, "must stand before us with a wonderful clarity, such continuous clarity that nothing they do strikes us as improbable behavior for just that character, even when the character's action is, as sometimes happens, something that came as a surprise to the writer himself." Patricia Highsmith says much the same: "One must know what these characters look like, how they dress and talk, and one should know even about their childhoods, though their childhoods do not always need to be written into the book. All this is a matter of living with one's characters and in their setting for some period of time before writing the first word. The setting and the people must be seen as clearly as a photograph—with no foggy spots."

Vividness like this must be achieved. Most characters begin as little more than an evanescent flicker in your mind. You start with that flicker. One early step for endowing it with some concreteness would be to endow it with a few vital statistics. John Braine suggests "the briefest possible biographical notes on your characters—age, physical appearance, occupation, income, education, war service if any, marital state, ages of children if any, and so on." It is surprising how resonant such bare-bone facts may become as they occur to you. Once you have a few of them, you may begin to sense something subtler: exchanges, wishes, and relationships—the essentials of personality. You may begin to get a glimpse of what your evanescent flicker is going to do when she or he happens to meet another evanescent flicker, somewhere, somehow.

USING MODELS. It may surprise you to know that it isn't essential—or even very important—that you know all that much about your model, even when you are shaping a really important character. The function of the model is only secondarily to supply information. Its prime function is to get you off to a good start, to propel your imagination forward and give it direction. Asked how much he'd researched Henry Ford to include him as a character in *Ragtime*, E. L. Doctorow answered: "Just enough." Often a quick impression is more useful that any detailed information, precisely because it suggests more and says less. E. M. Forster has some good advice: "A useful trick is to look back on [your model] with half-closed eyes, fully describing certain characteristics. I am left with about two-thirds of a human being and can get to work. A likeness isn't aimed at and couldn't be obtained, because a man's only himself amidst the particular circumstances of his life and not amid other circumstances. . . . When all goes well, the original material soon disappears, and a character who belongs to the book and nowhere else emerges."

William Styron remembers that when he was writing *Sophie's Choice,* "The kernel of my character, Sophie, was a real person, a person who looked and walked and talked very much like the Sophie I created. She was a young woman who disappeared from my life almost as quickly as she came. The story itself is really an improvisation . . . her real destiny—I don't know what it really was at all."

As Thomas Mann's wife recalled: "The remarkable thing about him [was that] he got the complete picture of a person immediately. . . . He didn't observe people for the sake of portraying them afterward. Once he had seen someone, he had a mental image of him, and when a fictional figure came along whom this someone matched, the someone popped up again, but not intentionally. There is no question of that. That's the way it was with the Krull family. Asked about his models, Thomas Mann answered, 'Oh, I once watched them for half an hour on a Rhine steamer.'"

John Gardner pointed out that it is almost impossible really to copy a model straight from life: "[E]xcept as creatures of the imagination, characters in fiction do not exist. It is true that Mrs. Eustace may be based on, say, Trollope's Aunt Maude. But except in the writing of a biography (and, strictly speaking, not even there), a writer cannot take a character from life. Every slightest change the writer makes in the character's background and experience must have subtle repercussions. I am not the same person I would have been if my father had been rich, or had owned elephants."

And if you insist upon taking a fictional character straight from life? Be my guest—but be warned that, even apart from a lawsuit, the roman à clef can be a treacherous form. It falls between the stools of nonfiction's authority and fiction's imaginative power. Meanwhile, if you decide to portray a living person in terms that you even suspect may be actionable, my advice would be like that of many editors. First, examine your conscience. Do you really *have* to go ahead with this? If the answer is yes, by all means, go ahead. Say what you have to say. Show what you have to show. Lay it all out. Don't pull your punches and don't slip into the dull fakery of "thin disguises." When you are done, but well before publication, tell your editor everything. But I mean *everything*—not least what embarrasses *you*. And show every single questionable passage to a competent attorney, fully explaining each and every point of even conceivable vulnerability. Then take that attorney's advice. In America, most authors' fears of libel are unfounded. Our freedom of expression really is pretty broad. Even so, a truly libelous passage can get you into some truly hot water.

While thin disguises tend to make thin characters, composite traits can merge, meld, and make something new. The simplest and most basic way to stimulate your imagination is to put a familiar fact into an unfamiliar context. It's a trick that can sometimes be turned by using little more than a switch in grammar. As Doris Lessing says, "It's amazing what you find out about yourself when you write in the first person about someone very different from you." A model from real life can be utterly transformed by just one fictitious fact. Good scholarly evidence now suggests that Mark Twain based his greatest character, Huckleberry Finn, not on one but two poor boys with the gift of gab. Model one came from Twain's boyhood hometown of Hannibal, Missouri. Biographers have known the identity this wily youth for a very long time. He was white. Model two was a kid Twain encountered after he was famous, not long before he began writing *Huckleberry Finn.* This model was a waiter in a hotel where the great man was staying, a jabbering little wise guy whose lilting voice the enchanted Twain set out to capture in a magazine article of the period. It was his first stab at Huck's voice. This boy was black. Does this composite of white and black suggest something to you? Consider the theme of *Huckleberry Finn,* how Huck is white and his companion and secret sharer, Jim, is black, and how together they are in flight, except that they are fleeing *down* the Mississippi, running the wrong way, into slave country.

COMPOSITES. As Flaubert famously remarked: "*I* am Madame Bovary." There's no doubt he meant it, but we also know that the wretched heroine of his great novel is based on (at least) two real women. One was a trapped and embittered housewife named Delphine Delamare, a bewildered provincial hopelessly snared in debt, a mediocre marriage, adultery, and the sticks. It was Delphine Delamare's real suicide that put the idea for the book into Flaubert's youthful head. The other model was an articulate, very with-it, knowing, brilliantly connected Parisian sophisticate named Louise Colet—*precisely* the woman poor Delphine Delamare would have given anything, *anything,* to be. When Louise Colet met Flaubert, he was a madly ambitious young man with big ideas and no CV, in search of some large project to make his name, very unsure of himself, and more than a little depressed. Louise Colet was older than Flaubert and way ahead of him in her career. They began a passionate, complex love affair through which Flaubert broke his depression and found a little of that missing confidence. He began to weave their relationship through his entire experience of writing the book. So, who is Madame Bovary again? All of the above, and none. Made from others, she is herself.

One of the most familiar characters in modern American fiction, Don Corleone in Mario Puzo's *The Godfather,* is an astonishing composite. It turns out that Puzo wrote his famous book without having any firsthand knowledge of the Mafia. "I'm ashamed to admit that I wrote *The Godfather* entirely from research. I never met a real honest-to-God gangster. I knew the gambling world pretty good, but that's all." Who, then, served as the model for the Don Corleone Marlon Brando played? Puzo looked closer to home. "Whenever the godfather opened his mouth, in my own mind I heard the voice of my mother. My mother was a wonderful, handsome woman, but a fairly ruthless person."

LIVING YOUR CHARACTERS. To create a character is to play that character's part in your mind, and acting is a good metaphor for the process. As Richard Rhodes says: "Inventing fictional characters... [is] like improvisational acting. All your characters are you, virtuals of you; writing is a controlled process of splitting into virtual personalities in the safe haven of the page. I can't tell you how to do that except to say that it feels like self-hypnosis and probably is. Controlled meditation helps. Once you've invented a character and gotten to know her, you relax into the role and she appears." Rhodes adds: "The haunting is voluntary." It is a mixture of magic and technique. The novelist Desmond Barry tells how, when he was writing about Jesse and Frank James in his first novel, *The Chivalry of Crime,* the Booker Prize winner Peter Carey walked him through a writer's equivalent of the Stanislavsky method of acting. "He said, okay. Don't think about writing. Just imagine yourself into the scene. Walk into the room. What do you see? He just said, do it, do it. Walk into the room. So I walked into the room. What do you see? So I described everything that I could see in the room. Then he said, how do you feel? Who is that person? What does she make you feel like? It was this whole process of . . . visualization." Incidentally, Peter Carey supplies a fine sketch using much the same method in his own novel, *The Unusual Life of Tristan Smith.*

KNOWING YOUR CHARACTERS. Always remember that you "know" vastly more than you think you know. Impressions, even fleeting impressions, are in their unsuspected way a kind of knowledge, too. In one of his most famous remarks, Henry James advised young writers: "Try to be one of the people on whom nothing is lost." This line appears in a particularly brilliant passage in which James is discussing, precisely, how much more we "know" than we think we know. "I remember an English novelist, a woman of genius, telling me that she was much commended for the impression she had managed to give in one of her tales of the nature and way of life of the French Protestant youth. She had been asked where she learned so much about this recondite being, she had been congratulated on her peculiar opportunities. These opportunities consisted in her having once, in Paris, as she ascended a staircase, passed an open door where, in the household of a *pasteur,* some of the young Protestants were seated at table round a finished meal. The glimpse made a picture; it lasted only a moment, but that moment was experience. She had got her direct personal impression, and she turned out her type. She knew what youth was, and what Protestantism; she also had the advantage of having seen what it was to be French, so that she converted these ideas into a concrete image and produced a reality. Above all, however, she was blessed with the faculty which when you give it an inch takes an ell, and which for the artist is a much greater source of strength than any accident of residence or of place in the social scale. The power to guess the unseen from the seen, to trace the implication of things, to judge the whole piece by the pattern, the condition of feeling life in general so completely that you are well on your way to knowing any particular corner of it—this cluster of gifts may almost be said to constitute experience, and they occur in country and in town, and in the most differing stages of education. If experience consists of impressions, it may be said that impressions *are* experience, just as (have we not seen it?) they are the very air we breathe. Therefore, if I should certainly say to a novice, 'Write from experience and experience only,' I should feel that this was rather a tantalizing monition if I were not careful immediately to add, 'Try to be one of the people on whom nothing is lost!' "

There it is: *The power to guess the unseen from the seen, to trace the implication of things.* James is right, of course: This is the "experience" from which fiction comes. Most of the time, you will be using experience from an untapped and until now barely noticed fund of knowledge already in your mind. Of course, that "inner" knowledge will have to be buttressed and corrected by the kind of knowledge you acquire "out there": You will also need information you can confirm. Yet it's generally best to move from impression to information, rather than the reverse. First imagine your character. Then dig up the facts you need to confirm or correct the picture you have. Christopher Tilghman shrewdly observes that when you are imagining people every day, month after month, "Sooner or later you're going to know who they are and how they would behave. It just isn't that complicated. . . . I've been working on a novella for a couple years about the Shakers. I haven't researched the subject; I don't want to. I finally gave the novella to Caroline [Tilghman's wife], who . . . had done a lot of research on the Shakers. She kept on saying, 'How did you know that?' And I'd say, 'I didn't know it, but there's just no other way for it to work out.' And I don't think that's because I have some great intuitive power. I think it's because if you spend six months thinking about how a community—in this case, a celibate community of ninety percent women and ten percent men—would organize itself, how it would behave, what kind of people you'd find there, then more often than not you're right. My advice to anyone writing about something researchable is, write it first, then research it."

VOICE

A character's voice is the *sound* of her or his identity. It is the sonic fingerprint of personality. There are few better ways to capture the essence of a character than to pin down the cadences and catches, the music and mannerisms, the whole resonance of how that figure speaks. See your characters, yes; but remember that your medium is words. You must hear them, too. When you've caught how someone speaks, you will know much about what she or he is likely to say—and knowing that will, in turn, tell you much about what she or he is going to do. Once you have caught the voice, maybe you won't have to "make up" the character's story after all. Maybe the character will tell you the story all by herself. "I shrink from saying this," Robertson Davies said, ". . . but I hear the story, I am told the story." Toni Morrison says much the same thing. After she reaches a certain point, "I have the characters to go to for reassurance. By that time they are friendly enough to tell me if the rendition of their lives is authentic or not."

If you can capture a character's voice by mimicking it out loud, wonderful—but it's enough to hear it in your mind's ear. Silent or spoken, mimicry will sweep you into your character as few things can. As for dialogue, read every line and clause of it out loud. Nobody's listening. You're not up for the Academy Award. Go ahead. It must be fully satisfactory to the ear. "If you can't speak it aloud," says John Braine, "it's no good." John Steinbeck advised the same: "If you are using dialogue—say it aloud as you write it out. Only then will it have the sound of speech."

Novelists from Dickens to Philip Roth have been wonderful mimics, and mimicry infuses their art. Dickens loved acting and reading from his work, and his famous performances were a natural outgrowth of his process of creation.

Once you've captured a character's voice, you can talk to that character. You can ask questions and get the character to explain, either to you or to others. You can interview your character—and the whole story may come blurting out. Is there something you don't understand? Ask the character to write you a letter and explain. As Anne Lamott says, "When you don't know what else to do . . . you might try telling part of your history—part of a character's history—in the form of a letter." The letter can be from you to your character, or from your character to you, or from one character to another. Allan Gurganus ended up using one such letter in *Oldest Living Confederate Widow Tells All*. "When I started . . . I recognized . . . that I was writing in the voice of an ungrammatical woman. She said 'ain't' a lot. She was very colloquial in her speech, and yet I was confused because I thought she was from an upper-middle or upper-class small-town family. That interests me very much, to have a character who can go anywhere but chooses a particular perspective. I was confused about why she was saying 'ain't,' so I typed 'Why I say ain't' at the top of the page. And that became a chapter which was my explanation to myself."

DIALOGUE AND INNER SPEECH

Film and television have convinced too many writers that heaps of dialogue make novels more like movies and therefore good. This is an amateur's fantasy, and it has induced some writers to surrender the few advantages they have over cinematic storytelling. The moviemaker is stuck with what the camera can see and the microphone can hear. You have more freedom. You can summarize situations. You can forthrightly give us people's histories. You can concentrate ten years into ten words. You can move anywhere you like outside real time. You can tell us—just tell us—what people are thinking and feeling. Yes, abundant dialogue can lighten a story, make it more readable and sparkle with wonders. But it is pitiably inadequate before what it is not suited to do. Exposition, for example: the "five w's"—the who, what, when, where, and why of a given situation. Jimmying this information into a visual background through performance and dialogue is cumbersome stuff. As Edith Wharton put it, "When, in real life, two or more people are talking together, all that is understood between them is left out of their talk." People do not usually remind each other of who they are and where they come from when they chat.

If you have the happy knack of doing dialogue easily, you are almost sure to overdo it. Trollope knew the temptation well and warned against it. "It is so easy to make any two persons talk on any casual subject with which the writer presumes himself to be conversant! Literature, philosophy, politics, or sport may be handled in a loosely discursive style; and the writer, while indulging himself and filling his pages, is apt to think he is pleasing his reader. I think he can make no greater mistake."

Wharton's old-fashioned advice on this subject is generally sound. "The use of dialogue in fiction seems to be one of the few things about which a fairly definite rule may be laid down. It should be reserved for the culminating moments, and regarded as the spray into which the great wave of narrative breaks in curving toward the watcher on the shore."

But it is possible to use your character's voice in much more than dialogue. A voice can color the world. Even when you write in the third person, a character's voice can permeate any passage, and if you are writing in the first person, it is easy to glide imperceptibly between a rather impersonal expository tone and a more intimate personal voice. In *Gatsby*, when Nick Carraway is describing, say, the car ride from West Egg into New York, his first-person voice slips from sounding like the WASPy upper-class nice guy he is and tends to sound rather more "like a novel." But when everybody settles in at the Plaza Hotel, Nick's voice becomes just a little confessional, and he sounds like himself again.

This merger of the "voice of a novel" with the voice of a character is one of the form's most potent techniques, and only fiction has it. In third person—or even in the first—you can use the prose to mimic the otherwise inarticulate inner speech of a character, and you can do it, lightly, in small ways, or you can drench everything in the sound of the character's mind, articulating thoughts she or he would never be willing or able to put into words. Flaubert speaks *for* Madame Bovary. He colors his own magnificent prose with the cadences and sound of her faltering, confused, meretricious language. He gives voice to her mind even—especially—when her language is unspoken, saying what Emma is incapable of saying, merging her words with his and articulating what she will go to her death without ever quite being able to grasp.

There are two ways to do this. One is to provide the characters' "stream of consciousness" in first-person soliloquies. The classic citations are in Joyce's *Ulysses*. These are sublime. Yet, because it is in the first person, most fictional stream of consciousness is rather cumbersome and inadaptive. Indirect discourse in the third person is a more usable and supple method. In it, the narrating voice of the novel begins to sound like the character's voice and mind, and articulates her or his otherwise inarticulate thoughts.

Narrowly defined, "indirect discourse" is a grammatical convenience that sidesteps direct quotation by presenting spoken words in the third person. Direct discourse: " 'I refuse to go,' Maurice replied." Indirect discourse: "Maurice replied that he refused to go." When we speak of indirect discourse as a method in fiction, however, the phrase acquires a much broader application. Most of our thoughts and feelings are not immediately bound to language. We almost always feel an emotion and connect to a thought well before we can *say* precisely what either one is. The art of indirect discourse—broadly defined—lets you put this inarticulate aspect of any character into the character's own words. It speaks with a voice that is neither theirs nor yours, but which reaches beyond the characters' explicit words and thoughts to become the voice of the fiction itself, making consciousness a unity.

THE SYMPATHETIC AND
THE UNSYMPATHETIC

"I once asked Ethan Canin," Anne Lamott reports, "to tell me the most valuable thing he knew about writing, and without hesitation he said, 'Nothing is so important as a likable narrator. Nothing holds a story together better.'" And no less an authority than Anthony Trollope would seem to agree. "Rochester's wretched thralldom to his mad wife, in *Jane Eyre*, is a tragedy. But these stories charm us not simply because they are tragic, but because we feel that men and women with flesh and blood, creatures with whom we can sympathize, are struggling amidst their woes. It all lies in that. No novel is anything, for the purposes either of comedy or tragedy, unless the reader can sympathize with the characters whose names he finds upon the pages."

Not everyone agrees. Tom Wolfe, whose work stands so very close to satire, rejects the need for likability. When *The Bonfire of the Vanities* was attacked for its unsympathetic characters, Wolfe responded: "I . . . looked back at novels about cities that I admire tremendously, John O'Hara's *BUtterfield 8*, Zola's *Nana*, and Balzac's *Cousin Bette*, and it's hard to find any major character in them who is sympathetic in the usual meaning of that term."

What is sympathetic may not be likable. What is likable may not be admirable. And any combination of the above may or may not be interesting. Yet Wolfe sounds a little perplexed and adds this footnote to his case against lovability: "Somewhere I ran into a theory which I'd never heard of before, that without love from the author a character is not noble. I was being called incapable of love for the characters. Actually, I was in awe of the characters. I couldn't very well love them."

In truth, you are going to feel all kinds of responses to your characters, and your prose is likely to be, one way or another, an invitation to the reader to join in those feelings. They may or may not include sympathy and love. Wolfe says he feels "awe" for his characters. (Isn't there more than a little amused contempt as well?) In satire, loathing can be as useful as love.

Whatever feeling you ask the reader to join, let it be strong. If your talent is connected to your passion, it will all find expression in a thousand signs, in turns that will be too multiple in meaning for one simple value judgment. The real issue isn't whether you love or hate your characters. The real issue, whatever the bond, is the vitality and force of what you do feel. Love is doubtless the highest peak on the range, and Wolfe's critic was right about one thing: If you really experience a character's nobility (*your* kind of nobility, something *you* take seriously), the glow of it will be felt somewhere in your prose. But not all characters are noble, and many passions other than love must flow through what you do if it is to live. This may have been what Chekhov had in mind when he advised a colleague: "Love your characters—but not aloud."

5

INVENTING YOUR STYLE

Style is the relationship between writer and reader, and it is the vehicle through which you say whatever you have to say. It is the way you get your story told, and it therefore consists of all your language and the whole manner you bring to its use. Style is always much more than décor or ornament, and it is always more than the way you dress up your story. It is the complete sound of what you write. Not just the fancy parts. All of it. And as you write, you are going to have to "invent" it—invent in "our" sense—by working once again in that realm that lies between making it up and finding it.

Writers often talk about "finding their voice," and that is indeed just what it feels like. In fact, most writers have to "find their voice" many times over, since each new project, with its changed subject and set of demands, will call for some change in manner and inflection. But it is a little misleading to speak of the "voice" in the singular. Yes, the style you end with will have a kind of synthetic unity, but most styles are in fact composites of many voices. Some are lifted from the writer's own voiceprint. Some are echoes of other people. Many belong to characters in the story. A few may be the classic voices of fiction itself. Some intensely conscious stylists claim complete control over their manner and seek any number of special effects: Nabokov is the classic example. Others disdain "style"—"I wish my prose to be transparent," says V. S. Naipaul. "I don't want the reader to stumble over me; I want him to look through what I'm saying to what I'm describing. I don't want him ever to say, 'Oh, goodness, how nicely written this is.' That would be a failure." Most likely, your working MO, like that of most writers, will turn out to be some personal, idiosyncratic combination of both: a merging of focused control and loose letting it happen. So be it. However you put it together, your prose is going to have some sort of style, whether you like it or not. Once your story is fully in place, once you've said your say, your style will also be in place. It can't help but be there. Maybe you'll fuss over it and maybe you won't. But you'll never write a single successful sentence without it.

That's because style is the unseen something that makes any given sentence able to stand up all on its own. In one of her many wise remarks, that sage woman Eudora Welty once suggested that style is whatever lifts what a writer has to say out of the "subjective" into the "objective." That is, style is what enables the writing to rise from its murky, confused preexistence as mere possibility and achieve the shining status of the autonomous and the written. Style therefore marks your prose not only with "you," but with whatever makes it stand apart from you, whatever makes it say what *it* has to say, and say it right, talking back to you as it does. "Born subjective," Welty said, "we learn what our own idea of the objective is as we go along." Your style is what your writing will sound like after you have finally finished the seemingly endless internal argument over the rightness and wrongness of every detail on every page. It is nothing more, but also nothing less, than this rightness. When it is finally there, it will seem somehow always to have been there, waiting to tell you what ought to be.

Meanwhile, style stamps your writing with your identity—

and this too it will do partly unconsciously, whether you do or don't try, and whether you like it or not. The way even impersonal prose is made uniquely the writer's own is one of the durable mysteries of writing. Truman Capote said: "I don't think style is consciously arrived at, any more than one arrives at the color of one's eyes. After all, your style *is* you. At the end the personality of a writer has so much to do with the work. The personality has to be humanly there. Personality is a debased word, I know, but it's what I mean. The writer's individual humanity, his word or gesture toward the world, has to appear almost like a character that makes contact with the reader. If the personality is vague or confused or merely literary, *ça ne va pas.*" Patricia Highsmith went a little further: "Most beginning writers think that established writers must have a formula for success. . . . There is no secret of success in writing except individuality, or call it personality. And since every person is different, it is only for the individual to express his difference from the next fellow. This is what I call the opening of the spirit. But it isn't mystic. It is merely a kind of freedom—freedom organized."

The elusive way style makes your personality visible—the way *it* "invents" what we might call your "prose personality"—contains a seeming paradox. Style is a created, man-made thing, and yet it finally emerges as naturally as breathing. Or put it another way: To work, any style must seem "natural"—"natural" to you—and yet its "natural" voice or voices can be achieved only through effort and polish. Style is indeed the very voice of individualism in prose, yet it can be found—be "invented"—only through the writer's self-surrender within that large community of voices that, in any language, comprises literacy. Style is the personality of your writing, and you find your personality in prose, as in life, through interaction with others.

The problem that defeats all too many novices is that they hope—and foolishly, in their dreams, really believe—that their own voice, the one they've always had, the "natural" one they use in their daily talk, the voice they use to make a date or call home to say they'll be back a little late, will be able somehow, all on its own, to endow their writing with a workable prose style. Naively, very understandably, and fatally, they lean way too hard into the "natural" side of style's inevitable bonding of the natural with the artificial. This can be carried to crazy lengths. I have not just sometimes but often run into hopefuls who avoid reading work by other writers not so much out of laziness as out of fear: fear that another voice or style, if it is strong enough, interesting enough, alive enough, might somehow mess up the wonderful "natural" purity of their own.

What these writers don't get is that the only way to find "their" voices is among, and through, the voices of other people and other writers. Sure, you have your own voice, and it has its individual voiceprint. The problem is that you are not talking; you are *writing*. And what you write is not talk: It is prose. Talk and prose work are two different entities, and when it comes to writing, chat won't cut it. And the sound of prose, even the prose of your own voice, is something you have got to *hear*.

Many writers tune their ear for prose by starting their day with a prose stimulant—a good, hot, steaming cup of strong, perfect prose. "I'll read something," says Maya Angelou, "maybe the Psalms, maybe, again, something from Mr. Dunbar, James Weldon Johnson. And I'll remember how beautiful, how pliable the language is, how it will lend itself. If you pull it, it says, 'Okay.' I remember that, and I start to write." Mary Gordon has an elaborate ritual: "Before I take pen to paper, I read. I can't begin my day reading fiction; I need the more intimate tone of letters and journals. From these journals and letters—the horse's mouth—I copy something that has taken my fancy. . . . I move to Proust; three pages read in English, and the same three in French. . . . Then I proceed to the fiction I am reading seriously, the one I'm using as a kind of tuning fork, the one I need to sound the tone I will take up in the fiction I'm writing at the time. . . . I copy paragraphs whose heft and cadence I can learn from. And some days, if I'm lucky, the very movement of my hand, like a kind of dance, starts up another movement that allows me to forget the vanity, the folly, of what I am really about." Paul Johnson, one of the most prolific essayists in England, turns to given masters for given needs. "Every writer will have his own prose-stimulants. Mine are the King James Bible, Bacon, Milton, and Hobbes. Some Swift and Hazlitt; a little Gibbon; Byron's letters continually. I read Jane Austen for her subtle ironies, so wonderfully under control, and her ability to advance a story swiftly while never appearing breathless. I study Waugh for his unusual capacity to combine stylistic luxury with strict economy of words." It would do you no harm to have on hand your own stimulants, loved passages of the prose that matters most to you, prose that sings the way you want to sing. It is not that you are going to copy this stuff. You are going to strengthen and guide your own voice with its sound in your ear.

Of course, there's going to be some intimate if unconscious link between your speaking voice and the prose you "invent," but what sounds most "natural" in your prose will not necessarily be talky. Almost nobody, even the most conversational writer, *really* talks the way she or he writes. Just try reading any transcript of tape-recorded talk. It almost always comes out sounding thin, feeble, repetitious, and boring to the point of numbness. Here is how Toni Morrison puts it: "I don't trust my writing that is not written [as opposed to dictated into a tape recorder], although I work very hard in subsequent revisions to remove the writerliness from it, to give it a combination of lyrical, standard, and colloquial language. To pull all these things together into something that I think is much more alive, and representative. But I don't trust something that occurs to me, that is spoken and transferred immediately to the page."

But why? Why should okay talk, when transcribed, not turn out to be okay prose?

Because talking and writing are different in just the way listening and reading are different. That difference affects everything. As Fran Lebowitz says, "In conversation you can use timing, a look, inflection, pauses. But on the page all you have is commas, dashes, the amount of syllables in a word. When I write I read everything out loud to get the right rhythm."

Moreover, most talk has precious little staying power. Once removed from its immediate context, it always fades and usually dies.

But most important of all, the *focus* of talk is totally different from the focus of prose. A talker focuses on the relation between her or his subject and the listener—and that listener is always a real person, physically (okay, telephonically) on the scene, present, part of the exchange. No third party is contemplated. Prose, on the other hand, must focus on an absent and, in fact, "invented"—"invented" in our sense—figure known as "the Reader." Prose—all prose—addresses this absent but imagined figure and shapes itself and that figure and its needs in an unseen relationship between them. In "our" sense, it both "invents" and is "invented" by that absolutely necessary yet invisible personage, that disembodied, Protean, purely imaginary being. The tone of the prose is created by the feel of the relationship between what we might call the persona of the Writer and the persona of the Reader—invented beings, both.

In talk, the Reader's persona does not exist—while creating the Reader's persona is an essential (if often unconscious) part of the writer's work. Of course, you want to have not the Reader but lots of readers, plural: lots and lots of real people "out there" who will pick up your work and, by reading, slip into the persona your prose has invented for them—real people taking up the Reader's role. Yet as you work, you can have only the vaguest and usually contradictory and confused idea of who all those real people might be. Instead, your prose must address—and "invent"—only one: *the* Reader. It doesn't matter whether you want your work to reach millions or only a small select coterie: Your prose is going to invent some kind of reader through its tone of address, through its manner of speaking, through the way it makes contact, and through the feeling of its exchange.

You create the Reader with your style, in a word. It is your manner of sharing, and only after you have created the Reader can real people come along and subtly, or not so subtly, imagine themselves in the role of the being you have invented. They will doubtless imagine this as semiconsciously as you imagined it for them. No matter. The pleasure of this delicate but potent experience of release from the real self is one of the prime pleasures of the text.

To illustrate: The same person may one day read and thoroughly enjoy Mark Twain's *Huckleberry Finn,* only to turn the next day with equal pleasure to Henry James's *The Wings of the Dove.* The voices of these two novels could hardly be more unlike, and one major way they are unlike is that each addresses an utterly different Reader. The persona to whom Huck Finn yammers away about Aunt Sally and Pa is a very different persona than the one to whom James presents the half-heartless second thoughts of Kate Croy over the death in Venice of Milly Theale. Yet the real Reader of either book can effortlessly "become" the persona of either book. It happens without a second thought. It is like playing a role—albeit passively, almost unconsciously. One becomes the Reader while also remaining oneself. Every writer's Reader differs. The Reader of Virginia Woolf is exquisitely attuned to every nuance. The Reader of Elmore Leonard has a mean, tough, get-down mind. The Reader of George Eliot has a masterful understanding, always alert to new ways to extend a menaced but magisterial grasp over the motives and details of daily life. The Reader of Emily Brontë feels the shudder of every slamming door and stifled sob. The Reader of Philip Roth is ready to listen to someone talk him through the craziest stories, while the Reader of Henry James, as T. S. Eliot put it, has a mind so fine no idea can violate it. The Reader listening to Nick Carraway tell *The Great Gatsby* is, like Nick, an awfully decent upper-class American, and the Reader of *On the Road* is leaning forward in the backseat, passing a joint back and forth while the car streams down a two-lane blacktop under the vaulted starry night.

This invention of "the Reader," the secret sharer of your every syllable, is a defining element of style. Like everything else in your writing, it will be pieced together from all kinds of remembered scraps and tags of language: books, voices, people, moments of wonder, whatever. It ends up as style: That is, it ends up as *a relationship*, and that relationship is always between two invented beings, exactly as, at this moment, I am inventing you and you are inventing me. As a writer, you have a great deal to say about what this relationship is to be. But it is not entirely in your hands. It is ultimately a collaboration, an exchange, and it is best described by the adjectives that describe human exchange. Whatever the relationship, it should offer the real person reading your prose the gift of some larger, richer consciousness.

YOUR VOICE, AND MAKING IT SOUND GOOD

John Wray, whose fine debut novel, *The Right Hand of Sleep*, went on to fully deserved international critical acclaim, once told me that "the first thing I realized, way back when I first began to work on the book, was that if this thing had any hope of being good, I had to make it at least *sound* good. At least in my own ears, it had to do that much. Of course, sounding good wouldn't necessarily make the book *be* good, but maybe if it did sound good—really good—the sound might pull the story along with it and help carry the novel the whole distance. That helped me. That made it possible for me to work."

This remark might strike you as a confession to superficiality. Absolutely not. It is a penetrating insight into how style works as a basic tool for invention. A voice can be exactly the lever you need to lift a story into existence, functioning in very much the same way that the story itself leverages a character into life.

We've already noticed that the *sound* of a character's voice may cue you over what the character is going to say. It's not a long step from knowing what a character will say to knowing what that character will do. Likewise, knowing what a story will sound like is closer than you may think to what that story is going to be.

"Making things sound good" brings us to the tricky issue of influence. You are going to be influenced. Whether they know and admit it or not, all writers without exception work under the influence of other writers. Don't ask whether you are going to be influenced by other writers. Ask how. You learned to talk from other talkers, and the talk of others is still teaching you. It's where you got your fluency, your accent, your vocabulary, your slang—just about everything—and all these things are continually refreshed by—more talk. Well, in just the same way, other writers will teach you how to write, and they are going to keep on teaching you as long as you keep going.

I know, I know—this sounds frustrating. You aren't *looking* for other writers' voices. You're looking for your own. And you should be. But precisely because style is an exchange, the place to find your voice is among the voices of others and through the love of them.

Let me illustrate. Let's say you love the hard-boiled voice of Raymond Chandler's prose. You want to try something like it, and you don't quite know how. You have nothing but the voice. It may be all you need. A Chandlerlike voice is capable of telling only certain kinds of stories about certain kinds of people. Yet the people Chandler knew and wrote about—his era, his kind of California, even his kind of crime—all of these things have vanished from the face of the earth. You cannot retrieve them. But you do have that voice. Whatever it has, whatever it is, remains alive, alive in your love of it, inside you, somehow or other. That alone offers you the basis of a persona. You can't turn it into Philip Marlowe of course. Marlowe has long since been invented. But the voice may lead you to some equivalent in *your* world.

You find your voice in, against, through Chandler's voice, as Walter Mosley did when he created Easy Rawlins.

Or let's suppose you are infatuated with Virginia Woolf's mature style, as Michael Cunningham must have been when that voice inspired him to write his best-selling novel *The Hours.* The voice in *Mrs. Dalloway,* like the voice of Chandler, can and will tell only certain kinds of stories about certain kinds of people. The real Michael Cunningham lives a very long way from Bloomsbury in 1922. The people in the pages of *Mrs. Dalloway* are long gone. Cunningham's childhood as an army brat was remote indeed from the one lived by the brilliant, troubled daughter of Sir Leslie Stephen at Hyde Park Gate. Yet something in the promptings of that Bloomsbury voice gave Cunningham the focus he needed to invent and find in his late-twentieth-century Greenwich Village persona the reader and writer needed to produce *The Hours.*

Note that neither Mosley nor Cunningham especially resembles his "mentor." They love them. The tie that binds is not resemblance but passion. And when you fall in love with any writer, it is usually the style you fall for. As the critic Terry Teachout writes: "Sometimes it's only a passing fancy ... sometimes it's far more serious. . . . Sometimes it's with a stranger, sometimes an old friend whom I suddenly come to see in a different light. But no matter who the objects of my literary affection may be, the nature of our relationship is the same: I want not merely to enjoy but to become them, to absorb their stylistic essence and be changed by it." Just as you can find yourself only through the coordinates of your human relationships with others, so will you find your voice, your style, your sound, only by zoning in on it through and among the voices of others, the styles and sounds that matter to you and sing silently in your own mind.

Yet any voice you're likely to love will probably have already been made a little remote by time. What you love, as Mosley loved Chandler and Cunningham loved Woolf, will already be turning into literature. In the process, it will have become slightly dated. This dated distance is both an obstacle to be overcome and an opportunity for you to invent. It doesn't matter that you can't *become* Raymond Chandler or Virginia Woolf. (Would you *want* to?) The voices of the English language, both spoken and written, and in all their countless varieties, change in subtle and unsubtle ways not just from generation to generation, but from year to year. An unsupple, unimaginative effort to resurrect the dead, a *crude* effort to "become" them can only result in some too "literary" style—and, as Truman Capote said, *ça ne va pas.*

But love of the other voice can help you find your own voice. Any voice, including your own, must be a mixture of past and present. That's how all language works. You are going to echo the talk that taught you to talk, and you are going to echo the prose that taught you to write. But what you do with any language must sing with some excitement that is yours and yours alone. As John Gardner pointed out, what is "yours" has to be different from any generation before you. "A good novelist creates powerfully vivid images in the reader's mind, and nothing is more natural than that a beginning novelist should try to imitate the effects of some master, because he loves that writer's vivid world. But finally imitation is a bad idea. What writers of the past saw and said, even the recent past, is history. It is obvious that no one any longer talks like the characters of Jane Austen or Charles Dickens. It is perhaps less obvious that hardly anyone under thirty talks like the characters of Saul Bellow and his imitators. The beginning novelist can learn from his betters their tricks of accurate observation, but what he sees must be his own time and place. . . ."

Who better to comment on this stylistic transition between the generations than Martin Amis, the celebrated literary son of a celebrated literary sire? "My father said to me that when a writer of twenty-five puts pen to paper he's saying to the writer of fifty that it's no longer like that, it's like *this.* The older writer, at some point, is going to lose touch with what the contemporary moment feels like. . . . When my father started writing, he was saying to older writers—for instance, Somerset Maugham—it's not like that. It's like *this.*"

This is absolutely true. The quiet nerviness that makes a young writer mutter to a Somerset Maugham, or a Saul Bellow, or a Kingsley—or Martin—Amis, "It's no longer like *that,* it's like *this,*" is indispensable to that writer's identity as an artist. There is a shade of Oedipal defiance in it, a defiance driven by both refusal and love. No style can be forged in isolation. Style, as we've seen, is an interlocking set of relationships: relationships to your Reader and to your story, but also to your language. That means a relationship to the voices of the past. But it takes two to have any relationship, and a writer's relation to her or his language is not egalitarian. The language may be way bigger than you are, but you must lead.

And watch out for what is too easily derived. Throughout the late 1980s and well into the 1990s, the most commonly imitated writer of short stories in the workshops I taught was Raymond Carver. (In the early '80s it was Donald Barthelme). Ironically, what those many young writers were imitating in their Raymond Carver knockoffs was the indelible force of Carver's chronic, and rather touching, awkwardness. Why? Well, for one thing it was easy—all too easy—to imitate. An obscurely stymied, fumbling, tongue-tied quality marks Carver as a stylist, just as it marked him as a man. In every story, you can feel him straining against his own inarticulateness. It's part of his harsh pathos and power. Yet two generations of young writers, some of them much more at ease with themselves than poor Carver ever got to be, set out to imitate the groping, uncertain eloquence of this man who was so radically uneasy in his own skin: the blurting monosyllabic eloquence of the hurt mind at 4:00 A.M.

Carver couldn't *help* his style: He couldn't make the words work any other way. What gave Carver his great force and influence was anything but virtuosity—the man was the antivirtuoso of his era. It was the obdurate, fumbling force of his personality.

Hemingway, the most imitated writer of the twentieth century, would have understood. "What amateurs call a style is usually only the unavoidable awkwardness in first trying to make something that has not heretofore been made. Almost no new classics resemble other previous classics. At first people can see only the awkwardnesses. Then they are not so perceptible. When they show so very awkwardly people think these awkwardnesses are the style and many copy them. This is regrettable."

Let the "awkwardnesses" Hemingway speaks of be not your mentor's but your own. You must be guided by your own excitement, your own sense of felicity, and your own happiness with what comes out right. John Updike, with perhaps the best ear of his generation—*the* virtuoso—speaks of the key role of this sense of rightness and how it functioned in his early work. "Most came right the first time—rode on their own melting, as Frost said of his poems. If there is no melting, if the story keeps sticking, better stop and look around. In the execution there has to be a 'happiness' that can't be willed or foreordained. It has to sing, click, something."

THE SPECTRUM OF STYLE

Like the Milky Way, the stylistic register of English prose spans from horizon to horizon on a continuum of dazzling breadth and depth. It rises from an endlessly varied low style of sub- or semiliterate street talk, climbing up through an incomparably well-developed, various, and supple middle style—the many modalities of educated discourse—and from there soaring into the apex of the language's most lofty rhetorical possibilities: the language of Shakespeare, Milton, and the authorized version of the Bible; the many voices of poetry and the novel in its high lyricism; the grand rhetoric of the great historians, critics, and philosophers.

The art of fiction is the one and only variety of writing that is free to move at will through and among all three levels of the rhetoric of the language without apology or discomfort. As a novelist or short-story writer, you are free to squat down as low as you like and scoop up the luscious stuff of talk. Yet you can also mix and match that talk with the more dignified middle style: the principal mode of exposition—that is, the supplying of information—in English, as well as the voice that dominates the main line of its fiction from Jane Austen to V. S. Naipaul. Finally, if you can keep your ear tuned to it, you will also hear, if only in the distance, the grandeur of the high style, the sound of English being magnificent, the modality with which through the centuries our language has been able to touch, and to name, the sublime.

These three levels move across a range of infinite variety. Simply put, the high style is defined by the language's long history of exceptional eloquence. It is the rhetoric of the courtly, the poetic, the reverential, and the magnificent. It seeks to inspire awe; it bypasses easy talk and forthrightly aspires to grandeur. The high style is almost definable as language that nobody would use in ordinary speech; language lifted into the tonalities of poetry, romance, scripture, vision, history, tragedy, and prophecy.

At the opposite end of the rhetorical range is the low style, rooted in the sounds of speech. Its distance from literacy measures the depths of its lowness. The rhetoric of *Huckleberry Finn* is "lower" than that of *The Catcher in the Rye* simply because Huck is illiterate and Holden is not. Low style lives on talk, and the lower it gets, the cruder and crumbier the talk: get-down and loose, direct, unliterary, unguarded if not uneducated, and straight from the streets. The low style is what you hear in the redneck voice of Huck Finn and in the nattering busybodies of Eudora Welty and the foulmouthed louts of Denis Johnson.

In the middle comes, of course, the "middle" style. This is the voice of lucid, literate expository prose. In place of low-style color and intensity, it offers the educated, self-aware, consciously masterful plain prose that, not incidentally, bases itself in the talk of the middle- and upper-middle classes. The middle style is what you hear in the lead story of the morning paper, and some variant of it is the voice of almost all nonfiction published in the language. Hemingway made himself the most influential writer of the twentieth century by, around 1925, setting a new standard for the use of the middle style in fiction. But the range is broad. Stephen Crane wrote by radically simplifying the middle rhetoric of his time; Henry James wrote by elaborating, and elaborating, and elaborating it.

The high style? In the nineteenth century, the great American masterpiece of the high style was *Moby Dick.* As for the twentieth century, the standard place to look is in James Joyce and in all the many writers who fell under Joyce's rhetorical spell. Among Americans, by far the most consequential of these is William Faulkner. Faulkner's incomparable, magnificently self-intoxicated yet far from flawless ear fills all his novels between *As I Lay Dying* and *Absalom, Absalom!* with echo after echo of the rhetoric of English at its most magnificent. This grandeur is based and mixed—Faulkner picked up the knack from Joyce—with an impulse to lift up and transfigure the lowest of low talk. High style has a natural affinity for the low style: As with Lear and the Fool, low tends toward high, and high tends toward low. As a modern phenomenon, this tendency is already visible in *Moby Dick,* but in the twentieth century it was Joyce who really drove it home. Yet it's audible in, say, Céline's *Journey to the End of the Night,* which seeks to lift Parisian street talk to the level of prophecy. Kerouac's *On the Road* reaches for the same with hipster jargon. Very much the same thing is true of Dickens, who, like Faulkner, mixes and moves between the language of the street and the sublime with wonderful panache—cadenzas of street talk, roaring outbursts of theatrical grandeur, dark flights of Gothic spookiness, and other breathtaking displays of oratorical virtuosity. Both writers base themselves—nominally—in the middle style, even though the middle style, I tend to suspect, bored them both. But then the middle style bores lots of people. Tom Wolfe is one, as we shall shortly see.

The middle style is the primary, and dominant, medium for almost all expository and discursive prose in the language, and it has been for three hundred years. It is ubiquitous, and its range is so broad that it is rarely recognized as a style at all. Since it is everywhere, we treat it like air. Of course, some air—say, Virginia Woolf's criticism—is so pure it intoxicates. Some air has a tendency to stink. The middle style can be written shoddily or brilliantly. It has endless possibilities and variants. You are reading it at this moment. The middle style can be pitched to a highbrow, middlebrow, or lowbrow level. Its highbrow variant is what you hear in *The New Yorker,* and it is no accident that the most influential manual of writing ever published in America was written in part by a founding editor of that magazine. I refer of course to William Strunk Jr. and E. B. White's *The Elements of Style,* which succinctly codified the middle style in its tonier twentieth-century American mode, once and for all.

And it has always been linked to gentleman journalism. In a great passage from *The Lives of the Poets,* Samuel Johnson describes how it took shape in the late-seventeenth- and early-eighteenth-century prose of Joseph Addison. "[Addison's] prose is the model of the middle style; on grave subjects not formal, on light occasions not groveling; pure without scrupulosity, and exact without apparent elaboration; always equable, and always easy, without glowing words or pointed sentences. Addison never deviates from his track to snatch a grace; he seeks no ambitious ornaments, and tries no hazardous innovations. His page is always luminous, but never blazes in unexpected splendour.

"It was apparently his principal endeavour to avoid all harshness and severity of diction; he is therefore sometimes verbose in his transitions and connexions, and sometimes descends too much to the language of conversation; yet if his language had been less idiomatical it might have lost somewhat of its genuine Anglicism. What he attempted, he performed; he is never feeble, and he did not wish to be energetick; he is never rapid, and he never stagnates. His sentences have neither studied amplitude, nor affected brevity; his periods, though not diligently rounded, are voluble and easy. Whoever wishes to attain an English style, familiar but not coarse, and elegant but not ostentatious, must give his days and nights to the volumes of Addison."

These paragraphs give us the stylistic ideal of *The New Yorker* at the late-twentieth-century apex of its influence two hundred years before the fact. Its longtime editor, William Shawn, might have had them in his office, engraved on a plaque.

While high and low style tend to reach for each other, the middle style generally stoops to the low mainly when quoting dialogue and stands on its tiptoes to reach the high only rarely, and usually only for a soaring moment or two. Take a look at the way Virginia Woolf typically ends the essays in *The Common Reader*. Here is great criticism written in the middle style. Its sound is the sound of highly literate talk deployed in the most impeccable modern British manner. That fluting, masterful, intensely articulate voice stays squarely inside the conversational middle range all the way through almost every essay—except at the very last moment, when Woolf often likes to end on a kind of high-style one-phrase stinger. (It's a trick she may have picked up from Addison.) Take this one, about Charlotte Brontë: "She could free life from its dependence on facts, with a few touches indicate the spirit of a face so that it needs no body; by speaking of the moor make the wind blow and the thunder roar." Or of George Eliot: "She sought more knowledge and more freedom till the body, weighted with its double burden, sank worn out, [and] we must lay upon her grave whatever we have it in our power to bestow of laurel and rose." Those last little clauses about thunder and laurel are sudden subtle snatches at sublimity. They rarely last for longer than a few words. The effect is always very grand.

The novel and journalism were nourished in the same cradle, and the middle style is their common parent. The style has marked style in fiction from Jane Austen to Nadine Gordimer and V. S. Naipaul. To be sure, what is called the "art novel" in English—Joyce was its great early-twentieth-century master, and Nabokov its prime mid-twentieth-century exponent—loudly disdains fiction's shared roots with journalism, but even these grand advocates can hardly turn their backs on the tremendous impact of the middle style on fiction, and from the form's earliest days until yesterday afternoon. Jane Austen herself, at the turn of the nineteenth century, was the first to perfect it as a narrative medium. George Eliot and Trollope are eminent among its nineteenth-century masters. It is the voice that talks to us about love and money in that famous first sentence of *Pride and Prejudice.*

Because the middle style, as Samuel Johnson pointed out, is conversational, it is endowed with a seductive ability to maintain a balance between impersonal clarity and the individual voiceprint of any writer who happens to be using it. When Hemingway writes in it, you *hear* Hemingway. When Jane Austen writes in it, you *hear* Austen. When George Eliot writes in it, you *hear* George Eliot. This is as true of Judith Krantz as it is for John Steinbeck as it is for Henry James. We don't hear their literal voices, of course; but we hear their voices as prose.

The style is equally adaptable for class and gender. It has no trouble sounding upper class (as in Virginia Woolf or Henry James); middle class (as in Somerset Maugham or Kingsley Amis); or working class (as in Richard Price or Stephen King). It has no gender inflection—a fact that may partly explain why, from the start, many of the style's greatest masters have been women.

It can boast of many other virtues, some of them rather Boy Scout–ish. It prides itself on being accurate, fair, clear, attentive to others, truth telling, and reliable. It is also *cool.* It insists upon retaining maximum control not only over its facts but also over its feelings and relationship to the reader. Indeed, quiet control is its fetish. Truman Capote, who served his apprenticeship at *The New Yorker* and wrote a minor masterpiece of the middle style, *In Cold Blood,* called it being "in control." "I mean [by control] maintaining a stylistic and emotional upper hand over your material. Call it precious and go to hell, but I believe a story can be wrecked by a faulty rhythm in a sentence—especially if it occurs toward the end—or a mistake in paragraphing, even punctuation."

There is not one word in Capote's remark with which William Shawn would have disagreed.

Yet all these fine strengths come with one massive drawback. A manner that declines ever to become unduly excited is a poor vehicle for conveying—as opposed to talking about—overwhelming passion. Here is Richard Rhodes writing, in the middle style, about the big problem with the middle style. "The Strunk and White voice—good standard English—is the voice of academic discourse, the voice in which most college papers are expected to be written . . . the voice of scholarly articles and books, those at least not strangled with jargon. It's actually an English voice more than an American, descended from the prose style favored by Victorian and Edwardian historians at Oxford and Cambridge. It's supposed to be a spare, cool voice, rational rather than emotional, but since reason and emotion come inextricably bound together in people and in words, it often sounds simply inhibited."

Faulkner, Walt Whitman, Solzhenitsyn, Kerouac, Dostoyevsky, Poe, Céline—all these figures are too large, too passionate, too driven, too possessed by their material, too overwhelmed and overwhelming, ever to settle for the middle style. Most of them would despise it, and its ideals, as suburban complacency. Imagine handing *The Elements of Style* to a Kerouac, or a Solzhenitsyn, or a Whitman, or a Céline. Imagine the burst of contemptuous laughter that would greet such a gift.

But then many writers loathe the middle style. At the beginning of his career, back in the days when he was plotting his grand attack on *The New Yorker,* it positively turned Tom Wolfe's stomach. "The voice of the narrator, in fact, was one of the great problems in non-fiction writing. Most non-fiction writers, without knowing it, wrote in a century-old British tradition in which it was understood that the narrator shall assume a calm, cultivated, and, in fact, genteel voice. The idea was that the narrator's own voice should be like the off-white or putty-colored walls that Syrie Maugham popularized in interior decoration . . . a 'neutral background' against which bits of color would stand out. *Understatement* was the thing. You can't imagine what a positive word 'understatement' was among both journalists and literati ten years ago. There is something to be said for the notion, of course, but the trouble was that by the early 1960s understatement had become an absolute pall. Readers were bored to tears without understanding why. When they came upon that pale beige tone, it began to signal to them unconsciously, that a well-known bore was here again, 'the journalist,' a pedestrian mind, a phlegmatic spirit, a faded personality, and there was no way to get rid of that pallid little troll, short of ceasing to read. This had nothing to do with objectivity and subjectivity or taking a stand or 'commitment'—it was a matter of personality, energy, drive, bravura . . . style, in a word. . . . The standard non-fiction writer's voice was like the standard announcer's voice . . . a drag, a droning. . . .

"To avoid this I would try anything."

To avoid that, Wolfe invented the style that made him famous.

READABILITY

Anthony Trollope remarked, "Of all the needs a book has the chief need is that it be readable." Not everyone agrees. Not everyone even understands. Too many people think readability means nothing other than easy reading. If pressed, many would claim that it leads to "dumbing down." Yet even its partisans identify readability mainly with clarity. Trollope, for example.

"It is the first necessity of [the novelist's] position that he make himself pleasant. To do this, much more is necessary than to write correctly. He may indeed be pleasant without being correct,—as I think can be proved by the works of more than one distinguished novelist. But he must be intelligible,—intelligible without trouble; and he must be harmonious. . . . It is not sufficient that there be a meaning that may be hammered out of the sentence, but that the language should be so pellucid that the meaning should be rendered without any effort of the reader;—and not only some proposition of meaning, but the very sense, no more and no less which the writer has intended to put into his words."

Well, Trollope is only half right. Nothing in this prescription would apply to Dickens, and yet Dickens has always had vastly more readers than Trollope. Dickens is not always "pellucid," he is not always harmonious, and he is not always pleasant. Yet people read and read.

This is because what really makes for readability is not clarity but *attitude:* the attitude of your prose toward our elusive friend the Reader and the role you invent for that invented being in your invented world. It is in precisely that relationship to the Reader that you will find most of the classic faults of style: pretension, condescension, servility, obscurantism, grandiosity, vulgarity, and the like—even academicism. That's why most serious faults of style can be described in language relevant to human relations. Is your style frank and open? Or does it have some unstated agenda? Is it out to prove something it does not or cannot admit? Is it trying to impress? Show off? Or maybe, on the contrary, is it kissing up? Or groveling? Is it maybe a just a tad passive-aggressive, with a mumbling half-audible voice that is unwilling to explain? It is trying to convince? Overwhelm? Help? Seduce? Give pleasure? Or is the aim perhaps to inflict pain? Would it like the Reader to be abashed, ashamed, punished? Is it ready to give? Or would it prefer to take? What balance does it find between the two? There is no area of the writer's work that is more responsive to the psychology of human connection than style.

But the relation to the Reader is not the only arena for trouble. Style triangulates the reader and the subject, and its flaws can also lie in its relation to the subject. In fact, flaws in that relationship have been viewed as the leading cause for faulty style throughout Western history. That fault was first noticed and condemned in the first century A.D., when the writer known as Longinus attacked it as "frigidity." John Gardner explains: "The fault Longinus identifies as 'frigidity' occurs in fiction whenever the author reveals by some slip of self-regarding intrusion that he is less concerned about his characters than he ought to be. . . . Strictly speaking, frigidity characterizes the writer who presents material, then fails to carry through—fails to treat it with the attention and seriousness it deserves. I would extend the term to mean a further coldheartedness as well; the given writer's inability to recognize the seriousness of things in the first place, the writer who turns away from real feeling, or sees only the superficialities in a conflict of wills, or knows no more about love, beauty, or sorrow than one might learn from a Hallmark card. With the meaning thus extended, frigidity seems one of the salient faults in contemporary literature and art. It is sometimes frigidity that leads writers to tinker, more and more obsessively, with form; frigidity that leads critics to schools of criticism that take less and less interest in character, action, and the explicit ideas of the story. . . . Frigidity is, in short, one of the worst faults in literature, and often the basis of other faults. . . ."

———

Speaking of faults, your fiction is not dependent upon a "flawless" style. As a matter of fact, style—in the sense of a highly developed and polished prose manner—is not even a necessary element of greatness: Line for line, Truman Capote generally wrote English more felicitously than even George Eliot, and much more felicitously that Dostoyevsky is said to have written Russian. He is not a greater writer than they are. As Somerset Maugham put it: "One fusses about style. One tries to write better. One takes pains to be simple, clear, and succinct. One aims at rhythm and balance. One reads a sentence aloud to see that it sounds well. One sweats one's guts out. The fact remains that the four greatest novelists the world has ever known, Balzac, Dickens, Tolstoy, and Dostoyevksy, wrote their respective languages very indifferently. It proves that you can tell stories, create character, devise incident, and if you have sincerity and passion, it doesn't matter a damn how you write. All the same, it's better to write well than ill."

Well, we could easily get into a rousing argument about Dickens's and Tolstoy's "indifferent" prose, but Maugham does have a point. In place of unfailing stylistic elegance, each of these writers had a large-spirited and unequivocal absorption in the world he was creating, and that absorption mobilized their enormous linguistic gifts to make a world in which the Reader can move with unprecedented freedom. Raymond Carver speaks of it in his poignant, fumbling way. "Some writers have a bunch of talent; I don't know any writers who are without it. But a unique and exact way of looking at things, and finding the right context for expressing that way of looking, that's something else. *The World According to Garp* is, of course, the marvelous world according to John Irving. There is another world according to Flannery O'Connor, and others according to William Faulkner and Ernest Hemingway.... Every great or even very good writer makes the world over according to his own specifications.

"It's akin to style, what I'm talking about, but it isn't style alone. It is the writer's particular and unmistakable signature on everything he writes. It is his world and no other. This is one of the things that distinguishes one writer from another. Not talent. There's plenty of that around. But a writer who has some special way of looking at things and who gives artistic expression to that way of looking: That writer may be around for a time."

6

THE STORY OF THE SELF

Fact, Fiction, and the Autobiographical Muse

Like the difference between the sexes, the difference between fiction and nonfiction is obvious, omnipresent, crucial, and not always as important as everyone says. There are of course moments when that difference is almost the only thing that counts. But in most things, and most of the time, the two opposites are more alike than they are different. They walk on the same two legs, breathe the same air, and see the same world through the same eyes. They are different in their sameness. They are the same in their difference. Fiction and nonfiction are united in difference, and that fact is nowhere more obvious than in the realm of autobiography.

The simplest definition tells us that fiction is "made up," while nonfiction sticks to the facts. That definition is plain, true, and quite misleading. In all writing, facts and imagination serve each other in a symbiotic partnership. Every kind of narrative—be it pure fiction, pure nonfiction, or something in between—has no choice but to embrace its facts *through* the imagination. The nature of that partnership assumes various forms, but it is always there. Yes, a historian will use the imagination to embrace the facts in a very different way than will a science fiction writer. But both must make the merger. To see facts as the adversaries of the imagination and the imagination as hostile to facts is simply to roll down the superhighway of received opinion to defeat.

Every writer senses this unity of fact and fiction somehow. It lurks near the secret heart of many a project. There is an unwritten novel silently brooding over most works of nonfiction, just as there is a true story lurking in the shadows of almost every novel or short story. The two hover near each other. To embark on one is to sense the other. This is because of their common source in the merger of imagination and fact. Reach into it and you will touch something alive, something central to the whole art of storytelling.

To illustrate, just consider these three basic truths about memoir as a literary form.

- *Every Memoir Must "Invent" Its Story.* I mean "invent" in our sense, of course. No crude collection of cold facts has ever once told a story all on its own. *Every* story, be it fiction or nonfiction, must be found among the facts and then be shaped from them. Moreover, no story, be it fiction or nonfiction, ever really exists until it has been *told.* That invention, be it in fiction or nonfiction, is a search only a storyteller can make.

- *The Subject of Your Memoir Cannot Be "You."* Not you all alone, anyway. A memoir must be about you and *something*—and that something should usually be your relationship to something intrinsically interesting and bigger than you. With a memoir, until you have found a genuine subject, you will have nothing at all—because *"you" are not a subject.* Neither are *"you"* a story. You are a *person.* As you shape your story and subject, you'll find that "you"—the amorphous, endlessly multifaceted, imperfectly perceived, living, changing, real you—will start taking shape on the page as a recognizable yet quite distinct, even faintly alien *persona:* a "you" for the page, a "you" that you must both find and make up in exactly the same way you invent your subject and your story.

• *Your Memoir Cannot Recapture the Past.* Yes, of course, it will be *about* the past, and of course you will try to summon up and depict the past as effectively as you can. But the past is no more a story than you are. It is the past. The past can supply you with events that your memory may link up in a web. But only you can invent their story, and that is something you're going to be doing now. The story, though it may seem implicit in the facts, must be put together from the past in the present. The past is not static; it is linked to the present; it is in a state of constant, dynamic change. It must be seen through the eyes of the persona you "invent" here and now to play the part of the "you" that lived, and vanished, back then. All this will make your memoir a new creation, a tale never told before.

These three truths are basic. Trust me: Counterintuitive though they sound, each one is real. And each one links the memoirist to the writing of fiction.

FACTS AND FICTION

The intimate bond between fiction and nonfiction is almost as old as literature. Writing in 322 B.C., Aristotle noticed that "A poet differs from a historian, not because one writes verse and the other prose . . . but because the historian relates what happened, the poet what might happen." We have repeatedly spoken of "digging up" a story. Toni Morrison calls it a kind of "archeology." "On the basis of some information and a little bit of guesswork you journey to a site to see what remains were left behind and to reconstruct the world that these remains imply." When Morrison reads the slave narratives of the eighteenth and nineteenth centuries, she digs up—discovers—what they suggest, an acquired memory that she can use in fiction or nonfiction or both, and she freely links the historical "archeology" of the slave narratives to the more personal "archeology" of her novels, "dug up" from within herself. "I can't tell you how I felt when my father died. But I was able to write *Song of Solomon* and imagine, not him, and not his specific interior life, but the world that he inhabited and the private or interior life of the people in it. And I can't tell you how I felt reading to my grandmother while she was turning over and over in her bed (because she was dying, and she was not comfortable), but I could try to reconstruct the world that she lived in. . . . These people are my access to me; they are my entrance into my own interior life. Which is why the images that float around them—the remains, so to speak at the archeological site—surface first, and they surface so vividly and compellingly that I acknowledge them as my route to a reconstruction of a world. . . ."

Morrison concludes: "Fiction, by definition, is distinct from fact." And yet, she says, "the crucial distinction for me is not the difference between fact and fiction, but the distinction between fact and truth. Because facts can exist without human intelligence, but truth cannot."

Maya Angelou says much the same thing. "I am an autobiographer as opposed to a fiction writer. In my case I have to remember facts and try to use my talent or my art or my creativity to tell the truth about the facts. I submit that there's a world of difference between truth and fact. Fact tells us the data: the numbers, the places where, the people who and the times when. But the facts can obscure the truth."

Does this sound a little *too* counterintuitive? Surely nonfiction has to rest on a foundation of fact, and surely those facts have to be reported accurately. Absolutely. Yet mere accuracy alone cannot define the truth that Morrison and Angelou are talking about. What defines the *truth* of the facts—as distinguished from their accuracy—is the *story*. The *story* is your principle of selection; the *story* is your standard of relevance; the *story* is your test of meaning. Yes, every fact in your story must be able to survive the tests of accuracy. But only the story can be tested for that broader criterion of the truth, its *authenticity*.

When you are writing a memoir, you will live with these realities in a particularly intimate way. Since so many of your facts will belong to you alone, they will be immune to the standard tests of accuracy. In fact, your own personal perspective amounts to almost a kind of fiction in itself. Here is William Zinsser in *Inventing the Truth: The Art and Craft of Memoir*, his indispensable collection of memoirists commenting on their art: "Memoir writers must manufacture a text, imposing narrative order on a jumble of half-remembered events. With that feat of manipulation they arrive at a truth that is theirs alone, not quite like that of anybody else who was present at the same events." Frank McCourt clinches the point: "An autobiography is not the attempt to recreate the facts of your life—your memoir is your impression of your life. The facts are there, but then what impression did they leave?"

Take a look at any memoir that you know and love. Open it at random. On any given page, how much of the writing is devoted to strictly reporting "facts"? Surprising, isn't it? Most of the page is given over to interpretations, dramatizations, and insights—*impressions*—that are frankly and obviously the writer's own. Some of it may even read rather like fiction. There will be narration, description, and maybe even dialogue. In the narration, scenes will be shaped, action shown, and events brought toward climax and conclusion. In the description, people will be characterized, places, times, and moods caught and held, motives and manners examined. Finally, there will be dialogue. Depending on the writer, there may even be a lot of dialogue.

And all of it is "invented." In a court, witnesses are ordered to stick to facts and offer no conclusions. You are not in court. Here, we *want* the conclusions of the witness; we *want* your guesses; we *want* your fantasies and dreams. Russell Baker loves Mark Twain's memoirs *Roughing It* and *Life on the Mississippi.* "Nobody understood better than Twain that a memoir is not a biography, but an art form. What a pleasure to watch him improve dull stretches of arid fact with inventions of the mind."

It is perfectly possible to fill page after page with Baker's "inventions of the mind" without ever once departing from the facts. Suppose you describe a hailstorm by saying "the hail strafed our house like machine-gun fire." That's not much of a simile, but it does embellish the hailstorm without departing from its reality. It is still nonfiction. But suppose you are faithfully reconstructing an angry conversation that really happened and suddenly you think of a wonderfully cutting remark one person *might* have said. It is *perfect.* It illuminates *everything.* It *could* have been said. It just wasn't. And you know that it wasn't.

You have arrived, by a perfectly natural and easy path, at the edge of a magical world. There is nothing shameful in the temptation to enter it. It would be so *easy* to depart from the facts and still tell . . . a quite real *kind* of truth. Not the literal truth, but *a* truth: the *un*factual truth. That perfect but never-spoken line, the one you "made up"—or was it "found"?—is infinitely more revealing than the banal nothing that really got said. It is not only more dramatic, more luminous, more interesting, and more moving than the real line—it is also more *truthful.* There is a bright light glinting in your eyes. It is the light of fiction's truth.

And you have a decision to make.

YOUR PERSONA: FACT OR FICTION? It is commonplace for critics to complain about "self-indulgent" autobiographical novels and memoirs, and you must indeed guard against this obvious risk. As Henry Louis Gates Jr. says: "When you write an autobiography or a memoir you're indulging yourself in your own sentimentality. So I found ways to guard against that: by using irony and wit and self-deprecation, and also by being honest, or revelatory, about pain and fear."

Yet when autobiographies fail, "self-indulgence" does not strike me as the usual cause of death. More often, the fatal flaw lies with the main character, all right—but "self-indulgence" is the least of it. The problem lies not in the excess of the author's persona. It lies in its *absence,* or more exactly in its failure to be persuasive, vivid, and truly imagined. Virginia Woolf saw this with her usual unerring vision: "Here I come to one of the memoir writer's difficulties—one of the reasons why, though I read so many, so many are failures. They leave out the person to whom things happened. The reason is that it is so difficult to describe any human being. So they say: 'This is what happened'; but they do not say what the person was like to whom it happened."

In most of these failures, there is a vague, uncharacterized, undefined, and very dull blur of words filling the page where a living, breathing central figure ought to be. Peripheral characters and distant situations often work beautifully: The author has no trouble seeing *them* whole. It is the dreary un-persona at the center—undeveloped, undramatic, and unseen—that sinks the enterprise. The figure that occupies the most space isn't really depicted at all. The prime job in any autobiography consists in shaping a sharp, firm, vital persona—a *character*—out of the amorphous mass of Everything we call "you." It's a very tricky transformation, and it's usually fumbled—not through self-indulgence, but through a failure of the imagination. A failure to imagine *yourself.* The writer slips into a fatal error. After all, she or he muses, why work on *myself*? I don't need to "invent" *myself*! Do I?

Take a look at *The Liars' Club* or *Angela's Ashes.* In each, the autobiographical persona is spread across every page. Neither feels in the least self-indulgent. Yet a surprising number of the contributors to William Zinsser's *Inventing the Truth* freely confess that their first drafts sank over just this issue. Just as Virginia

Woolf said, they did have a story—but they missed themselves. Russell Baker remarked about the first draft of *Growing Up:* "I had made a grievous mistake in trying to write a book about myself in which I didn't appear."

A failure of imagination like this is often a failure of craft. Consider this simple question: How *old* is your persona? Is she or he "you" now? Or "you" then? You probably will want your persona to be a composite of both. Well, what can that composite of past and present consist of except an "invention"? As Woolf pointed out, you want to "make them include the present—at least enough of the present to serve as a platform to stand upon. It would be interesting to make the two people, I now, I then, come out in contrast. And further, this past is much affected by the present moment. What I write today I should not write in a year's time."

As for fiction, a vast amount of the major fiction of the last century is *defined* by its invention of a fictional persona who is quite transparently based on the author. Stephen Dedalus is a fictional character, but who has ever for one second seen him as anything but a persona for James Joyce? In *A Portrait of the Artist as a Young Man,* Joyce "invented" a character for one novel and the author of another: *Ulysses.* In *In Search of Lost Time*—the vast autobiographical masterwork that many view as the twentieth century's greatest novel—Proust invented a "Marcel" to lead him through his epic meditation on memory as redemption. Ernest Hemingway shaped the "Hemingway hero" from the fighter in his lifelong losing battle with himself. Why do we suppose that the greatest fantasist of the twentieth century, Franz Kafka, gave the protagonists of *The Trial* and *The Castle* the surname initial *K*? With rare ingenuity, Philip Roth has spun fiction upon fiction from the personas of an autobiographical self. So has Woody Allen. So has Garrison Keillor. So, for that matter, has almost every major comic in broadcasting. Fiction rings change after change on the "facts" of autobiography. The varieties are endless.

In one astonishing case, Virginia Woolf's great autobiographical novel *To the Lighthouse,* the author's "persona" is the most "made up" character in an array of faithfully depicted real people. *To the Lighthouse* shows us Virginia Woolf's real girlhood summers. It gives us portraits of her real siblings and, above all, her real parents—the latter so precisely recalled to life that Woolf's sister Vanessa Bell saw the Ramseys as virtual resurrections of their parents. It is Virgina Woolf herself who is hard to find in the novel. The "invented" painter, Lily Briscoe, through whose eyes Woolf contemplates her own childhood, has replaced Woolf herself as the observer at the center of the book. Here is a very grand precedent for an instructive experiment. To "fictionalize" an autobiographical story, try giving us everyone just as they were—everyone except *you.* Replace "yourself" with an interested stranger.

Most of Colette's fiction is quasi-autobiographical, and she frequently gave the starring role to a creation named "Colette," an invented being who is in many ways wiser, better, more sensuous, more focused, and more fully present to life than her creator. This "Colette" is both less *and* more than the "real" Colette. Or consider *In Search of Lost Time.* In that novel, "Marcel" is psychologically saner, sexually less tortured, and morally more together than his creator. He is also, in some uncanny fashion, a more penetrating and sensitive observer than Proust himself, a being endowed with even more astonishing powers of insight and eloquence than the sublime neurotic who took to his bed and finally starved himself to death on coffee and brioches in order to invent him. The created "Marcel" endowed the real Proust with the sanity and balance he needed to produce his book. How is it *possible* that a creation on the page can be more eloquent, more insightful, and even more *intelligent* than her or his maker? The answer is both mysterious and simple. It is easy enough to see how a persona might be morally superior or kinder or saner than her or his creator. Any "character," properly conceived, will give you access to some part of yourself that is "superior" to "you," superior even in intelligence, even in insight, even in ability to reach the truth. Without "inventing" that character, you might never reach the part of yourself that is capable of these things.

—

During the 1990s, memoir was swept into an intensely fashionable vogue that ran through much of the publishing world. To name only three best-selling performers, Frank McCourt's *Angela's Ashes,* Mary Karr's *The Liars' Club,* and Kathryn Harrison's *The Kiss* all met with commercial success so dazzling that pundits, blinded by the glare, convened to declare the autobiographical novel a thing of the past, a dead duck. Up and down the street of commercial publishing, editors commissioned memoirs galore.

Then a glut of not-so-successful memoirs appeared.

Yet the memoir vogue does have something to teach. It is not how to get rich, and not that autobiographical fiction is dead. It teaches the *power* of observed reality. It shows that large transfusions of real life freshly observed can revitalize tired literary forms. Facts seen in a new way are a wellspring from which prose recovers its spent force.

And they always have been. The war between tired fantasy and robust fact is the heart of the comedy in *Don Quixote.* In 1719, readers of *Robinson Crusoe*—that first "survivor" story—bought a novel "based on a true story." "Truth is not only stranger than fiction," Somerset Maugham remarked, "it is more telling. To know that a thing actually happened gives it a poignancy, touches a chord, which a piece of acknowledged fiction misses. It is to touch this chord that some authors have done everything they could to give you the impression that they are telling the plain truth." During the 1970s, Tom Wolfe praised the rejuvenating power of facts to advance "the New Journalism" while delivering a terrible beating to some high-toned received opinion about the novel and its supposed superiority to journalism. Yet by the late

'80s, Wolfe was marshaling *identical* arguments—identical almost word for word—to advance *fiction,* or at least the kind of richly researched, portrait-filled, sociologically loaded fiction that he writes so well. Hypocrisy? Not in the least. For years, the psychological barriers between journalism and fiction had mesmerized Wolfe: The theme recurs again and again, all through his early work. But by the late '80s, things had changed. Wolfe had at last found his own path from nonfiction to fiction in a transition that was not a death-defying leap over some yawning chasm, but more like a couple of modest half-steps over one rather blurred squiggly line right at his feet. He calmly stepped over that line, and it turned out that he could take most of his wise and witty precepts about writing, and all his great talent, with him.

Other writers swear by a different mix of imagination and fact. Martin Amis dismisses Wolfe's view: "Tom Wolfe . . . said that writers are neglecting the real world. . . . He suggested a ratio of 70 percent research, 30 percent inspiration. But the trouble is that the real world probably isn't going to fit into the novel. In a sense, it's better to do the research in your mind. You need detail, you need pegs, but you don't want too much truth, you don't want too much fact. I would reverse the ratio: 30 percent research, 70 percent inspiration. Perhaps even 30 percent research is too much. You want a few glimmers from the real world, but then you need to run it through your psyche, to reimagine it. Don't transcribe, reimagine. Mere fact has no chance of being formally perfect. It will get in the way, it will be all elbows."

So, who is right, Amis or Wolfe? Both. Neither. Every artist can and must find her or his balance between the factual and the imagined. Lewis Carroll would have had something else, and very different, to say about the mix. Dickens would have something else again. There is no right answer, no program.

But there is always some mix, and that mix tends to define both the style of the work and its particular kind of truth. What did Chekhov say was absolutely indispensable to the writing of fiction? "Truth in the description of characters and things." Trollope likewise insisted that what connects the reader to the page is factual truth: "It all lies in that. No novel is anything . . . unless the reader can sympathize with the characters whose names he finds upon the pages. Let an author so tell his tale as to touch his reader's heart and draw his tears, and he has, so far, done his work well. Truth let there be,—truth of description, truth of character, human truth as to men and women. If there be such truth, I do not know that a novel can be too sensational." So does Stephen King: "Now comes the big question: What are you going to write about? And the equally big answer: Anything you damn well want. Anything at all . . . *as long as you tell the truth*."

Finally, truth in even the most fantastic fiction—that is, its authenticity—rests somewhere, somehow, on bedrock of fact. This bedrock may be obvious, or it may be all but invisible. It may be plain as the print on the page, or it may be carefully concealed. *War and Peace* has a forthright relation to historical fact, but *Alice in Wonderland* is just as firmly rooted in the reality of a little girl named Alice Liddell. A grounding in fact is written all over *The Bonfire of the Vanities;* a rather different grounding in fact is not quite so plainly lurking in *The Shining,* and yet another grounding in fact becomes quite mysterious in *The Waves* or *The Castle.* But the grounding in fact is *always* there. Somewhere.

This is all the more obviously so in autobiography, be it fiction or nonfiction. In either form, we generally feel the way it has been taken from the life without ever quite explicitly defining it. Anyone immersed in Jack Kerouac or Marcel Proust—or for that matter, that fine autobiographical novel *Winnie the Pooh*—will read sensing, *knowing,* that in some way much of what's happening on the page is taken from real life. Yet precisely this awareness of fact is what heightens the awareness of fiction. We sense the transformation, we are enthralled by it, and that magic, in turn, supplies the fiction with the authority and "poignancy" of fact that Maugham talks about. When, in *The Guermantes Way,* Proust describes the death of "my" grandmother, we read in half-conscious moral certainty that "the" grandmother in question is, of course, the real Proust's real grandmother. And we are right. Yet nobody would dream of saying that this fact diminishes the imaginative power of the account. On the contrary. The sick-room, the hissing oxygen tanks, the muttering doctors, the hovering, and the hurrying: Proust gives us all the facts, and our sense that he himself must have lived through them all heightens their power. In fact, when the facts get a little bizarre—as when the grandmother's voice begins involuntarily to "sing" under oxygen—we feel the force of lived experience confirming what we might at first be tempted to disbelieve. Yet "facts" do not dominate this great passage. The death of "the" grandmother in Proust is a transfiguration, and transfiguration is its true theme. That is what we care about.

Eudora Welty wisely notes that it is fiction's relation to its facts that endows it with its "honesty." Yet each writer will use her or his own kind of facts in her or his own way. In her own work, Welty relied upon the facts of time and place to make the story "honest." *They*—the Mississippi Delta, the Depression—ground the story; *they* are what must be not only true but accurate. "Time and place make the framework that any story's built on. To my mind, a fiction writer's honesty begins right there, in being true to those two facts of time and place. From there, imagination can take him anywhere at all." But other writers ground their honesty in other kinds of facts. The "honesty" of *Alice in Wonderland* consists in being true to the personality of Alice Liddell. The "honesty" of Michael Crichton's novels is based in the authority of their compulsively researched fact. It is as though Crichton's precision about every morsel his characters eat, every garment they wear, the very bricks in the buildings they live in, is precisely what permits the fantasy to fly off into his techno-dream. Sometimes the writer is true simply to a voice. When Henry Louis Gates Jr. wrote *Colored People*, his guide was the remembered voice of his father.

So each writer must find his or her own way to be "true" to the facts. Suppose you've decided to write an autobiographical story. Let it be fiction or memoir; I don't care which. Certain facts from that event will be dispensable. You can just skip them. Other facts, if you are writing fiction, will be changeable: It won't hurt the project—it will help—to change them or punch them up or play them down or turn them around. Other facts, however, will be essential and unchangeable. They *must* be honored. Drop them or change them, and you might as well drop or change the whole project. *Those* are the facts that are your grounding. *They* form the core of what you are doing. *They* define your principle of relevance, your "honesty."

It's the same with your persona on the page. But if you try to put in *all* of yourself—that unencompassable shoreless sea of you and your experience that we call "you"—you will fail. Trust me. You will fail. You must find some balance between a freestanding "invented" character on the page—a being with a distinct, limited, significant set of traits—and the real person called "you." Here your own "honesty" may be tested by the rules of fact versus truth. You may endow yourself, as Colette and Hemingway did, with your own real traits in improved—even perfected—form. This enhancement of the self through invention can be, as in the case of Proust's "Marcel," transcendent. Or it can be the basis of nothing but phoniness and vanity: fraud. Leave out or change certain things, and you may open a vista on the truth. Leave out certain *other* things, and you will be just plain lying. Perhaps you are the only person on earth who will ever know that you are lying. But you *will* know.

And it's a grim business, trying to live your life while waiting to be found out.

POSSESSING THE FACTS

Who better to comment on the link between fiction and fact than Shelby Foote, who is at once a powerful and accomplished novelist and a major historian. "There is no great difference between writing novels and writing history other than this: If you have a character named Lincoln in a novel who's not Abraham Lincoln, you can give him any color eyes you want. But if you want to describe the color of Abraham Lincoln's, *President* Lincoln's, eyes, you have to know what color they were. They were gray. So you're working with facts that came out of documents, just as in a novel you are working with facts that come out of your head or most likely your memory. Once you have control of those facts, once you possess them, you can handle them exactly as a novelist handles his facts. No good novelist would be false to his facts, and certainly no historian is allowed to be false to his facts under any circumstances. I've never known, in at least a modern historical instance, where the truth wasn't superior to distortion in every way."

Two phrases stand out among these very wise words. Foote speaks about "*getting control* of the facts" and about "*possessing*" the facts. Mere information is *never* enough. But then, neither is mere imagination. Two reliable signs of a healthy imagination are a hunger for facts and a will to satisfy that need. If you do not feed your imagination with facts, it will starve. It will try to feed on itself—and that will make it sicken and maybe even die. Yet mere facts alone are useless. We live in a limitless universe of them; most of them are dead as doornails. You must assimilate the facts with enough richness and confidence to make them live on a page. Merely experiencing them, merely reading about them, merely registering them—in life, in print, or on the screen—will never be enough. *You must make them yours.*

This will take time—and a funny mixture of conscious and unconscious effort. You must first get a firm grip on the fact. Then you must turn it over and over in your mind until it is fully, both consciously and unconsciously, in your possession. Visualize. Conceptualize. Remember. Invent a context. Give it language. The job will be done only when the fact is talking to you, even in your dreams.

Provided that you have managed really to get control of a fact, provided that you have genuinely taken possession of it by clinching this whole process in language, *it doesn't matter where you got the fact in the first place.*

All this puts our old friend "write what you know" in a special light. "Nothing is sillier," John Gardner pointed out, "than the creative writing teacher's dictum 'Write about what you know.' But whether you're writing about people or dragons, your personal observation of how things happen in the world—how character reveals itself—can turn a dead scene into a vital one." Gardner is on to the true distinction. Do not write what you know. Write what you have come to take control of and possess as your own. Let your facts come from the South Bronx or the twelfth century: They will live when, and only when, you have taken imaginative possession of them. Yes, personal experience is always a kind of guide, but let's be honest: Mere personal experience is, generally, quite dull. You are in the business of "exceptional happenings." Once you have taken imaginative possession of a fact, its *source*—whether you got it at the high point of your life or from the phone book—will not really be important. What counts is how you have made it yours.

—

The exact way you do this is up to you. It often happens only in the process of writing itself. Samuel Eliot Morison, the great historian of Columbus's journeys, sailed a small craft across the Atlantic twice, renavigating the original routes. Writing a memoir of his family, Ian Frazier learned to ask, "What story does this object tell? Often I had to leave what I had at home and go to the public library, or go to the place where a particular event happened. To understand what you have in the way of ephemera you have to be ready to do a whole bunch of different things to invest them with meaning.

"For instance, I made an angel food cake. My grandmother was famous for her angel food cakes. It's hard to make an angel food cake. . . . Doing some of these tasks made me understand her better and gave me an authority to write about her."

Whether you are showing us Vienna in 1938, or your own living room yesterday afternoon, your imagination must have taken possession of the facts through curiosity, arousal, excitement, and love. Here is Shelby Foote again: "Everything I have to say about the writing of history was summed up by John Keats in ten words in a letter, more or less like a telegram put on the wire nearly two hundred years ago. He said: 'A fact is not a truth until you love it.' You have to become attached to the thing you're writing about—in other words, 'love it'—for it to have any real meaning. It is absolutely true that no list of facts ever gives you a valid account of what happened."

THE TOOLS OF MEMORY

In his great memoir, *Speak, Memory,* Vladimir Nabokov notes, "The act of vividly recalling a patch of the past is something I seem to have been performing with the utmost zest all my life." Memory is second only to language itself among a writer's most important tools, and by an ironic turn, it will play a particularly important role in helping you take possession of any fact that happens to lie outside your own personal experience. Memory is as essential to the writing of fiction as to memoir.

This is because memory alone has the sovereign power to tell us *what things felt like.* Using it profitably, however, means assigning it tasks it can perform. Memory, and memory alone, can tell you what things felt like, looked like, smelled like, sounded like. *Only* your memory, imaginatively transposed to fit the facts you have, can tell you what it felt like to be hit on the head by a rock when you were eleven years old. Likewise, *only* your memory can tell us what felt like to be hit in the head by a rock in eighteenth-century London. Memory is indispensable, magical, at summoning scenes and supplying detail. Its ability to recall the textures of experience, to resurrect the senses, to open up totally fresh and unexpected links between things and places and times and sounds, is little short of sublime. Its capacity to restore to you whatever appears in the bright box of recall will serve you every day of your writing life.

On the other hand, your memory will lose all this power and become a bumbling incompetent when it comes to *comprehending* what you recall. Memory doesn't have the capacity to comprehend anything. It *only* remembers. And even a quite good memory is likely to be a very poor source of facts. Without the guide of a written record, memory is likely to bollix expository facts badly. Memory makes associations, but it is likely to fail in the search for the structure that you need to give your recollections shape. Your organizing narrative intelligence must do that. Nor can memory, unassisted, show you a story's meaning. It is a feeble philosopher. *You* must do these things.

Above all, memory meanders, and meandering is what memories do best. All too many memoirs—novels, too—fail because the writer hopes that this meandering can serve as a substitute for a structure. As a result, the piece rambles from memory to association to recollection to random thought. It grows confused, then lost, then pointless, and finally boring. You will be lucky to get even a vague contour of things from pure recollection. The miracle of Proust goes well beyond his dazzling capacity for recall: More impressive even than that is his ability to subsume all that recollection in one controlling, stylistically coherent narrative flow, and nothing more persuasively demonstrates the power of his controlling intelligence.

"To write a novel," says John Braine, "is, above all, to remember. You must learn to be quiet, to compose yourself, to let the memories enter. Apart from the time which you spend writing, you must have quiet periods, during which you can empty your mind of the day's events, shut off the present. Quiet places aren't

necessary. Even solitude isn't necessary. You only need time."
Sometimes the search for a memory can be strenuous. Hemingway begins *Death in the Afternoon* by speaking of a trip to Madrid to recapture the precise experience of witnessing, in a bullfight, a bull's horn goring a man's thigh so deeply one could glimpse bone.

The best advice I have known on the question of how to focus the memory comes from the writer and memoirist Ian Frazier. When you are trying to nail down a cluster of memories, Frazier says: GET ONE THING RIGHT. "I began with the premise that I wanted to get at least one thing right. My analogy comes from hunting. When you're in a field and a whole bunch of quail go up, if you're a beginner you put your gun to your shoulder and just go BANG. You see all the birds and you shoot at them all and you don't get one. If you want to get a bird, pick *one* bird and shoot it. . . .

"So, first, get one thing right—one thing that you really want to say. Once you get it right, look at it and see what it implies, because that one detail or observation that seems so beautiful to you can often point to narrative. It can be the first step in a sequence of equally evocative details. It's like a seed crystal. . . ."

So as you try to recollect a thing, don't try to remember *everything*. You will be overwhelmed, swamped, by "everything." Try to remember *one* thing, but get that one thing exactly right. Let it be your "seed crystal." Once you have that one thing mastered, see what grows from it. One of the most wonderful and rollicking passages in *Speak, Memory* is about the Frenchwoman who served as governess for all the little Nabokov children in the lost and distant Russia of Nabokov's childhood. Nabokov got his access to the huge resources in his memory bank on the woman the children called "Mademoiselle" through one detail, which, as if following Frazier's advice, brought her back to him. That detail was Mademoiselle's *hands:* "In our childhood we know a lot about hands since they live and hover at the level of our stature; Mademoiselle's were unpleasant because of the froggy gloss on their tight skin besprinkled with brown ecchymotic spots. Before her time no stranger had ever stroked my face. . . . All her mannerisms come back to me when I think of her hands."

FIRST STEPS TOWARD STORY

Depending on your openness and your talent, you will be crowded with scrappy narrative possibilities. You may cringe at some of them, and if, like me, you have a strongly critical temperament, it will be easy to find a nasty label for almost anything that comes into your mind: This is clichéd, this is sentimental, the other is embarrassing, stupid, overdone, boring, unoriginal. These are the killer words, and what they kill is creativity. They will be all too eager to crowd into your mind, clamorous and jeering and arrogant, assuring you that they are your friends, your guardians, the proof of your fine discernment, and—oh yes, about this silly little idea you have—right on target.

Well, of *course*, they are on target—at *first*. Every idea is vulnerable to ridicule *at first*. The miracle is that any of them make it through the critical gauntlet to the finish line. You must learn to accept this vulnerability, and even more: You must learn to defend your ideas from those who are inclined to go on the attack, even if one of those attackers is yourself. Any idea that moves or excites you deserves the privilege of at least a month or so in your notebook totally protected from critical abuse. Because almost any idea can be killed by that abuse in the first stage.

Above all be very careful about bandying that treacherous label "unoriginal."

Any story idea that happens to strike you will be unoriginal in *some* way. This is good, not bad. Familiarity may form the bedrock of interest. Let's say you ran away from home when you were young. Like tens of millions of others. Like the Prodigal Son. Your story is one of the commonplaces of human experience, and not incidentally an Ur-story, a founding myth of the culture. Does that make it a cliché? Maybe, and maybe not. Maybe your audience can be made to care not despite but *because* of those millions of runaways, not despite but *because* of the Prodigal Son.

In her impressive book *When Memory Speaks,* Jill Ker Conway argues that all our lives are caught up in latent yet astonishingly powerful basic narratives; "life stories" that we have consciously or unconsciously accepted as our own. "All of us live with a life history in our mind, and very few of us subject it to critical analysis. But we are storytelling creatures. So it's very important to examine your own story and make sure that the plot is the one you really want. . . . As a young person it's important to scrutinize the plot you've internalized and find out whether it accurately represents what you want to be, because we tend to act out those life plots unless we think about them."

And even if we do, these "life stories" are not necessarily clichés: They can ground you and your experience in the collective history of your type and kind; they can make you a participant in the collective history of a narrative. They are likely to be shaped by the classic deep narratives of humanity: the primal stories of quest; redemption; exile; struggle and war; homecoming; rebirth; romantic love. Doubtless we can and should use consciousness to shape them. That *is* possible. We *can* change the plot. A little. Yet as Russell Banks understands, these "life histories" look very much like destiny. "Early on, you intuit and start to create patterns of images and narrative forms that are bound to be central to American mythology. If you start to plug the imagery and sequences of your personal life into these patterns and form, then they are going to feed the way you imagine your own life. Before long, writing will turn out, for the writer, to be a self-creative act. The narrative that early on attracted me was the run from civilization, in which a young fellow in tweeds at Colgate University lights out and becomes a Robin Hood figure in fatigues in the Caribbean jungle. That fantasy is a story for myself. It also happens to be a very basic American story, as well as a basic white-male fantasy. A wonderful reciprocity between literature and life evolves. It seems to be inescapable."

7

WORKING AND REWORKING

Early Drafts and the Techniques of Revision

Every writer must be taught how to write every book she or he writes, and the teacher is always the book itself. Writing becomes good by accretion. It builds on itself; it picks up its own cues, it takes its own suggestions. You rarely if ever start out knowing exactly what you are doing or what is to come, and by the time you reach the middle, you rarely know how you are going to get out alive. The project must be your guide, and it will not be finished teaching you the job until the day you type the final page. Then, if you're lucky, it will let you go.

The stages through which the project leads you to this enlightenment are its successive drafts. I have read all too many *almost* good pieces of work, published and unpublished, that betray their promise simply and solely because their authors did not have the stamina or the determination or the time to run them through another draft or two.

We have said from the beginning that all writing lives off a two-stroke heartbeat of release followed by taking control. Another term for this rhythmic alternation between letting go and taking hold is *revision,* and as David Remnick, the editor of *The*

New Yorker puts it, "revision is all there is." There are writers who imagine that doing a single draft is somehow a sign of superior skill. This is simply untrue. The biographical facts are clear: Most writers, including the most proficient and greatest, produce their work in many drafts, and do so from the start of their careers until the end. It is not even true that as you become more confident and skilled, the number of drafts you do will decrease. Sometimes the reverse is true: When he was my student, Madison Smartt Bell wrote brilliant prose and invariably wrote it in a single draft. It's my impression that his first published novels were not greatly revised from their first drafts. Yet as this born virtuoso's career has made him steadily more accomplished, Bell has become more, not less, of a reviser.

I'm convinced that many novices and even some professionals resist revision not out of laziness or self-delusion, but simply because they do not know how to do one. Nobody is born knowing how to revise, but though they are rarely taught, revision's basic techniques are eminently teachable. You will develop your own methods, of course, but for heaven's sake, don't try to reinvent the wheel of revision all alone. In this chapter we'll be talking about first drafts and the basic methods of revision. In the next we will speak about middle drafts and finishing.

THE DEFINITION OF A "DRAFT"

A "draft" is a version of your whole project written out from beginning to end. It can be the draft of a whole short story, a whole novel, a whole memoir, a whole chapter, a whole essay, a whole anything. The operational word is *whole*. A completed movement from beginning to end defines a draft. Until you have gone that whole distance, you will not have a draft. Don't kid yourself about this: In the days of the typewriter, it was commonplace to crumple up twenty-six pieces of paper revising a single page. Those were not twenty-six drafts. That was one rather rocky page.

SINGLE-DRAFT WRITING. True single-drafters are a small minority among writers, but their ranks include some pretty distinguished people. When Kurt Vonnegut reaches the end of the first draft of a book, he has a finished book, ready to set in type. When Susan Sontag completes a page (in her fiction at least), she moves on to the next page, and the next day to the next, writing, she says, "as life is lived." The youthful John Updike confessed that "I . . . don't change much, and have never been one for making outlines or taking out whole paragraphs or agonizing much. If a thing goes, it goes for me, and if it doesn't go, I eventually stop and get off." Cynthia Ozick is a single-drafter. When she completes one sentence, she proceeds to the next, and the next, and the next, and she does not turn back. "I don't have to revise at the end," says Shelby Foote, a classic single-drafter. "Revision is heartbreaking." "Rewriting a whole book would bore me," said Anthony Burgess. It's said that Thomas Mann produced his page or two every day mainly as a single-drafter—though I can point to a passage in his diaries where he sketches plans for crucial revisions in *The Magic Mountain*. Single-drafting is not necessarily anything like careless writing or even rapid writing. Far from it. Flaubert spent five years devoting days to a single paragraph and many hours to a single line. And he fashioned the perfection of *Madame Bovary* in what amounts to a single draft.

For obvious reasons, most single-drafting crawls forward at a very slow pace, and it is often anything but haphazard. Yet for the most famous single-drafter of more recent times, speed was of the essence. Jack Kerouac turned his refusal to revise into a kind of arch-romantic principle. Though there is conclusive evidence that Kerouac did revise *On the Road*, he claimed to see revision as *immoral*—as a kind of dishonesty, an insult to karma. "By not revising what you've written," he said, "you simply give the reader the actual workings of your mind during the writing itself: You confess your thoughts about events in your own unchangeable way...." Just to prove that he himself wouldn't stoop to it, he typed much of his work, as fast as he could make his fingers fly, on long rolls of Teletype paper that left him with a single, unending page.

Kerouac's wild run down the shock corridor of his paper roll is not the way most successful single-drafters work. Most revise as they go, and revise a lot. They are the ones who leave their wastebasket stuffed with twenty-six dead page tens. The single-drafter, crawling to perfection, may finish a page or two a day. Three would be a lot. Such a pace may not be your rhythm. As John Irving, a multiple-drafter, says, "I write very quickly; I rewrite very slowly. It takes me nearly as long to rewrite a book as it does to get the first draft." Some parts of any work will come more easily than others. You may sail through certain pages and never need to touch them again. But a fast first draft— *pace*, Kerouac—will almost always need extensive revision. It will have all sorts of virtues, but a fully developed structure and polish are not likely to be among them.

Plan on a second draft.

MULTIPLE DRAFTS. So how many drafts should there be?

As many as it takes.

There is no rigid norm, but the usual rhythm is about three. The only draft that really matters is the final one, but somehow the three-draft rule of thumb does seem to correspond to some fundamental rhythm in the process. First comes conception. Second comes development. Third comes polishing. Bernard Malamud put it this way: "The first puts [the story] in place. The second focuses, develops, subtilizes. By the third most of the dross is gone.... First drafts are for learning what your story or novel is about. Revision is working with that knowledge to enlarge or enhance an idea, to re-form it.... The first draft of a book is the most uncertain—where you need guts, the ability to accept the imperfect until it is better." And Malamud added, in a phrase that will reach the heart of every multiple-drafter: "I love the flowers of afterthought."

For obvious reasons, short stories are likely to go through more drafts than novels. Ray Bradbury speaks of doing six or seven drafts of his stories (and calls them *"pure torture"*), while Raymond Carver said his "real work" on a short story began after three or four drafts. (Carver, incidentally, was passionate about revising. "It's something I love to do, putting words in and taking words out.")

Does this seem overwhelming? Well, yes, writing is a big job, but there may be some consolation in knowing that one or maybe two of these drafts may go quickly. In fact, one defining trait of any draft you do will be its speed.

FAST DRAFTS AND SLOW DRAFTS

As we have said, you may be someone who does your first draft very quickly. If that is true, your second draft should probably be slow moving. If, on the other hand, you crawl through your first draft—or even if you bog down in it—you would be well advised to capitalize on the inner mastery over your material that this long slow crawl has unconsciously built up in you by moving as fast as you can through the next draft. If the one draft is fast and reckless, the next should probably be slow and painstaking: Where one is sketchy, the next should be crystal clear; where one rides on its self-permission, the next should be self-critical. Where one is guesswork, the next should be researched. A fast draft will be filled with gaps, unproven premises, incoherent ideas, and things that don't work. Raymond Carver wrote his first drafts as fast as he could, skipping over difficulties, simply to get to the end. "Some scenes I save until the second or third draft, because to do them and do them right would take too much time on the first draft." Frank O'Connor used to cite Guy de Maupassant's advice on first drafts: "Get black on white. . . . I don't give a hoot what the writing's like; I write any sort of rubbish which will cover the main outlines of the story, then I can begin to see it. . . . I just write roughly what happened. . . . It's the design of the story which to me is the most important, the thing that tells you there's a bad gap in the narrative here and you really ought to fill that up in some way or another. I'm always looking at the design of a story, not the treatment."

The first draft is likely to be a fast draft, and that is what many writers recommend. On the other hand, there are writers who cannot tolerate the surrender of control over their material that a really fast first draft requires. Almost all writers of fast first drafts have in common a willingness—even a need—to accept a certain self-surrender as an essential part of their working lives. But your first draft doesn't *have* to be fast. Speed does not work, either psychologically or creatively, for everyone. Philip Roth's starts are notoriously slow. You may quite willingly crawl through a first draft, only to move like the wind through the second or third. There is a kind of slow draft that I tend to call the "research draft." This may or may not be the result of a great deal of outside research: It is in either case a draft in which information overwhelms story. It can be a piece of historical fiction or a piece that deals with some very unusual setting or set of people, something that requires the writer to master a special world, as García Márquez did with his Latin American dictator. It can and often does happen in a memoir. Alfred Kazin, Eileen Simpson, and Russell Baker are only three among many contributors to *Inventing the Truth* who produced laborious, even lumbering, first drafts of their memoirs. They may have had to. They had to wait for the second draft to reach the point of intimacy with their own story that permitted that story to "write itself." And it may work that way for you, too.

The desirability of alternating fast drafts and slow drafts was borne in on me so often that it became in my mind almost a kind of rule. Here is a classic scenario: I have encountered it many times, but the first time I encountered it was in my second year of teaching, and if I handled it properly, it was only through the luck of a novice. A young woman came to me with a mountain-ous mess that she wanted to make her senior project, a manu-script on which she had been slaving away for a long time about her unhappy marriage. And we began work together, struggling to make progress; struggling to organize the sprawl of pages into some sort of forward movement. It was slow going. I would make a suggestion. We would discuss it. The next week that suggestion would come back—in the form of a further complication in the mess. Characters seemed piled up pointlessly. Solutions were tried, and then discarded, and then tried again. The pages were filled with a lot of anger, a lot of working things out, a lot of re-sentment and lost love recurring again and again as the pages crawled forward. Whatever was hashed had to be rehashed. The project, along with the writer's spirits, seemed to be sinking under the weight of what I was too inexperienced to know was an ab-solutely classic case of slow-draft inertia. I tried to be helpful and sustaining, but I had begun to entertain some carefully concealed doubt about whether this thing could ever be pulled together. Meanwhile, the dreaded deadline was getting nearer and nearer. It was inflexible. The writer worried. She struggled against sink-ing into the stagnant sea of her own pages. She was losing faith. I was losing faith. That was the one thing neither of us could say.

Finally, at the end of a conference very near the deadline, I took a deep breath of my own and, on an intuition, said to her: "Look, you *know* what your story is. It's a very vivid, upsetting, interesting, passionate story, and it's all yours. In this manuscript you have explored every nook and cranny of it. Many, many times over. There is nothing left to explore. Now I have to tell you that you can't turn this in. You've worked hard, I know, but I'm sorry: What we have here is just too much of a mess. I hope you know and believe that I am fully on your side. I have one last piece of advice: Forget what you've done. Forget this whole draft. Never look at a single one of these pages ever again. Don't even try to fix them. You don't have time to fix anything. Go home, sit down in front of a totally blank page one, remember what you have to say, and *just say it*."

Tough talk. The deadline was so close it was breathing fire. My student left my office panicked and no longer even secretly warding off despair. She understood that this was *it*. No more long, rambling talks about the meaning of it all. No more struggling through yet another stab at the seventh chapter. No more fixing up this or that. Time's *up*. She had a huge mess of a manuscript, the work of months and months and months, and I had just taken her last shred of faith in it and finished it off. This draft just would not cut it. I had all but told her it was no good, and she believed me. What could she hope for now other than to get her miserable degree and somehow get out of school in one piece? And who *cared* anymore, anyway?

My student vanished for three, maybe four weeks. No more visits to my office. No more messages on my machine. Not a trace of her anywhere on campus. Whenever I thought about her, I would grow glum and groan inside, wondering if I had done the right thing and fearing I had not.

On the very last minute of the very last hour of deadline day, a bleary and disheveled young woman stumbled into the department secretary's office and tossed down on the desk a manuscript as if she were throwing in a towel.

The manuscript was sent to me. It was thin. I've forgotten how many hundred pages were in the tattered stack of the first draft, but this thing was clean and slender, quite compact. I went to my office and sat down to read. And the first page was ... crisp. Fresh. Smart. Not bad at all. I read on. But this was ... *good*. Maybe even—*very* good. Where was all that rambling, ranting prose we had struggled with so long? Where was the wilderness in which we had been wandering lost so very recently? This thing sparkled. There wasn't a dull paragraph. It was nimble; it was alive. The story was the same narrative, all right. I was reading about the very same miserable marriage we'd already explored in such depth, but speed—*desperate* speed—had made it clean, clear, direct, and swept on its own story. Somewhere around page thirty, I remember leaning back in my chair and starting to laugh— laugh—over how good it was turning out to be. I laughed in a baffled mixture of astonishment, relief, and joy. She'd *done* it. One of her thesis readers, a famous novelist not known for treating student manuscripts with kid gloves, began her report: *"This novel is wonderful. . . ."* An important publisher bought and published the book within a year. The author inscribed my copy with a sentence three words long: *"Just say it!"*

What is the lesson of this little tale? It is not, I assure you, that every book can or should be written in three desperate weeks. It is that some people cannot "just say it" until they have gone through the long, introspective, suffering, sometimes all but stagnant process of first-drafting that produced that elephantine unsubmittable first draft. Some things may have to be mastered both internally, and on the page, before you can "just say it."

I am aware of course that many writers, including many novices, use neither a fast nor a slow first draft, but something in between. The more usual method is a stop-and-start forward crawl. Richard Price describes it well. "Typically, what I'll do is write a page, reread it, edit it, write half a page more, and then I'll go back to the very first thing I wrote that morning. It's like the nursery rhyme 'The House That Jack Built,' where you go back to the first line of the poem and go all the way through, adding a line each time, and then back to the first. So, I don't know whether I'm editing, reediting, or writing something new, but it's kind of a creeping, incremental style of writing. I always sort of half-know where I'm going."

"The House That Jack Built" is a perfectly reasonable way to combine revision and first-drafting. I use a variant of it myself. But it does come with certain liabilities. It loses the advantages of speed: beating your inner censor, coming unblocked, getting narrative momentum. Moreover, "The House That Jack Built" tends to favor beginnings. You go back to the start again and again; you reach the end, exhausted, once. This will show. If you work this way, remember that you will need to give very special attention to the end.

SHOWING A FIRST DRAFT

Most mentors agree: A rough first draft should be for your eyes only. Stephen King calls the first draft a "closed-door draft." If you are a student working with a teacher, or if you are in a workshop, this may not be possible. Your first draft, be it fast or slow, is likely to be cluttered with stuff you won't want others to see: your haste, your wild guesses, your blunders, your raw fantasies, your embarrassment. It's the rare reader anywhere who can see past these things to the piece's potential.

Keeping the door closed can be hard. You naturally want to connect; you want to show the stuff that seems good. It would be nice to have somebody tell you you're not crazy. Resist these temptations. The wrong feedback now can flatten you with a touch. Even a fully justified criticism can intrude on what must be a personal process, and of course blundering criticism will only mess up everything. King puts it nicely: "Give yourself a chance to think while the story is still like a field of freshly fallen snow, absent of any tracks save your own." You will have a use for another pair of eyes soon enough.

Okay, what *should* you do after you finish a rough first draft?

First, feel good. It's quite true that you are not done yet, but this is a real accomplishment just the same. You have come a long way—longer than you may suppose. Some version of your story is down on paper. It is real. It is there. Your story is now within your grasp in a way it has never been before.

Have a glass of champagne. Celebrate. Enjoy the glow.

Then give it a rest.

You will need a little distance from the draft; it will help to come to it cold, and so a little time off, tinkering with another project can be healthy. It should not be long—just a decent cooling period. Resist the temptation—which will be strong—to read and compulsively reread what you have. Various writers suggest various periods of time off. A week? At most a couple of months? Not more. You are not trying to *forget* this draft, you trying only to get enough distance from it to see it again later through fresh and rested eyes. You are trying to get away from your role as writer so you can be your own first reader.

After this time of rest, prepare yourself to read through the whole draft. This should be done in one sitting or something as close to it as you can arrange. If this is a story, a chapter, or even a short novel, do a whole read-through at once. If your project is too long for that, plan on as few sittings as possible This is a very special moment. Be calm. Give yourself plenty of time. Close the door and keep it firmly closed. Get your notepad and Post-its handy.

And get ready for a bumpy ride.

There are not many rapid mood swings like the ones you are about to go through. The goal, says Richard Bausch, is to "read it with the cold detachment of a doctor looking at an X ray." Lots of luck. If you are an even ordinarily self-critical writer, you will come across lots of things that will make you want to scream. Sloppiness. Stupid blunders. Incomprehensible passages. Boring passages. Embarrassments.

Do not panic. Your twin friends, the sense of rightness and wrongness, are going to be your guides, and they are going to be busy. What you hear that voice—*wrong, this is wrong*—don't cringe, just make a simple note: "wrong," "cut or improve," "needs work," "sentimental." And keep going. And then there will be some surges—*good, this is good*—but don't celebrate; just make a one-word note—"good"—and keep going. Resist the impulse to start serious revision right now. If you're suddenly overtaken by a visionary brainstorm that lifts everything to a new level, okay, write it down. But you are reading here. So don't write, read. Feel the exact quality of your own reading involvement. Do you forget yourself and read ahead, absorbed and involved? Congratulations. Mark the passage "good." Is that absorption suddenly broken by the familiar voice: *wrong, wrong*? Congratulations again. Are you bored? Does your mind wander? Are you skimming? Good again. Boredom is *always* pointing to trouble. If I don't cut it on the spot, I note boring passages with a one-word acronym: MEGO—"My Eyes Glaze Over." Above all, resist the impulse to overreact. Fight down both panic *and* ecstasy. You are going to fix all these problems. Just keep making those terse notes. Get to the end.

When you are done, *do not make a judgment.* Your manuscript is not ready to be judged. It is ready to be improved. Besides, your judgments may not be very sound right now. Your head will be swarming with a mass of conflicting and even bewildered responses. You will have your notes on the page. And you will have, when the inner tumult subsides, something you have not really had until now. You will know your story. At least you will know it well enough to be ready to take full possession of it.

TAKING CHARGE OF THE STORY. The most typical problems are sketchiness, shallow characterization, undepicted action, and vague description—not to mention a wavering, unclear voice. You are going to attend to all these things.

But begin by taking charge of your story. Though even a completed first draft will rarely provide you with full mastery over your story, you have now managed to tell the story once. True, that's only once, but it does give you the *basis* for getting that mastery in the second draft. Do you remember our remark, a few chapters back, that since there are many ways to tell any story, you may have to tell yours several times before you settle on the right way for it? This may be the moment to try some of these retellings. You certainly do not want to retell the story each time in a full draft. Life *is* short.

This may be the moment to write a scenario. That is, you may be able to write a short but detailed précis or paraphrase of the story that's been forming in this draft. And that scenario may turn into a map for the second draft.

Note well: I'm suggesting you write your scenario *after*—not before—you finish your first draft. You were in no position to write a scenario before you'd done the first draft. You did not know the story well enough for that.

No story is really a story until it can be retold. Paraphrase is one of the mind's most potent instruments of understanding: What cannot be paraphrased has probably not been understood at all. Remember the early days, how you blushed and stammered and felt like an idiot when people asked you about your story? You began the first draft feeling, guessing, that you might have a story. That time is over. Your story lies before you, fresh territory. Now you need a map.

If you decide to do even one scenario, try several. Tell yourself your emerging story again and again until you have, in capsule, a potent credible version that is propelling you into the new draft. If you like, summarize your first-draft version in the first. Then try some other ways of telling it. Change the beginning, change the ending, shift points of view and perspectives. Keep each summary short and try never to devote more than a day's work to any one of them. You are not rewriting. You are summarizing; you are testing possibilities. If your project is a short story or novella, don't produce one syllable over 350 words. If you are writing a novel, the summary should not be more than 3,000 words. Even those numbers are probably too generous. Stick to the story. Don't talk to yourself *about* the story: Tell it to yourself in this concentrated form. Don't indulge in fancy meditations on the theme and do not theorize. But do include images and motifs and moments that you know drive the story forward, keeping them in a kind of shorthand that you'll clearly understand. Remember, this is just for you. A good model is Flaubert's scenario for *Madame Bovary*, which appears in the appendix of one of the best books I know about the writing of a great novel: Francis Steegmuller's *Flaubert and Madame Bovary*. It's true, Flaubert was (in *Madame Bovary*, anyway) a single-drafter who wrote his scenario before he did that first draft. But the document is especially useful because it so clearly shows how images and precisely visualized moments can serve as the pivots and stepping-stones for forward narrative movement, while some of the dramatic, even hectic scenes in the novel—Emma's suicide, for example—are noted in a couple of calm sentences. Work quickly. Don't get bogged down. With each new version, reconsider, change, tighten, revise. John Braine, from whom I learned this scenario technique, recommended doing a scenario a day, even it means you must defer dealing with this or that incoherence or problem until the next day. "If you write quickly—ideally producing a summary each session—this will be reflected in the finished novel. The narrative will have an organic unity; it won't be a bundle of loosely linked episodes. And it will flow compulsively; it won't stop and start, run and stagger."

When you are fully satisfied, you will have a map for your second draft.

RULES FOR REVISION

If you are about to begin a second draft, it is best to prepare yourself psychologically by realizing that you are about to rewrite—not polish, rewrite—your entire project. This will be obvious if you do the scenario and settle on one that differs significantly from what you have in the first draft. But in any case, you should plan on rewriting in depth.

If you imagine that a second draft can be created simply by sitting down and starting on page one to polish every line, stop: You are about to fall into a classic trap. You are not yet ready to polish anything. I've repeatedly seen novices slaving away at polishing rough first drafts before they had really taken charge of the shape and structure and character alignments of the story itself. They had not yet taken possession of the narrative voice, they did not yet really know who their characters were. Polishing happened to be the only technique of revision they knew, and so they were polishing, hoping that it would release the things they needed, the way rubbing Aladdin's lamp released the genie.

It won't. *Do not polish a mess.* Polishing can't give your story its shape. Polishing can't show you what action you need or reveal your characters' roles. Polishing can't even give you the *sound* of your dialogue or your voice. In a second draft, you are going to be hauling huge hunks of prose to completely new places, cutting whole chapters, banishing irrelevant characters, and adding new relevant ones. With or without the help of your scenario, you are going to be dealing with structure. It will be hard work, but the nice thing is that once it is done, it is likely to stay done. You will not be restructuring much in third or final drafts. That is when you'll be polishing.

And so—

REVISE FOR STRUCTURE FIRST. Redrafting should begin by solving the problem of sequence. Always. So should every revision, no matter how minor. Structure determines not only the large shape of the story; it also determines every section, every paragraph, for that matter, the smallest turns in the cadence of every sentence. There is an implicit sequence in *everything* you do. In any novel, or story, or chapter, or passage, there is a necessary sequence: of blocks of information, of events, of sentences. No other will do. You *must* find that sequence, and you must be looking for it all the time. Logic will give you some of it. Intuition will give you some more. The indispensable editorial impulse to simplify the order of things will give you more. As if with a safecracker's sandpapered fingertips, you must *feel* the tumblers of the right combination falling into place. That order, incidentally, is always there. If your ear is fine enough, it is always findable. Get it right, and the locked door will swing open.

DEVELOP THE UNDEVELOPED. Cutting out the bad parts is not enough. If you wrote a fast first draft, you should expect the second draft to be longer, more complex, and probably slower paced than the first. It will not necessarily be that way when you finish the third draft: This is the time for development. Virtually everything in a first draft needs to be made more vivid, more coherent, and more powerful. Your second encounter with your own prose should make you see *more,* not less. Act on every insight. Get them down. Fill paragraphs and pages with them. Bear in mind your great advantage over screenwriters: *You* don't lose momentum and audience if you dare pause to explain or savor something for longer than ten seconds. Provided it's interesting enough, dynamic enough, suggestive enough, you *gain* momentum through expansiveness.

REVISE FOR PLOT. Remember that the plot follows the story, and that while stories can be paraphrased and summarized, plots are nothing if not concrete. Now is the time to give your full attention to this concreteness, finding and getting down the exact *ways* the events in your story happen, and how those changes drive the story forward. Until now, given the amorphousness of your story, you have not been in a position to pay a great deal of attention to the "mechanisms" of plot. Now is the time to get these details right. How do the twists and turns of this story work, exactly? Aristotle spoke of the "reversals and recognitions" in every story. What are your "reversals and recognitions," and what is the precise way they take place? Somewhere in the course of doing the second draft, you must get complete clarity on every single one of them.

And, speaking of clarity—

REVISE FOR CLARITY. The single most destructive force dooming most first fiction to failure is simple unreadability. As we have seen, the heart of readability is your relationship to your reader. Clarity must be an essential element of that relationship. When I first began teaching, I sometimes imagined I was surrounded by young writers who, for some strange reason, were enchanted with obscurity and opacity as artistic modes, a bunch of Gertrude Steins and Mallarmés. I had never read large numbers of manuscripts in an early stage. Here was a lot of often strikingly well-written work in which I had real trouble grasping what was being said. At first I imagined that this obscurity was somehow intended. It almost never was. These passages were crystal clear to their authors. They could see it all, with all its nuances and details, plain as plain. Why couldn't I?

First drafts, even pretty good ones, can be excruciatingly hard for anyone but their authors to read. The primary issue, line by line, is not their higher meaning. It is their basic meaning. What is going on? Is John talking to Mary, or is he talking to Bill? Are we in Iowa or Guatemala? Nothing is so infuriating as not being understood, but if a reader of good basic intelligence does not know what you are talking about, you have a problem. Don't rationalize it by blaming the messenger for the message. Your reader is not stupid. You are not being understood, and it is *your* problem.

Sadly, your first readers may be reluctant to tell you the truth about your lack of clarity. It is a fact that many readers (especially in a school) will go to great lengths to conceal their bafflement over a piece of prose they don't understand. Rather than run the risk of being thought dense or uncomprehending or philistine, all too many readers, including many who should know better—editors, teachers, workshop members—would rather skip over an obscurity than admit they just don't get it.

Yet it is simply impossible to be too clear. Always, always make your writing a little clearer than you think it needs to be.

Does this make you nervous? Are you afraid some snob will sneer and call your writing "obvious"? Don't be. If clarity reveals that your scene is *really* too simple, if it unmasks your dialogue as *really* humdrum, then clarity will have done you a very great service. It's pretty easy to cut the "obvious." On the other hand, if your scene is rich and elusive and rare, clarity can only crown those virtues with perfection. Murk—mere murk—sinks. "If a man writes clearly enough," Hemingway said, "any one can see if he fakes. . . . True mysticism should not be confused with incompetence in writing. . . ."

It is time to leave the pretensions of the classroom behind: *No* piece of literature has ever been better *merely* because it is unreadable or obscure. Keep in mind always that "common reader" with whom, as Virginia Woolf reminded us, Dr. Johnson rejoiced to concur. I know, it will be galling when somebody you respect tells you that they "just don't get" that shimmering paragraph, the one you think may be the most mysterious and beautiful you ever wrote. You've got to get over it. They are doing you a favor.

THE 10-PERCENT SOLUTION

It's said that Fred Astaire once gave this advice to a young filmmaker: "Make it as good as you can. Then cut ten minutes." I hope Astaire really did make this remark, because it is at once profound and worthy of his debonair perfection. It belongs alongside Blaise Pascal's remark, in a letter, that he would make it shorter if he had the time.

There is a bit of wisdom about revision that I regularly pounded into the heads of each new generation of students, always imagining I had thought it up myself. It became so central to my teaching that the maxim came to be known around the school, with a smack of irony, as "Koch's 10-Percent Solution."

The 10-percent solution is absurdly, sublimely simple.

Cut it by 10 percent.

Cut *everything* by 10 percent.

If your story is 10 pages long, make it 9 pages long. Twenty pages? Make it 18. If your draft is 300 pages long, knock it down to 270. Do you have a bunch of pages—any bunch of pages—that needs work? They have not been worked on until they have been washed and preshrunk in the 10-Percent Solution.

Once in a rare while someone will come along for whom this rule is unworkable. I'd guess maybe one time in fifty. The best and wisest guide to all cutting is your own boredom. Elmore Leonard put it beautifully when he advised leaving out the boring parts. Do your eyes glaze over as you read? Cut. Are *you* not held? Cut. Been there? Done that? Cut, cut, and cut again. When you are bored—really bored—don't even *try* to fix the passage. Just cut. Is there maybe one lively sentence somewhere in there? Good. Save that one sentence. And then cut. Forget the transitions and the explanations: cut *bravely*. Are you afraid some boring passage is also essential? If it really is essential, it will eventually make its way back onto your page, though we hope in a more lively form.

Cut phoniness. There are going to be certain passages that you put in simply in the hope of impressing people. It is true of me, and it is almost surely true of you. I have maybe never known a writer of whom it is not true. But literary pretension is the curse of the postmodern age. We all have our favorite ways of showing off, and they rarely serve us well. When you have identified your own grandiosity, do not be kind. When Georges Simenon was an eager young wannabe in Paris, none other than Colette herself advised him that his prose was "too literary, always too literary." Thereafter, Simenon spent much of his amazing career cutting away his efforts to impress. "It's what I do when I write," he said, "the main job when I rewrite. . . . [I cut] every word which is there just to make an effect. Every sentence which is there just for the sentence. . . . Cut it."

I have since discovered that the 10-percent solution isn't mine at all. Stephen King, in *On Writing,* says he learned the rule from a rejection slip when he was in high school, back in 1966. One of his stories was returned to him with a rejection slip on which some wise editor had scrawled, "Not bad, but *puffy.* You need to revise for length. Formula: 2nd Draft = 1st draft − 10%." King wrote it out on a piece of cardboard and put it above his desk: "Second draft equals first draft—minus 10%."

Put that equation over *your* desk.

REVISE OUT LOUD

When it comes to line-by-line work, the ear is a wonderful editor—and usually a much sharper, smarter, and livelier editor than the eye. When she was a little girl, Dickens's daughter Mamie was once granted the unique privilege of spending several days reading and resting on a sofa in her father's *very* closed-door study while he worked. This was an opportunity granted to nobody else, but Mamie was getting over being sick, and she was her daddy's darling, and she promised to be quiet. As a grown woman, Mamie wrote a reminiscence of her time in the inner sanctum. As Dickens sank deeper and deeper into his work, she wrote, "Evidently not seeing me, he began talking rapidly in a low voice." From time to time, he would jump up, still murmuring, and rush to a mirror, where he pulled a variety of weird faces. Then he would rush back to the desk to mumble some more. Charles Dickens was *muttering* his prose onto the page. In fact, even when the master was away from the desk, when he was "searching for some pictures I wanted to build upon," he would whisper the emerging cadences aloud, "his eyes looking straight before him, his lips slightly working, as they generally did when he sat thinking and writing."

Take it from the greatest: You will *hear* what's right and wrong on your page before you *see* it. This precept is of course crucial for dialogue, but it is really true for everything. "My working rule with narrative prose," says John Braine, "is the same as for dialogue: If it can't be read aloud, it's no good." Once you've revised for structure, once you've done some basic cutting, it's useful to crown the whole process of revision by reading aloud. "You must learn to reread your own sentences," says Richard Bausch, "as a stranger might. And say everything aloud. Listen to how it *sounds*."

This work should go on behind closed doors. Your prose is not yet polished enough to be read aloud to anyone but yourself. An accomplished editor I know recalls, as an undergraduate, listening to his English professor read his papers aloud to him in private conference: "a very powerful way to get you to see what needs improving." You do not want to discover what needs improving in a performance.

REWRITE FROM MEMORY

Some bad prose is a tar baby. Touch it and you just sink deeper into tar. If your battle with some passage is leaving you bleary-eyed and frustrated, it's often best simply to return to your original inspiration and without so much as a backward glance, quickly write out the whole thing again, from scratch, and from memory. When you are mired in a manuscript, *rewrite from memory*. Scott Fitzgerald's notebooks are filled with this injunction. That is what, through dumb luck, I got my early student to do when she was mired in her impossible first draft. And it works for little things as well as big ones, as I learned many years ago from a wise magazine editor. I was doing a lot of work for her magazine, and so I often found myself in her office, trying to make something clear that, as we thrashed about, only became more snarled up. After a certain point in these discussions, the wise editor would lightly push the manuscript aside and calmly say, "Stephen, why don't you just tell me what you're saying here?" And I would

look up from the battered page. It was like breaking an evil spell.
I would lean back in my chair, and I would tell her. "Okay," she'd
answer. "That's clear. Let's say that." She would cross out the
mess and write down what I had said. Simple. I didn't know I was
rewriting from memory. But I was.

TRUST WHAT YOU HAVE

Cut, but don't cut out your heart. Don't banish something vital
from your page just because after a few tries it is still unsatisfac-
tory. When you first scribbled it down, it seemed so transporting,
so superb. So . . . what happened? Well, maybe it just hasn't happened yet. Don't let your chagrin over the mess you've made
make you forget that first excitement. Your job in revision is to
recapture that first excitement and know it again, no longer as a
promise but as a promise redeemed. From the very beginning,
the definition of your job has been to trust your own excitement
and make it pay off. It still is. Never condemn your own prose.
Redeem it. If you do, the original excitement will come back, but
it will come back fulfilled and alive with a power that will be new
to you.

8

FINISHING

Now that you are plunging into second, or middle, and finishing drafts, the time has come for you to strengthen your grasp not only on your story but also on its meanings. What is this story about? What is it saying? What does it imply? The meanings you deal with now will be the meanings that you "invented"— "invented" in *our* sense—as a consequence of inventing the story itself. You are finally, and for the first time, in a position to become really conscious and much more fully in control of what your narrative signifies.

This fine, fascinating, new set of insights and conclusions is going to help you revise. It is going to help you refine, develop, and find certainty over something much more important even than your story's meaning—and that is the story itself. When you started out, your hold on the narrative was—remember?— possibly pretty feeble. You may have been barely able to sum it up in a stumbling paragraph or two. And you were certainly in no position to expand upon what it all might mean. Back then, you were lucky to get the story told at all, and since you did not know it yet, that meant getting the story to tell itself through you. Yet as the emerging narrative has moved through the process of getting itself told, you doubtless noticed that every once in a while the story has suggested to you this or that significant implication. I hope you noticed and cared, and I also hope that the slow stirring of significance did not distract you from the unfolding of the tale. You would have been well advised to keep yourself a passive vehicle for both, letting the story lead.

But now things have changed. With the first draft in place, you are finally in a position to assess what this is all about. Something did stir, something did make itself felt in the first draft. "Your job in the second draft—" says Stephen King, "one of them, anyway—is to make that something even more clear. This may necessitate some big changes and revisions. The benefits to you and your reader will be clearer focus and a more unified story."

So the time has come to tighten your grip on meaning. Just don't make it a stranglehold. Confirm your understanding, yes, but don't make that understanding too narrow. Though you can and should have a solid command of the dominant ideas implicit in your story, it is unlikely that you will be able to grasp *all* the meanings and implications that your story is disclosing. In fact, it amounts almost to a test of the story's vitality that *some* of its meanings and implications, *some* of the overtones of its dominant ideas, will escape you. Some themes will be fully formed in your mind, while others may flicker there half-obscure. The way they flicker may change as you revise, but it is unlikely that you will ever totally "know," in a fully conscious way, their whole significance.

Nor should you. As you work, what matters is to keep all your meanings, both the clear and the obscure, the explicit and the implicit, the dominant and the secondary, at work sustaining and enriching the story that they are helping you revise. You are not revising in order to clarify your ideas. It's the other way around. You are using these latent thematic ideas to help clarify your story: to make it more coherent, more compelling, more powerful, and—yes—more meaningful. But you are not trying to turn your story into an argument illustrated by an anecdote.

In narrative art, meanings are always subordinated to the story. They always emerge *from* it, rather than the other way around. There is nothing anti-intellectual in this basic truth of the art. It is perfectly possible to start out with some strong general thematic idea and then look *through* it for some narrative that will make it live. Yet even a writer like Chinua Achebe, who almost always begins his novels building on some strong "general idea," makes it a point to pursue that idea *through* the story, and not the reverse. "Once the novel gets going, and I know it is viable, I don't then worry about the plot or themes. These things will come in almost automatically because the characters are now pulling the story." In the first draft, your initial idea is likely to develop and change in unexpected ways. It may even be transformed, as Dostoyevsky's original idea about alcoholics in Saint Petersburg was transformed in *Crime and Punishment*.

But no matter how you handle it, some part of the story's meaning is likely always to escape you. The meaning of a story usually takes the form of a kind of nimbus of implications and suggestions, some implicit and some explicit, all surrounding the narrative. Some of the "somethings" glowing within the halo of significance will have resonance and overtones that, even to you, may remain finally only half-definable and obscure, partly present and partly not, partly articulated and partly not.

This is as it should be.

You will never understand *everything* about your own story.

Meaning—understanding itself—is not a thing. It has no existence considered as a thing. Meaning exists only as an exchange, a transaction. It is therefore an event, and moreover an event that consists in some sort of relationship between people. In writing—all writing—this relationship is formally encoded in the implied relation between the writer and the writer's "invented" interlocutor, the Reader. After that, the actual transaction takes place *through* the invented identity of that Reader in the literal exchange between the work and the real human beings perusing it. That is an exchange over which you can hope for only partial control, at best. Each reader is going to bring to your page her or his own responses and fantasies and associations, and you cannot—you should not—have much control over how those things come into play.

This element of uncertainty—call it indeterminacy if you like—is going to be an omnipresent and inevitable formal aspect of the work because it is an omnipresent and inevitable formal quality of language itself. It is there in the relation that is implied between your prose and its "invented" Reader, and it is there above all in one of the prime attributes with which you have endowed that Reader: the Reader's *silence*. Implicit in this silence is the way the Reader's unspoken attention—and the Reader's imagined understanding—helps to shape and define the story itself, just as at this moment my words are being guided by my silent sense of how you are understanding me. This mute attention, this imagined experience of someone else hearing and grasping what you have to say, inevitably guides any writer's work. Your prose must be shaped in part by your understanding of how the Reader is *listening* to it. And this—all of it—is something you must also "invent."

Now, don't get me wrong. You must be clear in your meanings, and nothing here should be taken to derogate the importance of clarity. I am anything but an advocate of intentional obscurity or general indeterminacy of meaning in prose. I like, need, and demand significant coherence in everything I read. Life is simply too short for me to spend it wandering alone in the desolate wastelands of gnomic implication. You must make your story clear. Clarity is a measure of the coherence of your work, and as you move from draft to draft, that story—and its ideas, too—should grow steadily clearer, and clearer, and then clearer still.

On the other hand, the *vitality* of the work can partly be measured by the way *some* of its meanings and implications remain elusive, resonant but not pinned down, implicit in the Reader's elusive, silent, individualized comprehension. The dominant meaning of any strong piece of writing ought to be both clear—*and* too multiple and various to be entirely captured in any single statement. What, precisely, is the meaning—or the meanings—of Gulliver's imprisonment in the Land of Lilliput? Of Dorothy's voyage to and from Oz? Of the humiliation of Isabel Archer? Every reader experiences these narrative images as replete with "meaning," and a competent critic ought to be able to supply a perfectly plausible, albeit partial, summary of what those meanings might be. But these narrative images are too vital to be co-extensive with such a summary. They live silently in the mind; they generate meaning the way life itself generates meaning.

There is a crucial element of freedom implicit in the Reader's silence. By making your story alive—alive with narrative, and with meaning, too—you are giving something away and surrendering your hold on it. And by, as the saying goes, "taking your point," the Reader and your readers make it their own. Though you do give the story away, some part of it is going to remain forever yours, private, even incommunicable. But some other essential part of it is going to be handed over and lost; it is going to become the part of the inner life of the Reader, and also all the many real people whom you hope will become your readers. That's just part of the deal, an inevitable aspect of the exchange. What starts out yours, ends up theirs. As an artist, you are trying, as Shakespeare put it once and for all, "to please." What pleases is never *mere* meaning. What pleases is a coherent image of life, and life is always both communicable and incommunicable, simultaneously freely given away and present to us alone.

This helps explain, I hope, why some of the meanings of many stories are so often left unspoken. It is not that there is anything so wonderful in itself about unspoken significance. If you can put your finger on the exact moral of the story, by all means, go ahead and put your finger on it. If you can get the story explicitly to say what it means, for heaven's sake, don't hold back. Just say it. But for the reasons we've given, what a story "means" will usually involve exactly what the story is *unable* to put into words. The Reader's comprehension is finally silent, and so is yours. The last thing you should do is try to plumb the meaning of your story as if you were writing a term paper or critical article. You are not a critic or scholar of your own work. "It is hard enough to write books and stories without being asked to explain them as well," Hemingway once remarked in his testy way. "Read anything I write for the pleasure of reading it. Whatever else you find will be the measure of what you brought to the reading."

CLIMBING MOUNT PROBABILITY

Yet you will get a grip on your meanings only through revision. And since you are writing fiction, part of reaching that understanding will consist of convincing yourself of your fiction's imaginative truth. In chapter 3, I joined many mentors in urging you to embrace drama and improbability. A storyteller has to be a specialist in the unlikely. Fiction is made—depending on how you define them—from "exceptional happenings." Almost every really interesting story is rooted in the improbable in some quite striking way. And that is not merely because fiction is riddled with "improbability." So is life.

As Somerset Maugham pointed out: "The behavior of the persons in *Othello,* of Othello himself principally, but to a less extent of almost everyone in the play, is wildly irrational. The critics have turned themselves inside out to show that it isn't. In vain. They would have done better to accept it as a grand example of the fundamental irrationality of man. I am quite ready to believe that contemporary theatergoers saw nothing improbable in the behavior of any of the characters."

Yet the critic who attacks your story for being "improbable" is hitting it hard. And though I've advised you to embrace the improbable, you cannot leave it on your page in all its raw improbability. That would wreck the story. It is your job, usually through revision, to make the improbable credible and convincing. And from being credible and convincing, you must go on to make it inevitable.

This comes with work. I call it climbing Mount Probability. The path up to the summit of Mount Probability is revision, and the way you make the improbable convincing will say a great deal about the formal mode in which you work. A realist climbs Mount Probability by finding the exact realistic details. A fantasist finds the modes of fantasy that make the whole thing fly. The science fiction writer finds the right science; the librettist finds the grand aria that makes it all matter. Belief is very much a matter of tone: harmony, consistency, maintaining the appropriate persuasive voice, all of which will contribute to the mix of how you yourself believe in the material.

"But people don't act like that." Maugham pointed to the grave dangers coiled in that treacherous phrase. Our demand for probability grows more and more stringent. We balk at coincidence and accident. We invariably expect the characters who are presented to behave like ourselves. "People don't act like that?" True enough—*most* people don't act like that. Your story is not *about* most people. The true enemy of your fiction is not improbability but imaginative unbelief.

You have a climb ahead of you, out of the banal flatlands and into the heights of your own story. The scramble ahead may be tough and slow. At times you will face a sheer cliff. Other times there will be a ravine, deep and slippery and seemingly impassable. Some cliffs really will be too sheer to climb; some ravines really will be too wide to swing across. So you must find some other way around and up. Yet you must reach the top of your story. Step by step, foothold by foothold, you must ascend Mount Probability. Trust me: The view from the summit is dizzying, intoxicating.

THE END AND THE FINAL DRAFTS

Starting with Aristotle, mentor after mentor makes the same point: You cannot really know what you're saying until you reach the end. It's an unbreakable rule of narrative. You must come to a conclusion. A story turns into a real story only when the forces driving it come together and resolve. If there is no ending, there is no story. If you are writing without moving toward an ending, you are probably just piling up narrative information and—it's an all-but-dead certainty—being a bore.

Yet many writers neglect endings. They get lazy. Or hasty. For one thing, work on the first half of any project in fiction, especially any novel, is likely to be more time intensive and demanding than the second half. As Tom Wolfe says, "If you've . . . written forty percent of a novel . . . you have worked out the most difficult problems. You know your characters by now. You know the real course of your plot. You know how you're going to create suspense." So the first 40 percent of your project's pages will absorb much more of your time than the last 5 or 10 percent. Habits of revision are part of it. If you revise to the rhythm of "The House That Jack Built," you will have been over the start a hundred times to your ending's once. Then there is deadline pressure. "Read the last chapter of that marvelous book *Nana*," says Tom Wolfe. "Here's a guy who is terribly tired or had a day and a half to finish . . . a book!"

Your ending may come to you at any time. It may have been vivid in your mind from sentence one. As we have seen, plenty of writers say they can't begin at all until they know how they are going to end. Or the end may occur to you sometime while you are at work on that crucial first 40 percent that Tom Wolfe talks about. That is what usually happens to Toni Morrison. "When I really know what [my story] is about," she says, "then I can write that end scene. I wrote the end of *Beloved* about a quarter of the way in. I wrote the end of *Jazz* very early and the end of *Song of Solomon* very early on. What I really want is for the plot to be *how* it happened." Even if you don't reach any early conclusions about how to end, you may well at least sense the *kind* of conclusion you're moving toward. Is this comedy or tragedy? Are we going to be left laughing or crying or thinking and feeling . . . something else? If so, what? Your sense of this will depend much more on intuition than intellect. The first test of an ending is the *feeling* of finality. It may be almost imperceptible at first. It may appear first only as a path, a hint, and a sense of direction. It must grow in force as you proceed, and at some point the force it gathers must be compelling force. After the feeling of finality, the next test of a potential ending's strength should be how strongly it manages, whether subtly or not so subtly, to serve as a narrative magnet, pulling all the major elements and events of the story toward itself.

Of course, one natural place to look for a story's ending is in what happens after the story's crisis. So of course the placement of the climax matters. Patricia Highsmith said, "I am not sure every book has a special event that could be called a climax. Some plots will have an obvious climax, a surprise or something *boulversant.* If this is so, then it is well to decide whether it should come in the middle, at the end, or three-quarters through a book. Some books may have two or three climaxes of equal importance. Some climaxes should be the last thing in a book, because after them, there is nothing to be said, and the book should end there, with a bang." While the crisis usually comes rather late in the story, it is always a kind of pointer pushing you toward the end.

A story can be defined as a sequence of events that leads to an outcome or ending. That means you should begin to have some clear intuition of what your ending might be by the time you are fairly deep into the first draft, and certainly before the halfway point. The ending should have started to make itself felt in some way by the time you get through that opening 40 percent Tom Wolfe speaks about. That is, by, say, page 8 of a 20-page story, or maybe page 70 or so of a 200-page novel. Mind you, I say the ending has to "make itself felt" in some way. It doesn't have to be crystal clear, and it doesn't have to be definitive, and you certainly don't have to know exactly what happens. But you should feel its power beginning to draw you toward it. If you are writing a novel and find yourself piling up chapter after chapter without feeling anything pulling you toward a potent end, you may well be simply lost.

If you are writing short stories, be particularly careful of the all-too-familiar (in fact, generic) ending that is so often called in creative-writing classes an "epiphany." This is the term James Joyce contrived to describe of the climactic or critical moments in his collection of short stories, *Dubliners:* moments of bleak lyricism in which the protagonist's depression condenses into a moment of intensity that reveals the impasse of her or his life. Joyce's academic prestige has made this impasse and the anti-lyric "epiphany" that defines it a classroom cliché, incessantly popping back to demonstrate yet again that weary old chestnut, the emptiness of modern life.

Modern life? The stories in *Dubliners* were all written well before the outbreak of the First World War. The "epiphany" that many decades of academicism has turned into a generic one-size-fits-all ending has become something worse than a cliché. It is just a bore. Watch out for it.

THE FINAL DRAFTS

Let's review the typical things that are accomplished in a slow middle draft. In this long labor, you must address every essential problem of credibility and coherence your story presents. Whatever feels wrong must be made to feel right. You must make your imagination credit every syllable on the page, whether it is about a descent into a coal mine or a visit to Munchkinland. With its holes and gaps, your first draft should have shown you exactly what research you need to do, and by the end of the middle draft that research should be done and integrated into the story. Every character, to be a character, must have a role: If each does not have a clear role by now, you have failed. And every character must have a personality. No more stand-ins, no more stick figures walking through the part. Then there is action: All the action must come in the right place and be believable. The dialogue has got to be right. No more laziness. Either those voices are really talking or they are silent. Back when you were beginning, you only sketched what things looked like or even how they happened. Now you have got to get them exactly right. Style and language? By the end of the middle draft—or drafts—you should have long since found your pitch and key and tune. You should be playing riffs on them at will. Above all, you should have climbed Mount Probability, and once you have reached its summit, you should be able to stand calmly looking down upon a breathtaking view, the first you have ever had, of your whole story. The whole thing should be laid out below you, every tiny house and driveway and footpath clear and in view.

The final draft is also called a polishing draft, and yes—now at last you should lavishly indulge your impulse to polish. Lots and lots of out-loud editing should be going on. Every clumsy, inexact phrase, every cliché, every dried stick of prose with its brown cluster of rustling dead words must be cut away and disposed of now. The time has come at last for your perfectionism. You need it now. The second-to-last draft of *The Great Gatsby*—the version Fitzgerald turned in to his editor, Maxwell Perkins—has been published in a revealing scholarly edition that shows exactly how, partly by using Perkins's suggestions, Fitzgerald was able to transform a quite good novel into a great one. We see exactly how he was able to endow that manuscript with the lustrous flawlessness that gives it preeminence. The final draft made all the difference in *Gatsby*.

And yet, since everything else is in place, the work now is likely to go quite fast. Fitzgerald zipped through the final draft of

Gatsby in six weeks flat on the resort island of Capri. You are going to be doing another fast draft, but remember that your quickness now should be a new kind of speed. Back when you were careening through your first draft, if you wrote recklessly, you could be proud of it. No more. Your speed now should not have a trace of haste or even a touch of recklessness. You should never be anywhere near being out of control. No more streaking past the demons of your self-doubt, no more lightning raids on your creative unconscious. Yes, keep up the momentum, but *festina lente*. Make haste slowly. Do not slump into inaction. But do not race.

Keep on researching until the last day. According to his wife, Katia, this is what Thomas Mann did. "When he was working on a book, he immersed himself to an extraordinary degree in the relevant subject matter, learning all he could right up until the book was finished. He got hold of everything worth knowing on the topic, collecting a mass of material, but as soon as the book was finished, he forgot it all again. He was no longer interested in it." Late research will function like all crowning touches, its relevance and usability, even at the last minute, will be instantly clear, leaping out at you. Indeed, some of the very best research of all is just such "last-minute" research, precisely because your sense of what is relevant now has a pitch of completeness and sensitivity it has never had before.

This done, the time has come to open the studio door. You are ready now to show what you have not only to those who love you. It's also time for some cold objectivity, and so maybe it should also be seen by a few who do not.

OTHER PEOPLE'S ADVICE

"The idea," says John Irving, "that what inspires you is untouchable either by your own revising or by an editor's thoughtful suggestions is a kind of hubris." We have said that you should write your first draft behind closed doors. But when you have moved beyond the first-draft phase, you would be very foolish indeed not to turn to other people for their opinions and advice. But how you go about this can be a very delicate business, and you must do it in a carefully considered way.

Let me begin by drawing a very simple but often overlooked distinction between criticism and editorial advice.

Criticism is an intellectual enterprise—and a branch of literature—that owes you and your project nothing. It is a form of discourse, a means of assessing and understanding literary and artistic work, and a way of thinking about what has been written. It is absolutely free to do all these things without the slightest reference to your welfare. Nothing obliges it to say anything good or useful about you or your work. It has taken no vow to "first, do no harm." Nothing—apart from intellectual honesty and common decency—prevents it from being, with a perfectly clear conscience, relentlessly and wholeheartedly malevolent.

Editorial advice, on the other hand, is a service. It owes you its entire existence. It is there *only* to help improve your work, and it has no more right to ignore your interests than a doctor has the right to ignore a patient's interests.

This distinction should be in your mind in every workshop you join and in every editorial exchange you have. If you are doing the advising, there may sometimes be tension between your critical opinion and your editorial opinion. You're getting science fiction and you hate it. You cannot stomach this kind of macho hero. The politics here make you want to scream. It happens all the time. As a teacher, I have more than once given what I hope was my very best, editorially and pedagogically, to projects—some of them damn good projects—that I would certainly have attacked or ignored had they come before me in my role as a critic.

There *is* a gray zone: warnings. It is a perfectly legitimate—and often vital—part of editorial advice to alert a writer to the kind of criticism she or he is likely to face. You can tell a writer that this macho hero is going to take a lot of heat, or that the politics here are going to get shredded in this or that journal. You'd be surprised how often writers miss such simple truths.

If possible, a writer should anticipate her or his critics. That is not always easy. Remember those nasty doubts from the early days? You should have been warding them off until now. Now is the time, privately, to let the dogs slip back into the compound and give them their day. Any story, any novel, any work of art is at least potentially open to some kind of attack. If you can antici- pate the ones that will be used against you, well and good. The time is now. "Only when a piece of work is done should the writer pile on the critical pressure," says Paul Johnson. "Then, indeed, he should reread it through the eyes of his worst enemies—on what particular weak points would they pick?"

Be tough with yourself. Do your imagined assailants have a point? About what? What are you going to do about it? If, in your heart, you even suspect that they may be right, you must act. You must not needlessly expose your work to attack. Most writers have a much clearer idea of a story's vulnerabilities than even the most hostile critic. You know where your story's jugular lies. If you can find solutions, if you can find a way to protect and strengthen your story, do it now. Find solutions. Consider con- cessions. Forge your defense.

If, that is, something really looks wrong. And only if. Never back away from a genuine strength merely because somebody somewhere might attack it. Protect your work; don't betray it. And remember, not every writer is endowed with a critical gift. As Eudora Welty points out, "Story writing and an independently operating power of critical analysis, are separate gifts, like spell- ing and playing the flute, and one person proficient in both has been doubly endowed. Even he can't rise and do both at the same time." As Toni Morrison puts it: "If you know how to read your own work—that is, with the necessary critical distance—it makes you a better writer and editor. When I teach creative writing, I always speak about how you have to learn how to read your work; I don't mean enjoy it because you wrote it. I mean go away from it, and read it as though it is the first time you've ever seen it. Critique it that way. Don't get all involved in your thrilling sentences and all that. . . ."

Even if you have a highly developed critical gift, you may well find the shift of gears between creation and criticism difficult. In a sense, your critical faculty has been in operation all along—it has always been at work in your sense of rightness and wrongness. But if you are going to flourish as an artist, your critical instincts should always give way to the richer creative energies of self-permission.

That done, open the door. It is now time to hear what other people have to say. To begin, you may well need some specialized readers. Let's say you have three scenes in a Midwestern small town, and you have spent exactly two days of your life in a Midwestern small town. You need to get yourself a Midwesterner with a clear, cool eye. Don't be afraid to ask: People are often flattered to have a role. Do you need a spy? A fireman? You may need to get hold of one or two.

You may also need some specialized advice of another kind: skilled editorial advice. It is easy to get lost in a middle draft, and when you are done with one, it may be helpful to get some good outside advice. "In my experience of writing," says Michael Crichton, "you generally start out with some overall idea that you can see fairly clearly, as if you were standing on a dock and looking at a ship on the ocean. At first you can see the entire ship, but then as you begin to work you're in the boiler room and you can't see the ship anymore. All you can see are the pipes and the grease and the fittings of the boiler room, and you have to *assume* the ship's exterior. What you really want in an editor is someone who's still on the dock, who can say, Hi, I'm looking at your ship, and it's missing a bow, the front mast is crooked, and it looks to me as if your propellers are going to have to be fixed."

READING A FIRST DRAFT. Different drafts call for different kinds of editorial advice. For example, the reader of a first draft should concentrate on large structural issues and on defining the elements—the roles of the characters, the general textures of the prose, the main movement of the story line—that must be addressed in the second draft. Detailed observations about the polish on the prose are obviously a waste of time. In addition, a good first-draft reader must be exceptionally sensitive to the possibilities of a project that is sure to be either still sketchy or, if it came from a slow draft, loaded with mind-blearing information that does not serve the story. The first-draft reader must see through first-draft faults and see the idea animating the whole project. Big questions count. Is this story tellable and worth telling? Is it too cumbersome? Or too simple? How long should it be? What is its proper scale? How interesting is it in its current form? Some bright ideas on structure or character or sequencing would do no harm, or perhaps a hint about what might build suspense and believability.

READING A MIDDLE DRAFT. By the time you ask people to read a middle draft, your book, like your needs, will be very different. By this time, you will, I hope, have addressed the clear weaknesses of your story and answered every question the draft raised in your own mind. By now your story should be coherent. You will have climbed Mount Probability, or at least be getting near the summit. By now, your story should have the right beginning, the right ending, and the right protagonist pretty much in place. The other characters should be doing what they have to do in pretty much the right way, at the right place and time. You have done much, if not all, of your research. Your expository problems—who, what, where, why, and when—should be solved.

And now . . . your solutions are the problem. The most typical fault of a middle draft is that it has lost the first draft's freshness and momentum. It is top-heavy. The *simplicity* of its story is buried under heaps of narrative information.

What you need now is help recovering that original spirit and momentum. The reader of the second draft should help you dig out the living thing that may be buried under all your work. What you may need now is a way to transform the mastery the second draft has given you back into freshness and speed.

Incidentally, every time you bring in outside readers, whether early or late, it's a useful idea to ask them to summarize the story for you. Nothing fancier than that. The reader may balk: Just *retell* the story? That's *it*? No big thinking about the theme? No grand observations or profundities about the characters? Just tell the *story*?

Right. *Just tell the story.* That summary can be the most useful thing you will hear. If the story you hear back is something other than the story you think you told—and you'd be amazed to know how often it is—you will have just learned exactly what you need to revise.

Naturally, different readers will say different things. When a value judgment is unanimous, be it favorable or unfavorable, something important has been said. It is of course possible—unlikely, but possible—that you are right and everyone else is wrong: After all, it *is* your story. But usually something everybody dislikes needs fixing. Unanimity is rare. "More likely," says Stephen King, "they'll think that some parts are good and some parts are . . . well, not so good. Some will feel Character A works but Character B is far-fetched. If others feel that Character B is believable but Character A is overdrawn, it's a wash. You can safely relax and leave things the way they are (in baseball, tie goes to the runner; for novelists, it goes to the writer). If some people love your ending and others hate it, same deal—it's a wash, and tie goes to the writer."

Finally, protect what you love in your writing. Somebody is sure to blunder against the one part that matters most to you;

sure to insult it, suggest you cut it, even sneer at it. Forgive them and reject what they say. In any given project, there is almost always something, or maybe some things, that are the secret heart of the work. These you must defend. As Ian Frazier puts it, "If the part you love is not there, it doesn't matter how much else you did. I've witnessed battles between writers and editors that you can't believe the intensity of. But the writer knows that if that point came out, the book wouldn't be his."

FINISHING TOUCHES

A final draft is one that has been cleared, one way or the other, of all the clutter typical of middle drafts. You should no longer be bogged down. The pure sweet shape of the story should be back up front, rolling forward, exciting, fully told, and alive. This draft was probably done quite fast—probably faster than the middle draft, and the job was probably a great deal easier than you thought and feared it might be. The 10-percent solution has been applied and reapplied. Every page has been read aloud, and every page sounds good. The boring parts have been cut away. Everything has fallen into place. This project finally knows what it is saying. You may not have quite reached the end, but you are close.

This is a tremendously fertile moment in the life of any project. Now that the basics are fully in place, the fine ideas of the finishing touches will start coming to you, and they can be invaluable and exhilarating. Whatever you touch turns better. Certainty grows and grows. Your project may have unfolded slowly. You may not have reached what Melville called "the inmost leaf," even of the story itself, until now. But now the book has taught you how to write it. Now you know. Philip Roth describes it: "The two years it generally takes to write a book means a long running start to get the pitch, and then the leap of the last three or four months. And I come out here nights then, or I'm taking a shower and halfway through I have an idea and rush off in my bathrobe to come back out here and have yet another go at the book. Those last months are wonderful."

After finishing the basic drafts of his memoir of his family, *Colored People,* Henry Louis Gates Jr. went into psychotherapy to retrieve the key inspiring memory. "As soon as I finished writing the book I realized that I needed to talk to a therapist. As it turned out, that therapy brought back a crucial event that I had completely repressed. . . . That incident explained everything: why I joined the church and why I always felt such a strong sense of guilt. The book was virtually in galleys when I recovered that memory, but I knew I had to insert it. Writing that episode was agony—dealing with something buried so deep that suddenly had come to the surface."

Now *that* is a very pure example of the finishing touch. Back when you began, you had no choice but to entrust your enterprise to forces and feelings that often seemed maddeningly vague. But now—at this late stage of work—you have brought yourself to a level of almost uncanny acuity and depth of focus. You have reached a honed grasp of the relevance and exactitude that shares with your groping early phase only that it too is difficult to put into words. But it is wonderful. The time is golden, and you have what feels like a golden touch. It can make you feel like the blessed of the earth. The architect Walter Gropius thought God is in the details. Well, God can certainly seem to be in those dazzling wonder workers, the *last* details.

When Truman Capote reached this phase, "I put the manuscript away for a while, a week, a month, sometimes longer. When I take it out again, I read it as coldly as possible, then read it aloud to a friend or two, and decide what changes I want to make and whether I want to publish it." Philip Roth is even more systematic. He does not show his work in progress until he is very near the end. "When I've finished what looks to me like the last draft of a novel, I give a copy of the manuscript to five or six people to read, my friend and editor Aaron Asher, and other friends whose literary judgment and taste I respect. Obviously I don't want to finish a book and then drop it into a void without hearing what *anyone* makes of it. These people read it, and then I go with a pencil and a pad and listen for two or three hours to what each of them has to say. Because the book is still in manuscript form they tend to be more candid and direct than they might be if I confronted them with a bound volume which I could no longer rework. What they give me is not only their criticism, but along the way they *describe* the book to me, and that is really the best of it—hearing words *unlike* those with which you have been describing the book to yourself as you went along, finding out how it register on an intelligence that's not your own."

Once you have assimilated what these carefully chosen readers have to say, you will want to move through the manuscript one last time, polishing and perfecting, and hearing the first sound in your ear of a real audience. The experience is in fact so gratifying that it is difficult to leave. Your project has taught you how to write it; you finally feel you have mastered it. At this final stage, you will have reached a level of comfort and confidence unimaginable when you started.

———

And then one day, unbelievably, you will be done. "You know it's finished," James Baldwin said, "when you can't do anything more to it." It will be different from the idea you had when you began. "No book," says Patricia Highsmith, "when it is finished, is ever exactly like the first dream of it." You will never be so close to this thing again, and it will be hard to say good-bye. When he completed his vast lifework, *The Decline and Fall of the Roman Empire*, Edward Gibbon felt great relief. The burden of a lifetime had been lifted. He felt inexpressible joy that he had managed to live long enough to complete his Herculean task. And then he felt overwhelmed by a wave of sadness. This was the work and partner of his life, the companion of his days. For years, since he was a young man, the best that he possessed as a human being had been poured into it. He had shared with it a tempestuous intimacy and a communion like no other. He had lived with it. He had loved it. He had given it everything. He had found and formed his being in it. And now the time had come to say good-bye.

Here is Virginia Woolf writing in her diary moments after completing *The Waves:* "Here in the few minutes that remain, I must record, heaven be praised, the end of The Waves. I wrote the words O Death fifteen minutes ago, having reeled across the last ten pages with some moments of such intensity & intoxication that I seemed only to stumble after my own voice. . . . & I have been sitting these 15 minutes in a state of glory, & calm, & some tears. . . . How physical the sense of triumph & relief is! Whether good or bad, it's done."

———

Except that it is never done. When one project is completed, there is another waiting. To finish is to be put into the position of beginning again and facing once again the process of reaching the elusive mastery of an idea's first perplexing promise. The composer Quincy Jones can remember the precise moment when, as a very small boy, he came across his first piano and made the tremendous, life-defining discovery that his small hands could touch its keyboard and mix and match sounds. Jones ends this story with a sigh, noting that he is still at that keyboard, still trying to figure it out.

Well, so are we all. Throughout this book, I have been addressing "you." Yet one of the people I've been addressing with that pronoun has been, of course, myself. I have spent my life writing, and I expect to end it writing. Writing is how I know who I am. I only wish I had somehow stumbled across something like this book when I was starting out. It would have spared me . . . well, let me not linger over what it would have spared me. When I speak of "you," I most certainly do mean you—but I am also addressing another me, the gangling wishful boy who long ago used money from his paper route to buy, along with his first hardcover book (*The Selected Writings of Gertrude Stein*), a then-current copy of *The Paris Review,* with its magnificent last interview with Ernest Hemingway.

The boy biked home and, sprawling on his bed, started out with the Hemingway interview.

> *Interviewer:* Are these hours during the actual process of writing pleasurable?
> *Hemingway:* Very.

The boy read on, and as he moved from answer to question to answer, he felt the world—the *whole* world—falling flawlessly and miraculously into place. A few years later, when he graduated from high school, his mom surprised him—the perfect dizzying unrepeatable *gift* of it!—with a brand-new Smith Corona portable typewriter. About a year later, he loaded that Smith Corona, along with the Stein and the *Paris Review,* onto a Greyhound bus headed for New York, and destiny.

Even before the PC age dawned, an IBM Selectric and an electric portable were acquired, and the graduation Smith Corona was at long last eased into retirement. But not before that youngster had written on it . . . let's see: two novels, a book on Andy Warhol, a ten-part PBS television series, and many hundreds of articles and stories. In my mind, its owner is still there before his gift, still a kid, still hunched over that manual keyboard, still trying to get the words right. He is so close to me that I could this minute stroll through the next door of an adjacent existence and greet him with a simple "Hi." He would look up from his work irritably, suspiciously, and I would sit down and start talking, trying to win his trust. This would not be easy. He doesn't know me from Adam, and trust, I fear, is not his strong suit. Still, I would try to get him to see that I am every bit as absorbed in the struggle to learn as he is, and that I always have been. I could tell him that I understand—better than he knows—where he's coming from. Gently, almost by stealth, I would try to convince him—God knows how—that I am on his side. I would let him know how much I hope that he might find it in his heart to permit me to remain on his side. Tact would be essential. I would never forget, but also never say, how needy he is, how frantically he prizes what he calls his "independence," and how *very* huffy he can get when the wrong person threatens that "independence" with what he thinks is the wrong kind of help.

But if I could get him to listen, I would sit down and tell him . . . everything you have just read in this book. Every clause, every word: a long conversation. As we talked, I would keep my eyes on that listening face of his, a face that a wise woman once told him was incapable of hiding anything. I am sure that as he listened to what I had to say, those youthful features of his would be frequently creased with flashes of annoyance. They would be impudent, disdainful, and unforgiving. He is a young man with all sorts of very grand theories, and not everything in this book is fully in accord with them. Yet I am pretty sure that many flashes of excitement and hope would cross that listening face as well. He always was—still is—a very hopeful guy. Moreover, I think that his irritation and hope would be marked by more significant signs of *recognition*—since I am reasonably confident that he already knows many of the things I say here. His knowledge is latent and obscure, but he has it, somewhere inside him. Not that he has mastered it yet. How could he? Mastery is a lifelong process, and this son of the springtime is still huddled over the Smith Corona, stranded forever in the wonderful beginning of things. But somewhere, somehow, he's in touch with it all. It's all inside him, all waiting. He needs only just a little prompting— just a few words to the wise. Then he'll get it. I'm sure of that.

I'm sure because the kid taught me everything I know.

POSTSCRIPT

Writing on the Craft

THE ANCIENTS

The Poetics, Aristotle. After some 2,300 years, the enduring miracle of *The Poetics* is how much in it is still right on target. Aristotle works by drawing distinctions between kinds of things, and of course the kinds of drama known to the boyhood tutor of Alexander the Great are pretty remote from those of the twenty-first century. Yet virtually every generalization Aristotle makes about story and plot remains alive and remarkably acute. Chapters V through XIV are indispensable. Pay special attention to Aristotle on "reversals and recognitions," on the artist's need to visualize the work and on "unity of action." While you're at it, notice Aristotle's comparisons of history and poetry. Here is someone who instinctively grasps the intimacy between fiction and nonfiction. It has been there, it seems, for a long, long time.

———

On the Sublime, Longinus. John Gardner was obsessed with morality in fiction, and it was Gardner who rediscovered in this classic first-century meditation on style a lesson for today. Gardner thought the sage known as Longinus had been the first to put his finger on the link between style and authenticity, and thus on the decay in quality that occurs when a work's language fails to generate a felt perception of its truth. Longinus calls this problem "frigidity," and the concept recurs in every one of Gardner's books on writing. Here's a question: Is what Longinus calls "frigidity" what we mean by "affectation"? If not, what *is* the difference? Here's another: Is Longinus's "frigidity" what we mean by "phoniness"? If so, what is the difference, if any, between "phoniness" and "affectation"?

CRAFT AND CONFIDENCE

Questions of confidence can never be separated from questions of craft. As Paul Johnson puts it, "In writing, as in all art, confidence is the beginning of skill." Sooner or later—usually sooner—almost every writer will feel her or his skill under assault from just plain old fear.

The two best books I know about confidence in writing are separated by four generations, and by a universe of sensibility. The first is Anne Lamott's *Bird by Bird*. Though *Bird by Bird* is filled with useful practical suggestions on literary technique, it sees even craft through the lens of an overriding concern for the writer's self-esteem. The book is like a twelve-step program in the recovery of self-confidence, guided by a big-sister type who stands up in the meeting and announces in a strong, vibrant voice: "My name is Anne Lamott, and I am a scared writer." The book is really about how to get going—and keep going—in the face of self-doubt, self-contempt, panic, competitive rage, the wish to flee, the inability to get to work, the conviction that you just can't do it.

Though Dorothea Brande's *Becoming a Writer* is a kind of companion volume to *Bird by Bird,* the two books could hardly speak in more different voices. Published in the early 1930s, Brande's book is impressed by the cutting-edge technology of "the talking pictures"; she urges writers to get hold of one of these newfangled contraptions, a portable typewriter. Yet *Becoming a Writer* sells on, year after year. Brande has next to nothing to say about craft as such. Yet as John Gardner notes in his introduction to a book he rediscovered, she seems to know everything about the writer's heart and mind, speaking straight to the prime fears and vulnerabilities of the profession. Brande has *exercises—useful* exercises—on how to deal with blocks and fear. And long before left- and right-brain science, she grasped the dual nature of the artistic personality, deploying real insight into how writers must train a bicameral psyche to find integration. *Becoming a Writer* is *Bird by Bird* from forty years before. Where Anne Lamott spills her guts, Brande is ladylike and rather buttoned up. Both are valuable. If you are blocked, if you have trouble producing, if you freeze and go stupid at the keyboard, if criticism leaves you too easily bruised, if you cannot get a clear perspective on your own work, if you feel just plain petrified, begin your therapy with one, or both, of these books.

THE TRADITIONAL MODERNIST TEXTS

Throughout most of the twentieth century, two manuals for writing fiction dominated academia, and they were in fact versions of each other. The lectures collected in E. M. Forster's classic study *Aspects of the Novel* (the Clark Lectures, Trinity College, Cambridge, 1927), really consist of Forster's jocose popularization of a much less lucid and amusing book by Percy Lubbock called *The Craft of Fiction.*

The academic prestige of these two handbooks for highbrows was likewise linked, and it remained quite exalted for decades. Forster was a doyen of Bloomsbury; Lubbock was a friend and acolyte of Henry James. Their books thus move in the loftier levels of the "good taste" of two eras. But as the late Victorian age and the 1920s recede into the remote past, time has pried open what may once have seemed hairline cracks in these books and left them gaping fissures.

The flaws were there from the start. Virgina Woolf herself, as her biography and diaries make clear, had serious reservations about Forster's Clark Lectures even when they were given and harbored really grave doubts about their source in *The Craft of Fiction.*

I agree with Woolf. Forster's winsome self-deprecation is irresistible, and the famous distinction between "flat" and "round" characters (so often cited, and so rarely read; see chapter 5) remains superb, undiminished by time. It alone makes *Aspects of the Novel* still worth the price of possession. But be wary. Forster is quite often way out of his intellectual depth. He drips with amused disdain for "mere" storytelling. First he sneers at it as "primitive," comparing it to the yammering of aborigines grunting around their fire. Next, he tosses this embarrassing image aside to seize, in delight, on an even more demeaning one: Storytelling, he says, is *worse* than primitive. It is *suburban.* Golfers— *feh!*—like stories.

Watch out for this nonsense. The truth is that Forster's own definition of *story,* in chapter 2, is feeble and confused, and Bloomsbury's general disdain for the "vulgarity" of storytelling is a dreary, and exhausted, modernist prejudice. Forster may or may not have been a snob first and an artist second, but he did suffer from Bloomsbury's inveterate habit of substituting "good taste"—meaning little more than high-toned and condescending taste—for thought, lived experience, and passion. Back when the Bloomsbury's main enterprise—the conquest of British highbrow attitudes—was still fresh, *Aspects of the Novel* must have sparkled with the new look. The look is new no more.

In America, academic deference maintained *Aspects of the Novel* as a classroom yardstick for "good taste" over nearly seventy years. It even kept Percy Lubbock's much duller book on at least the list for suggested supplementary reading. Lubbock idolized Henry James; he was the first editor of James's letters. He really was a little nutty on the subject of James. He believed James's late novels ought to be *the* measure of *all* modern fiction, without exception. In Lubbock's worshipful eyes, *The Golden Bowl* and *The Ambassadors* are not merely good, important, or even great novels. They are, to the exclusion of all other options, what being serious fiction had to be. Follow in their sainted footsteps, he suggested, or do not write at all.

Well, that was 1927, and time and reality long ago left Lubbock's doctrinaire nonsense dead in a ditch, survived only by two very tired classroom clichés: "Show, don't tell," and the slippery notion that fiction is unified not by unity of action but by its "point of view." During their fifty-year reign as platitudes, neither of these semitruths has served the art particularly well. And their claim to be "modern" has long since come and gone.

WRITERS ON WRITING

Writers on Writing: The Paris Review Interviews. The Paris Review's interviews with writers are the mother lode. From 1953 onward, *The Paris Review* has published the most consistently interesting and probing literary interviews one can find. They are indispensable to anyone thinking about literary craft and an incalculable contribution to literature.

The individual interviews have been collected in various forms. For a long time, a new compilation of all the recent interviews would appear every few years and then, after a reasonable run, go out of print. Since the late 1990s, the compilations have been more focused: *Playwrights at Work, Beat Writers at Work, Women Writers at Work,* and (as revised) *The Writer's Chapbook*—the latter a fine little compendium made up of short citations from the whole half-century-long range.

To think about the craft of fiction and the life of a writer is to read this work.

———

Letters to a Fiction Writer, edited by Frederick Busch. "If you had to really get down, really lay it out for some young writer, what would you say?" Editor Busch compiled this book from his conviction that every writer nurses in her or his innermost thoughts a core set of beliefs about the craft that would be best expressed in personal advice—like a letter—to some young hopeful. The result assembles thirty-two such letters to real and imagined young hopefuls, some written for the book, and some extracted from existing archives. Here Malcolm Cowley gives advice to John Cheever, Caroline Gordon to Flannery O'Connor, John Updike to Nicholas Delbanco, Shelby Foote to Walker Percy, and Ray Bradbury to Don Chaon—and many others give advice to hopefuls in general. The company is distinguished, and the letters are often captivating. Yet this is necessarily a browsing book. While there is something interesting in every contribution, it may take you a while to hit on the letter that seems addressed to you.

JOHN GARDNER

Since John Gardner's untimely death in a motorcycle accident in 1982, his books about writing fiction—*On Becoming a Novelist, The Art of Fiction,* and *On Moral Fiction*—have refused to go away, and are now nearly ubiquitous in the libraries of writers everywhere.

The three books go together, and you should read all three. They all have their faults. In *The Art of Fiction* (rather more often than in *On Becoming a Novelist*), Gardner can get badly tangled in his own prose. Too often he allows his professorial self (a key to his identity) to meander mesmerized, and seemingly forever, in pursuit of this or that recondite observation. Gardner can be schoolmasterish, peevish, and prescriptive. He can struggle too ferociously, trying to wrestle his personal prejudices to the mat of general truth.

Yet in all the books, Gardner's essential advice is remarkably sound. These are living insights pulled from lived experience; at their best, they are liberating, wonderful. Keep reading Gardner even when your eyes glaze over, because a moment is coming, quite likely soon, when he will suddenly open those same eyes a whole new world. The books are thoroughly intelligent, and in my opinion right more often than anyone would expect such a cranky and opinionated author to be.

What makes them all finally worthy of their eminence, and far better than their lingering bad rep, is their irresistible generosity of spirit. When *On Moral Fiction* first appeared, the book was almost shunned: Every novelist in America froze up. Oh, boy. Here we go again: the Reverend John has mounted his gloomy pulpit to glower, shake his finger, and damn us all as sinners. Well, okay, Gardner's hatred of *chic* and its easy successes did occasionally make him preachy and uncool. But the *chic* he attacked in *On Moral Fiction* has long since become passé. What remains is much more important: the generous and very decent thoughts of someone who understood—*really* understood—that writing fiction is a struggle to reach and comprehend something called the truth. To get this—*really* get it—is almost all you need.

MEMOIRS AND MANUALS OF THE CRAFT

Zen in the Art of Writing, by Ray Bradbury. If I had to choose one book for writers of that maddening and elusive form, the short story, I guess this would be it. Bradbury does not speak only to short story writers. Novelists, memoirists, all kinds of writers will learn useful things about situation and character and many other matters, but it's the book's insight into harnessing the power of the *image* in fiction that makes *Zen in the Art of Writing* stand apart. While this serves all kinds of writers, it serves writers of short stories at the most fundamental level, because the short story is the fictional form that relies most fundamentally on pure image. Nothing seems more baffling, or more tempting, than the latent power of an image glowing with intangible significance that seems unmoored to either characters or events. Getting past the baffles and tapping into that latent power takes a very special kind of imaginative discipline. I have never seen that discipline better described than Bradbury does here.

———

How to Write a Novel, by John Braine. I cannot say that I recommend every line of John Braine's book on the long form. The author of *Room at the Top* and *The Crying Game* had firmly fixed ideas of what the novel ought to be, and they gave Braine his confidence and brio. They also narrowed his range. Here and there, this manual lays down the law too harshly for my taste. The voice is occasionally ill tempered, rather too irritably sure of itself. Yet most of the advice in *How to Write a Novel* is thoroughly sound, and some of its ideas are outright brilliant. Those sound and sometimes-brilliant ideas, in turn, could change your life. Like any self-aware artist, Braine understood that the novel is a form with its own inevitable nature and its own inherent logic. Rather than vaguely invoke that inherent nature with the usual atmospheric flourishes, Braine sat down and hammered out on the page how they worked for him, and did so much of the time with memorable persuasiveness and point.

———

Narrative Design, by Madison Smartt Bell. The virtues of *Narrative Design* are multiple. It grasps the role of the unconscious mind in the writing of fiction and manages to make the case for it without sinking into romantic obscurity or mystification. *Narrative Design* also understands the role of structure—something everyone talks about and few understand—and analyzes it with exceptional force. Third, it applies its many detailed lessons in design and structure, *and* the role of the unconscious in them both, to twelve *short stories*. Without quite knowing they are doing so, most discussions of structure tend to become discussions of *novelistic* structure, and the short story's very different issues of structure and "narrative design" end up neglected. Finally, *Narrative Design* is well marbled throughout with a rich understanding, both critical and supportive, of writer's workshops and how they affect young writers.

———

Plotting and Writing Suspense Fiction, by Patricia Highsmith. Highsmith's title is a little misleading. Any writer of fiction will profit from this plain-talking compendium of advice from the author of *The Talented Mr. Ripley* and *Little Tales of Misogyny.* Highsmith's suggestions are aimed at the real problems of the craft, and they hit their targets with uncanny accuracy. An example: There's a notably lucid chapter distinguishing story development from plotting—fifteen pages that by themselves could save many a novelist many months of wasted time. Especially pertinent are the passages in which Highsmith walks the reader through solutions to her own problems—how she invented the climactic event in the first *Ripley* novel, for example, or how she developed the diabolical premise of *Strangers on a Train.* All this comes with crisp get-down wisdom on subjects that range from concept development and notebooks to vacations and naps.

———

On Writing: A Memoir of the Craft, by Stephen King. *On Writing* may be the single most useful and comprehensive book on the craft of writing that I have encountered. In addition to being a memoir of certain aspects of King's prodigious writing life—his boyhood and early struggle, the death of his mother, his last-minute save from alcohol and drug addiction, the crisis that came when he was almost killed in a road accident in 1999—*On Writing* is filled with forceful, cogent, usable advice on every aspect of the writing life. King's opinions are strong and assertive, but he is never prescriptive. The man really does think you should do it *your* way, not his. Any working writer will learn from *On Writing*. I know I did.

King is a lowbrow. He is almost demonically productive. He has a vulgar streak two miles wide. He is probably the most widely read and financially successful writer of fiction now alive. His prose can be very exciting, and it can be very spotty. His imagination is prodigal and hit-or-miss—but it is also unstoppable and, when it hits, irresistible. He is thoroughly intelligent about his art. As for the man's native talent, it is little short of stupendous.

Because we are all human, something in this inventory of traits is likely to annoy you. I recommend getting over it. This is a wonderful book.

———

One Writer's Beginnings, by Eudora Welty. You can learn something about writing from many memoirs, but now and then a memoirist lifts the form to a kind of self-reflexive incandescence. One such book is Vladimir Nabokov's *Speak, Memory*. Another is *One Writer's Beginnings*.

I once had the honor to introduce a reading by Eudora Welty in New York, before perhaps the largest, and certainly the most fervent, audience I've ever addressed. When that tall, stooped, admirable old lady stood up and calmly stepped forward carrying her book of stories, she walked into an inundating wall of applause, the tide of which flooded the room with one plain fact: This woman was *loved*.

The three sections of Welty's memoir are: "Listening," "Learning to See," and "Finding a Voice." Building her analogy between growing up and learning the craft, Welty fuses memoir with manual. It is impossible to read five pages of this book without encountering special insight. The intelligence is simple but penetrating, and it speaks in a firm, calm voice that gently fills the mind.

———

The Writing of Fiction, by Edith Wharton. When Edith Wharton's little-known book on the craft of fiction is good, it is very good. When it is bad, it . . . rides a hobbyhorse. Wharton's hobbyhorse in 1928 was her mistrust of the then-current literary avant-garde—Lubbock and Forster, for example. Mrs. Wharton looked at Bloomsbury, the modernist movement, and all that was being said and done in the name of her dear but departed friend Henry James with the grim suspicion that these upstarts might be about to leave her behind. Too much of *The Writing of Fiction* is motivated by Wharton's defensive but grand disdain for anyone who dared even to think of such a thing. Wharton was sure that (Proust aside) the approach to fiction promoted by the new moderns was skewed and unreal, flawed somehow. As she struggled to counter the new ideas, she did manage to say a number of things that are worthy of her genius.

And a number that are not. Edith Wharton lost the argument of 1928. Lubbock and Forster won it. Their "modernist" views became required reading, while *The Writing of Fiction* sank into obscurity. Wharton's views *were* bypassed, just as she feared. But now that the orthodoxy of Lubbock and Forster has crumbled—and *The House of Mirth* still stands—a fair amount of Edith Wharton's ringing counterstatements seem, if not fresh, at least sensible and sound.

FICTION AND NONFICTION

Inventing the Truth: The Art and Craft of Memoir, edited by William Zinsser. If you are writing a memoir, read this book in which ten superbly skilled people tell the tales of how they wrote theirs. You are sure to find a variant of your problems somewhere among theirs. Perhaps the most interesting large issue is the way so many of these talented people had trouble finding *themselves*— that is, their own personae—in the flood of information that pours through a first draft. Any memoir must be shaped from a massive—oceanic—wealth of personal information that is often accompanied by a rather indistinct, even feeble, sense of story. The one naturally overwhelms the other. How to deal with this problem is one of the mysteries cracked by several contributors to *Inventing the Truth.*

———

How to Write, by Richard Rhodes. *How to Write* casts a wide net: It is a straight-from-the-shoulder compendium of advice on the writing of both fiction and nonfiction, both of which Rhodes has written beautifully. He is as smart as anyone I've read on their relationship. Rhodes also excels at illustrating things by using his own work. His analysis of the opening paragraph to his own most famous book, *The Making of the Atomic Bomb,* could change your whole view of nonfiction. Later, in a particularly brilliant passage, Rhodes guides us, step-by-step, word-by-word, through the process of writing—precisely that brilliant passage. There is never anything narcissistic or pompous about how he does this; he so obviously is not showing off, so obviously only trying to help, that we're left with a kind of easy intimacy.

How to Write has other strong points. The chapter on research is perhaps the best I have seen. It merges practical advice with literary critical acuity in a very relaxed and successful way. It has a fine clarity and balance discussing point of view and voice. Every syllable strikes me as dead-on. And the chapter on the writer's business affairs—get ready for a *very* cold shower—is the straight stuff.

PUBLISHERS AND EDITORS

The Forest for the Trees: An Editor's Advice to Writers, by Betsy Lerner. This book offers a solid, sensible get-down talk about the practical realities of selling, editing, and publishing your work, written by a book editor and agent who is both wise *and* in the know. (It also is acutely insightful about the politics of MFA programs.) There is plenty here about the technique and lore of publishing as it touches on writers, and it is especially good on the personality types of writers as seen from the other side of the editorial desk. "The Ambivalent Writer," "The Natural," "The Wicked Child," "The Neurotic": Each of these chapters identifies a type in the *genus literatus,* and somewhere in them most writers will find X-ray insight addressed to her or him, and nobody else anywhere. This book will help guide you in your practical business. It will also help you feel less crazy and alone.

NOTEBOOKS

A Writer's Notebook, by W. Somerset Maugham. There is a technique to everything, even keeping a notebook. Maugham's notebook is one of the most instructive ever to have gotten out of the desk drawer and into print. ("I forget who it was who said that every author should keep a notebook but should take care never to refer to it. If you understand this properly, I think there is truth in it. By making a note of something that strikes you, you separate it from the incessant stream of impressions that crowd against the mental eye, and perhaps fix it in your memory.") This is not a diary: Maugham claimed he never made a note that he did not intend to use professionally. We see the first thumbnail sketches—five or six lines about a place or about a stranger who has crossed his path—that became his most famous and successful stories. But Maugham was also one of the great travelers, and his notes on places, from Soviet Russia during the 1917 revolution to the South Pacific, Hawaii, and Pago-Pago—in 1916!—are models of how to capture a setting and the atmosphere of a place and time. You hear the sound of Maugham's voice in every entry. Every entry is a snapshot in words. Everything is shaped and alive. It is all potential. It is all just waiting to happen.

NOTES

CHAPTER 1: BEGINNINGS

P. 4 *"The common conception . . ."* Martin Amis, interview by Francesca Riviere, in *The Writer's Chapbook*, ed. George Plimpton (New York: The Modern Library, 1999), 244.

P. 5 *"I start with a tingle . . ."* Isak Dinesen, interview by Eugene Walter, in *Writers at Work, The Paris Review Interviews*, ed. George Plimpton, 4th ser. (New York: Penguin Books, 1976), 17.

P. 5 *"Any book I write . . ."* Robert Penn Warren, in *The Writer's Chapbook*, 97.

P. 5 *"Sometimes, if things are going badly . . ."* Tom Wolfe, interview by Ralph Ellisa and Eugene Walter, in *Writers at Work: The "Paris Review" Interviews*, ed. George Plimpton, 9th ser. (New York: Penguin Books, 1992), 251.

P. 5 *"One must be pitiless . . ."* Joyce Carol Oates, interview by Robert Phillips, in *Women Writers at Work: The Paris Review Interviews*, ed. George Plimpton (New York: The Modern Library, 1998), 431.

P. 5 *"First and foremost, get writing!"* Samuel Eliot Morison. "History as a Literary Art," in *By Land and By Sea* (New York: Knopf, 1953), 293.

P. 6 *"hidden in a very somber . . ."* Isabel Allende, in *Writers Dreaming*, ed. Naomi Epel (New York: Carol Southern Books, 1983), 8.

P. 6 *"I am profoundly . . ."* Toni Morrison, interview by Claudia Brodsky Lacoar and Elissa Schappell, in *Women Writers at Work*, 347–48.

P. 7 *"It can be a voice, an image . . ."* E. L. Doctorow, interview by George Plimpton, in *The Writer's Chapbook*, 78–79.

P. 7 *"When I start something . . ."* Tom McGuane, interview by Sinda Gregory and Larry McCaffery, in *The Writer's Chapbook*, 89.

P. 7 *"minute and windblown . . ."* Henry James, preface to the New York Edition of *The Spoils of Poynton*, in *Henry James: European Writers* and *The Prefaces* (New York: Library of America, 1984), 1138.

P. 7 *"can be little or big, simple or complex . . ."* Patricia Highsmith, *Plotting and Writing Suspense Fiction* (New York: St. Martin's Press, 1990), 8.

P. 8 *". . . a pattern in the list, in these words . . ."* Ray Bradbury, *Zen in the Art of Writing* (New York: Bantam Books, 1992), 17, 19.

P. 9 *"When I started writing that story . . ."* Flannery O'Connor, in "Writing Short Stories," as cited by Raymond Carver in *Fires: Essays, Poems, Stories* (New York: Vintage, 1984), 16–17.

P. 9 *"[The book] began with a mental picture . . ."* William Faulkner, interview by Jean Stein, in *Writers at Work, The Paris Review Interviews*, ed. Malcolm Cowley, 1st ser. (New York: Viking/Compass Books, 1959), 130.

P. 9 *"I remember being on a train . . ."* William Trevor, interview by Mira Stout, in *The Writer's Chapbook*, 287.

P. 9 *"I think the first impulse . . ."* John Hersey, interview by Jonathan Dee, in *The Writer's Chapbook*, 85.

P. 10 *"I wrote it in one night . . ."* Eudora Welty, interview by Linda Kuehl, in *Women Writers at Work*, 173.

P. 10 *"It sounds dopey to say . . ."* Grace Paley, interview by Jonathan Dee, Barbara Jones, and Larissa MacFarquhar, in *The Writer's Chapbook*, 91–92.

P. 11 *"If I had to give . . ."* Gabriel García Márquez, interview by Peter H. Stone, in *The Writer's Chapbook*, 334.

P. 11 *"I have never claimed . . ."* W. Somerset Maugham, "Preface," *A Writer's Notebook* (New York: Penguin Books, 1984), 13.

P. 11 *"Writing teachers invariably tell . . ."* E. L. Doctorow, interview by George Plimpton, in *The Writer's Chapbook*, 34.

P. 12 *"What kind of experience . . ."* Henry James, "The Art of Fiction," in

Henry James, *Essays on Literature* (New York: Library of America, 1984), 52.

P. 12 *"I think you begin by..."* Stephen King, *On Writing* (New York: Scribner's, 2000), 158.

P. 12 *"As to experience...."* Edith Wharton, *The Writing of Fiction* (New York: Charles Scribner's Sons, 1925), 21.

P. 12 *"I begin by telling the truth..."* John Irving, interview by Ron Hansen, in *The Writer's Chapbook*, 85–86.

P. 13 *"Plug your nose and jump..."* Anne Lamott, *Bird by Bird* (New York: Pantheon Books, 1994), 4.

P. 13 *"As I always told my students..."* Richard Price, interview by James Linville, in *The Writer's Chapbook*, 95.

P. 14 *"Stories aren't souvenir T-shirts..."* Stephen King, *On Writing*, 163–64.

P. 14 *"When I used to teach creative writing..."* Kurt Vonnegut, interview by David Hayman, David Michaelis, George Plimpton, Richard Rhodes, in "The Art of Fiction, LXIV," *Paris Review*, no. 69 (spring 1977), in *Conversations with Kurt Vonnegut* (Jackson: University Press of Mississippi, 1988), 188–89.

P. 15 *"My characters write..."* Ray Bradbury, "Dear Don Chaon," in *Letters to a Fiction Writer*, ed. Frederick Busch (New York: Norton, 1999), 62.

P. 16 *"Beginning a book is unpleasant...."* Philip Roth, interview by Hermione Lee, in *Paris Review*, "The Art of Fiction," LXXXIV, in *Conversations with Philip Roth* (Jackson and London: University Press of Mississippi, 1992), 163.

P. 17 *"If I didn't know the ending..."* Katherine Anne Porter, in *Women Writers at Work*, 48.

P. 17 *"A writer should not see his craft..."* Paul Johnson, "The Craft of Writing," in *The Pick of Paul Johnson* (London: Harrap, 1985), 18.

P. 17 *"At one time..."* Truman Capote, interview by Pati Hill, in *Writers at Work*, 1st ser., 297.

P. 18 *"I retired from teaching..."* Frank McCourt, "Learning to Chill Out," in *Inventing the Truth*, ed. William Zinnser (New York: Mariner Books, 1998), 77.

P. 18 *"I used to think..."* Anne Lamott, *Bird by Bird*, 190.

P. 18 *"If it's a situation..."* Tom Wolfe, in *Writers at Work*, 9th ser., 241.

P. 19 *"Some of the freest writing . . ."* Sue Grafton, in *Writers Dreaming,* 62.

P. 19 *"I have never been blocked . . ."* Lorrie Moore, interview by Elizabeth Gaffney, in *Paris Review,* no. 158 (spring/summer 2001): 67.

P. 19 *"If you are struggling . . ."* Betsy Lerner, *The Forest for the Trees* (New York: Riverhead Books, 2000), 24–25.

P. 20 *"Never throw away . . ."* Patricia Highsmith, *Plotting and Writing Suspense Fiction,* 35.

P. 23 *"My ideal way to write . . ."* Eudora Welty, in *Women Writers at Work,* 178.

P. 23 *"Get it all down . . ."* Anne Lamott, *Bird by Bird,* 190.

P. 23 *"Write freely and as rapidly . . ."* John Steinbeck, interview by George Plimpton and Frank Crowther, in *Writers at Work,* 4th ser., 185.

P. 24 *"If I get into some . . ."* Christopher Isherwood, interview by W. I. Scobie, in *Writers at Work,* 4th ser., 219.

P. 24 *"What can we writers learn . . ."* Ray Bradbury, *Zen in the Art of Writing,* 13.

P. 24 *"I suddenly realized . . ."* Tom Wolfe, interview by George Plimpton, in *Writers at Work,* 9th ser., 239.

P. 25 *"From the beginning I have found . . ."* Russell Banks, interview by Robert Faggen, in *Paris Review,* no. 147 (summer 1998): 85.

P. 26 *"Courage, first . . ."* Maya Angelou, interview by George Plimpton, in *Women Writers at Work,* 303, 305.

P. 26 *"One of the marks . . ."* Katherine Anne Porter, interview by Barbara Thompson, in *Women Writers at Work,* 45.

P. 26 *"When I read women's . . ."* Toni Morrison, in *Women Writers at Work,* 351.

P. 27 *"One night . . ."* Gabriel García Márquez, in *The Writer's Chapbook,* 9.

P. 28 *"I believe that any . . ."* Joyce Carol Oates, "Writers on Writing," *New York Times,* 18 July 1999.

P. 28 *"I immediately started writing . . ."* Gabriel García Márquez, in *The Writer's Chapbook,* 9.

P. 29 *"Writing is a painful trade . . ."* Paul Johnson, *The Pick of Paul Johnson,* 11.

CHAPTER 2: THE WRITING LIFE

P. 31 *"Talent is insignificant . . ."* James Baldwin, interview by Jordan Elgrably and George Plimpton, in "The Art of Fiction, LXXVIII"

(*Paris Review,* 1984), in *Conversations with James Baldwin,* eds. Fred L. Stanley and Louis H. Pratt (Jackson and London: University Press of Mississippi, 1989.), 251.

P. 31 *"Talent, even of a very high order . . ."* Graham Greene, interview by Simon Raven, in *The Writer's Chapbook,* 38.

P. 31 *"I started out . . ."* Katherine Anne Porter, in *Women Writers at Work,* 36.

P. 31 *"I am compulsive . . ."* John Irving, in *The Writer's Chapbook,* 65.

P. 31 *"I assure you . . ."* Betsy Lerner, *The Forest for the Trees,* 27.

P. 32 *"I think I was born knowing it . . ."* P. D. James, interview by Shusha Guppy, in "The Art of Fiction CXLI," *Paris Review* no. 135 (summer 1995): 55.

P. 32 *"I was solitary . . ."* Robert Stone, interview by William Crawford Woods, in *The Writer's Chapbook.* 27.

P. 32 *"I did something . . ."* P. D. James, *Paris Review,* no. 135 (summer 1995), 55.

P. 32 *"I learned in this way . . ."* Anthony Trollope, *An Autobiography,* chapter III.

P. 33 *"First try to be something. . . . I still think . . ."* Lorrie Moore, cited by Betsy Lerner, *The Forest for the Trees,* 27–28.

P. 34 *"Writing a novel . . ."* Walter Mosley, "Writers on Writing," *New York Times,* 3 July 2000.

P. 34 *"Sit quietly and think . . ."* John Braine, *How to Write a Novel* (London: Methuen, 2000), 33.

P. 35 *"Do not think . . ."* Richard Bausch, "Dear Writer," *Letters to a Fiction Writer,* 28.

P. 35 *"These ideas have no . . ."* Walter Mosley, "Writers on Writing," *New York Times,* 3 July 2000.

P. 36 *"What's taken directly . . ."* Philip Roth, interview with Sara Davidson, in *New York Times Book Review,* 18 September 1977, reprinted in *Conversations with Philip Roth,* 103.

P. 36 *"The dreaming self . . ."* Russell Banks, interview by Robert Faggen, "The Art of Fiction, CLII," *Paris Review,* no. 147 (summer 1998): 75.

P. 36 *"The effort . . ."* Eileen Simpson, "Poets in Their Youth," in *Inventing the Truth,* 89.

P. 37 *"I witness with pleasure . . ."* Vladimir Nabokov, *Speak, Memory,* in *Novels and Memoirs, 1941–1951* (New York: Library of America, 1996), 506.

P. 37 "That robust reality ..." Vladimir Nabokov, *Speak, Memory*, in *Novels and Memoirs*, 422.

P. 37 "Searching for the unnoticed ..." Ernest Hemingway, interview by George Plimpton, in *Writers at Work, The Paris Review Interviews*, ed. George Plimpton, 2nd ser. (New York: Penguin Books, 1977), 236–37.

P. 39 *"When I'm writing ..."* Edmund White, interview by Jordan Elgrably, "The Art of Fiction CV," *Paris Review*, no. 108 (fall 1988): 70.

P. 39 *"Unless it be given ..."* Anthony Trollope, *An Autobiography*, Chapter XII.

P. 39 *"If a writer ..."* Ernest Hemingway, in *Writers at Work*, 2nd Ser., 235.

P. 39 *"I wanted to be a reader ..."* Toni Morrison, in *Women Writers at Work*, 348.

P. 39 *"If I had a nickel ..."* Stephen King, *On Writing*, 147.

P. 40 *"I read fiction ..."* Philip Roth, interview by Allen Finkielkraut (1989), in *Conversations with Philip Roth*, 124.

P. 40 *"Indeed, learning to write ..."* Eudora Welty, "Words into Fiction," in *The Eye of the Story: Selected Essays and Reviews* (New York: Random House, 1990), 134.

P. 40 *"The reader must ..."* Percy Lubbock, *The Craft of Fiction* (New York: Viking Press, 1957), 17–18.

P. 41 *"Read poetry ..."* Ray Bradbury, *Zen in the Art of Writing*, 39.

P. 41 *"I think of it as farming ..."* Michael Crichton, "A Time Traveler Returns, Still Restless," by Jane Gross, *New York Times*, 24 November 1999, 1, 3.

P. 42 *"I read everything ..."* Gabriel García Márquez, interview by Peter H. Stone, in *Writers at Work: The Paris Review Interviews*, ed. George Plimpton, 6th ser. (New York: The Viking Press, 1984), 327.

P. 42 *"being swept away ..."* Stephen King, *On Writing*, 146.

P. 43 *"Write, write, write ..."* Anton Chekhov, letter to Maria V. Kisseleva, September 1886, cited in David Magarshack, *Chekhov: A Life* (New York: Grove Press, 1952), 131.

p. 43 *"You are a 'beginner' ..."* Anton Chekhov, letter to Yezhov, September 1887, Magarshack, *Chekhov*, 131.

p. 43 *"Bellow also talked ..."* William Kennedy, interview by George Plimpton, in *The Writer's Chapbook*, 338.

p. 43 *"A bad novel is better than an unwritten novel . . ."* Paul Johnson, *The Pick of Paul Johnson*, 16.

p. 44 *"and because I'm feeling . . ."* Stephen King, *On Writing*, 155–56.

p. 44 *"I set myself a quota . . ."* Tom Wolfe, interviewed by George Plimpton, in *Writers at Work*, 9th ser., 251.

p. 45 *"Nothing surely . . ."* Anthony Trollope, *An Autobiography*, Chapter VII.

p. 45 *"The time to work . . ."* Ernest Hemingway, *Writers at Work*, 2nd ser., 226.

p. 46 *"Find the time to write . . ."* Ann Beattie, "Letter to a Young Fiction Writer," *Letters to a Fiction Writer*, 58.

p. 46 *"It's work . . ."* Philip Roth, interview by Jesse Kornbluth (1983), in *Conversations with Philip Roth*, 147.

p. 46 *"I write from . . ."* Philip Roth, interview by Ronald Hayman, in *Conversations with Philip Roth*, 118.

p. 46 *"I'm always reluctant . . ."* Gore Vidal, in *The Writer's Chapbook*, 74–75.

p. 46 *"To give the best of the day . . ."* John le Carré, interview by George Plimpton, "The Art of Fiction CXLIX," *Paris Review*, no. 143 (summer 1997): 56.

p. 47 *"If you want . . ."* Walter Mosley, "Writers on Writing," *New York Times*, 3 July 2000.

p. 47 *"I have never been able . . ."* Toni Morrison, in *Women Writers at Work*, 344.

p. 47 *"I write in spurts . . ."* Susan Sontag, in *Women Writers at Work*, 387–88.

P. 47 *"Writers say . . ."* Edmund White, interviewed by Jordan Elgrably, in *Paris Review*, no. 108 (fall 1988): 71.

P. 48 *"You can write any time . . ."* Ernest Hemingway, in *Writers at Work*, 2nd ser., 223.

P. 48 *"teach yourself . . ."* Richard Bausch, "Dear Writer," *Letters to a Fiction Writer*, 26.

P. 49 *"Ask a doctor . . ."* John Irving, in *The Writer's Chapbook*, 65.

P. 49 *"Your friends and family . . ."* David Bradley, "Letter to a Writer," *Letters to a Fiction Writer*, 73.

P. 49 *"I think writers, artists, are . . ."* Nadine Gordimer, in *Women Writers at Work*, 278.

P. 49 *"There is no known excuse . . ."* Richard Bausch, *Letters to a Fiction Writer*, 27.

P. 50 *"I learned from Hemingway . . ."* Andre Dubus, "Letter to a Young Writer," *Letters to a Fiction Writer*, 137.

P. 50 *"I have formed the habit . . ."* Nadine Gordimer, interviewed by Jannika Hurwitt, in *Women Writers at Work*, 279.

P. 50 "Be open . . ." Richard Bausch, *Letters to a Fiction Writer*, 27.

P. 50 *"I feel more confident and more satisfied . . ."* Anton Chekhov, Letter to A. S. Suvorin. September 11, 1888, in *Anton Chekhov's Life and Thought: Selected Letters and Commentary*, ed. Simon Karlinsky (Berkeley, Los Angeles, and London: University of California Press, 1972), 107.

P. 50 *"One luxury . . ."* John Irving, *The Writer's Chapbook*, 65.

P. 51 *"Engaging the jury . . ."* Scott Turow, "Writers on Writing," *New York Times*, 22 November 1999.

P. 51 *"You have to tell the story . . ."* John Mortimer, interviewed by Rosemary Herbert, "The Art of Fiction, CVI," *Paris Review*, no. 109 (winter 1988): 108.

P. 51 *"I taught at Stuyvesant . . ."* Frank McCourt, "Learning to Chill Out," *Inventing the Truth*, 75.

P. 52 *"I've always been convinced . . ."* Gabriel García Márquez, interview by Peter H. Stone, in *Writers at Work*, 6th ser., 317.

P. 53 *"I think you have a duty . . ."* Martin Amis, *Paris Review*, no. 146 (Spring 1998): 128.

CHAPTER 3: SHAPING THE STORY

P. 61 *"The writer's job . . ."* Stephen King, *On Writing*, 163–64.

P. 61 *"I hesitate . . ."* Robertson Davies, interview by Elisabeth Sifton, "The Art of Fiction, CVII," *Paris Review*, no. 110 (spring 1989): 47.

P. 63 *"When I'm beginning . . ."* John Irving, in *The Writer's Chapbook*, 65.

P. 63 *"dredging my mind . . ."* Virginia Woolf, *Diaries, Volume II, 1920–1924*, ed. Anne Oliver Bell, assisted by Andrew McNeillie (New York and London: Harcourt Brace and Jovanovich, 1978), 189.

P. 67 *"a long sustained streak . . ."* Truman Capote, Introduction to the 20th Anniversary Edition of *Other Voices, Other Rooms* (New York: Random House, 1968), xiii.

P. 67 *"I invariably have the illusion . . ."* Truman Capote, *Writers at Work*, 1st ser., 297.

P. 68 *"Plot is . . . the writer's jackhammer . . ."* Stephen King, *On Writing*, 164.

P. 70 *"Usually, with a novel . . ."* Russell Banks, interviewed by Robert Faggen, *Paris Review*, no. 147 (summer 1998): 62–63.

P. 72 *"If you asked anybody . . ."* John Mortimer, interviewed by Rosemary Herbert, *Paris Review*, no. 109 (winter 1988): 120.

P. 73 *"I should think that . . ."* Ernest Hemingway, in *Writers at Work*, 222.

P. 73 *"I had the story . . ."* Susan Sontag, in *Women Writers at Work*, 397.

P. 74 *" 'The cat sat on . . .' "* John le Carré, in *The Writer's Chapbook*, 182.

P. 75 *"You're looking, as you begin . . ."* Philip Roth, interview by Hermione Lee (1986), in *Conversations with Philip Roth*, 164.

P. 76 *"the artist's primary unit of thought . . ."* John Gardner, *The Art of Fiction* (New York: Vintage Books, 1991), 18–20.

P. 79 *"Don't have too many characters . . ."* Anton Chekhov, letter to his brother, Aleksandr Chekhov, Moscow, May 10, 1886, in *Letters of Anton Chekhov*, ed. Avrahm Yarmolinsky (New York: The Viking Press, 1973), 37.

P. 80 *"Neither novelist nor playwright . . ."* Edith Wharton, *The Writing of Fiction*, 84.

P. 82 *"However appropriate . . ."* John Braine, *How to Write a Novel*, 125–26.

P. 83 *"Finding the right form for your story . . ."* Truman Capote, in *Writers at Work*, 1st ser., 287–88.

CHAPTER 4: MAKING CHARACTERS LIVE

P. 86 *"find a character . . ."* Ray Bradbury, *Zen in the Art of Writing*, 7

P. 86 *"Character comes first . . ."* Shelby Foote, "The Art of Fiction, CLVIII," *Paris Review*, no. 151 (summer 1999): 73.

P. 86 *"The characters . . ."* Stephen King, *On Writing*, 164–65.

P. 86 *"My books tend to be based . . ."* Ibid., 164.

P. 87 *"In the first, the persons . . ."* Edith Wharton, *The Writing of Fiction*, 125.

P. 88 *"I think I can say . . ."* Chinua Achebe, in *A Writer's Chapbook*, 207.

P. 88 *"The same experience . . ."* Edith Wharton, *The Writing of Fiction*, 85–86.

P. 89 *"that one should always write about . . ."* John Gardner, *On Becoming a Novelist* (New York: W. W. Norton and Company, 1999), 43–44.

P. 90 *"A story does not achieve unity . . ."* Aristotle, Section VIII, *Poetics*.

P. 91 *"It is a truth . . ."* Jane Austen, *Pride and Prejudice*, Chapter 1.

P. 92 *"We are bounced up and down . . ."* E. M. Forster, *Aspects of the Novel* (New York: Harcourt, Brace, and Company, 1927), 122–23.

P. 94 *"Flat characters were called . . ."* Ibid., 103–04.

P. 95 *"I have this belief . . ."* Mary McCarthy, interview by Elisabeth Sifton (1962), in *Women Writers at Work,* 235, 236.

P. 96 *"Any story has . . ."* Christopher Tilghman, "Passion and Craft," *The Literary Review* (winter 1995).

P. 96 *"I never use anyone I know . . ."* Toni Morrison, in *Women Writers at Work,* 358.

P. 97 *"Mostly, real people . . ."* J. K. Rowling, interview with J. K. Rowling, Amazon.co.uk., http://www.cliphoto.com/potter/interview.htm.

P. 98 *"Absorbed in the fate . . ."* Henri Troyat, *Tolstoy* (New York: Harmony Books, 1980), 337.

P. 98 *"I divided myself . . ."* Ingmar Bergman, cited by Richard Rhodes, *How to Write* (New York: Quill, 1995), 98.

P. 98 *"desires to make . . ."* Anthony Trollope, *An Autobiography,* Chapter XII.

P. 99 *"The writer's characters . . ."* John Gardner, *The Art of Fiction,* 45–46.

P. 99 *"One must know what . . ."* Patricia Highsmith, *Plotting and Writing Suspense Fiction,* 37.

P. 99 *"the briefest possible biographical . . ."* John Braine, *How to Write a Novel,* 28.

P. 100 *"A useful trick . . ."* E. M. Forster, in *Writers at Work,* 1st ser. 32–33.

P. 100 *"The kernel of my character . . ."* William Styron, in *Writers Dreaming,* 273.

P. 100 *"The remarkable thing about him . . ."* Katia Mann, *Unwritten Memories,* ed. Elizabeth Plessen and Michael Mann, trans. Hunter and Hildegarde Hannum (New York: Knopf, 1975), 71–72

P. 100 *"[E]xcept as creatures . . ."* John Gardner, in *The Art of Fiction,* 45–46.

P. 101 *"It's amazing what you find out . . ."* Doris Lessing, in *Writers at Work,* 9th ser., 145.

P. 103 *"I'm ashamed to admit . . ."* Mario Puzo, *The Godfather Papers and Other Confessions* (New York: G. P. Putnam's Sons, 1972), 35.

P. 103 *"Whenever the godfather opened his mouth . . ."* Mario Puzo, Preface to second ed. of *The Fortunate Pilgrim* (New York: Fawcett Books, 1998), iv.

P. 103 *"Inventing fictional characters . . . The haunting is . . ."* Richard Rhodes, *How to Write*, 98.

P. 103 *"He said, okay. . . ."* Desmond Barry, interview with the author, March 2001.

P. 104 *"I remember an English novelist . . ."* Henry James, "The Art of Fiction," 52.

P. 105 *"Sooner or later . . ."* Christopher Tilghman, "Places and Visions: An Interview with Christopher Tilghman," in *The Literary Review* (Fairleigh Dickinson University), Winter 1995, vol. 38, no. 2, 247.

P. 106 *"I shrink . . ."* Robertson Davies, in *The Writer's Chapbook*, 113–14.

P. 106 *"I have the characters . . ."* Toni Morrison, in *Women Writers at Work*, 349.

P. 106 *"If you can't speak . . ."* John Braine, *How to Write a Novel*, 85.

P. 106 *"If you are using . . ."* John Steinbeck, in *Writers at Work*, 4th ser., 186.

P. 107 *"When you don't know what . . ."* Anne Lamott, *Bird by Bird*, 172.

P. 107 *"When I started . . ."* Allan Gurganus, in *Writers Dreaming*, 100.

P. 108 *"When, in real life . . ."* Edith Wharton, in *The Craft of Fiction*, 74–75.

P. 108 *"It is so easy . . ."* Anthony Trollope, *An Autobiography*, Chapter XII.

P. 108 *"The use of dialogue . . ."* Edith Wharton, *The Craft of Fiction*, 74.

P. 110 *"I once asked Ethan Canin . . ."* Anne Lamott, *Bird by Bird*, 49–50.

P. 110 *"Rochester's wretched thralldom . . ."* Anthony Trollope, *An Autobiography*, Chapter XII.

P. 110 *"I . . . looked back at novels . . ."* Tom Wolfe, in *Writers at Work: The Paris Review Interviews*, 9th ser., 248.

P. 111 *"Somewhere I ran into a theory . . ."* Ibid.

P. 111 *"Love your characters . . ."* Anton Chekhov, letter to Tetany Schepkina-Kupernik.

CHAPTER 5: INVENTING YOUR STYLE

P. 113 *"I wish my prose . . ."* V. S. Naipaul, "The Art of Fiction CLIV," *Paris Review*, no. 148 (fall 1998): 56.

P. 113 *"Born subjective . . ."* Eudora Welty, *The Eye of the Story*, 142.

P. 114 *"I don't think style . . ."* Truman Capote, in *Writers at Work*, 1st ser., 296.

P. 114 *"Most beginning writers . . ."* Patricia Highsmith, *Plotting and Writing Suspense Fiction*, x.

P. 115 *"I'll read something..."* Maya Angelou, in *Women Writers at Work,* 290.

P. 115 *"Before I take pen to paper..."* Mary Gordon, "Writers on Writing," *New York Times,* 5 July 1999.

P. 116 *"Every writer will have..."* Paul Johnson, "The Craft of Writing," in *The Pick of Paul Johnson,* 14.

P. 116 *"I don't trust my writing..."* Toni Morrison, interviewed by Claudia Brodsky Lacour and Elissa Schappell, in *Women Writers at Work,* 245.

P. 116 *"In conversation..."* Fran Lebowitz, in *The Writer's Quotation Book: A Literary Companion,* ed. James Charlton (Wainscott, N.Y.: Pushcart Press, 1985), 41.

P. 119 *"the first thing I realized..."* John Wray, interview with the author, 2001.

P. 121 *"Sometimes it's only a passing fancy..."* Terry Teachout, "Literary Crushes," *New York Times Book Review,* 12 September 1999.

P. 122 *"A good novelist..."* John Gardner, *On Becoming a Novelist,* 27.

P. 122 *"My father said to me..."* Martin Amis, *Paris Review,* no. 146, 115.

P. 124 *"What amateurs call ..."* Ernest Hemingway, interviewed by George Plimpton, in *Writers at Work,* 2nd ser., 231.

P. 124 *"Most came right..."* John Updike, in *Writers at Work,* 4th ser., 436.

P. 127 *"[Addison's] prose is the model ..."* Samuel Johnson, "Addison," in *Lives of the Poets.*

P. 128 *"She could free life ..."* Virginia Woolf, *The Common Reader* 1st ser. [annotated ed.], ed. Anderw McNeillie (New York and Orlando: Harcourt Brace & Co., 1984), 161.

P. 128 *"She sought more knowledge..."* Virginia Woolf, *The Common Reader,* 1st ser., 172.

P. 130 *"I mean..."* Truman Capote, in *Writers at Work,* 1st ser., 287.

P. 130 *"The Strunk and White voice ..."* Richard Rhodes, *How to Write,* 40–41.

P. 130 *"The voice of the narrator..."* Tom Wolfe, "Introduction," *The New Journalism,* eds. Tom Wolfe and E. W. Johnson (New York: Harper and Row, 1973), 17–18.

P. 131 *"Of all the needs ..."* Anthony Trollope. *An Autobiography,* Chapter XIX.

P. 132 *"It is the first necessity..."* Ibid. Chapter XII.

P. 133 *"The fault Longinus identifies . . ."* John Gardner, *The Art of Fiction,* 117.

P. 133 *"One fusses about style . . ."* W. Somerset Maugham, *A Writer's Notebook,* 291.

P. 134 *"Some writers have . . ."* Raymond Carver, "Introduction," *Fires,* 13.

CHAPTER 6: THE STORY OF THE SELF

P. 137 *"A poet differs from a historian . . ."* Aristotle, *The Poetics,* Chapter IX.

P. 137 *"On the basis . . ."* Toni Morrison, "The Site of Memory," in *Inventing the Truth: The Art and Craft of Memoir,* ed. William Zinsser (Boston & New York: Mariner Books, 1998), 192.

P. 138 *"I can't tell you . . ."* Toni Morrison, *Inventing the Truth,* 185.

P. 138 *"Fiction, by defintion . . ."* Ibid., 192.

P. 138 *"I am an autobiographer . . ."* Maya Angelou, in *Writers Dreaming,* 27–28.

P. 139 *"Memoir writers must manufacture . . ."* William Zinsser, in *Inventing the Truth,* 6.

P. 139 *"An autobiography is not the attempt . . ."* Frank McCourt, interview by Sarah Mosle, *New York Times Magazine,* 12 September 1999.

P. 140 *"Nobody understood better . . ."* Russell Baker, *Inventing the Truth,* 203–04.

P. 140 *"When you write an autobiography . . ."* Henry Louis Gates Jr., *Inventing the Truth,* 108–9.

P. 141 *"Here I come to one . . ."* Virginia Woolf, "A Sketch of the Past," in *Moments of Being* (2d ed.), ed. Jeanne Shulkind (San Diego/New York/London: Harvest Books, 1985), 65.

P. 142 *"I had made . . ."* Russell Baker, in *Inventing the Truth,* 33.

P. 142 *"make them include the present . . ."* Virginia Woolf, *Moments of Being,* 75.

P. 144 *"Truth is not only . . ."* W. Somerset Maugham, *A Writer's Notebook,* 248.

P. 145 *"Tom Wolfe . . . said that writers . . ."* Martin Amis, *Paris Review,* no. 146, 128–29.

P. 146 *"Truth in the description . . ."* Anton Chekhov, letter to his brother, Aleksandr Chekhov, Moscow, May 10, 1886, *Letters,* Yarmolinsky, ed., 38.

P. 146 *"It all lies in that. . . ."* Anthony Trollope, *An Autobiography,* Chapter XII.

P. 146 *"Now comes the big question..."* Stephen King, *On Writing,* 158.

P. 147 *"Time and place make..."* Eudora Welty, in *Women Writers at Work,* 176.

P. 149 *"There is no great difference..."* Shelby Foote, *Paris Review,* no. 151, 56.

P. 150 *"Nothing is sillier..."* John Gardner, *On Becoming a Novelist,* 71.

P. 150 *"What story does this object..."* Ian Frazier, in *Inventing the Truth* 169–70.

P. 151 *"Everything I have to say..."* Shelby Foote, *Paris Review,* no. 151, 57,

P. 151 *"The act of vividly recalling..."* Vladimir Nabokov, *Speak, Memory,* in *Novels and Memoirs,* 420.

P. 152 *"To write a novel..."* John Braine, *How to Write a Novel,* 42.

P. 153 *"I began with the premise..."* Ian Frazier, in *Inventing the Truth,* 178–79.

P. 153 *"In our childhood..."* Vladimir Nabokov, *Speak, Memory,* in *Novels and Memoirs,* 447.

P. 155 *"All of us live..."* Jill Ker Conway, in *Inventing the Truth,* 56.

P. 155 *"Early on, you intuit..."* Russell Banks, *Paris Review,* no. 147, 59–60.

CHAPTER 7: WORKING AND REWORKING

P. 159 *"I... don't change much..."* John Updike, interview by Charles Thomas Samuels, in *Writers at Work,* 4th ser., 452.

P. 159 *"I don't have to revise..."* Shelby Foote, *Paris Review,* no. 151, 55.

P. 159 *"Rewriting a whole book..."* Anthony Burgess, interview by John Cullinan, in *Writers at Work,* 4th ser., 332.

P. 159 *"By not revising..."* Jack Kerouac, interview by Ted Berrigan, in *Writers at Work,* 4th ser., 364. See also *Beat Writers at Work,* ed. George Plimpton (New York: Modern Library, 1999).

P. 160 *"I write very quickly..."* John Irving, in *The Writer's Chapbook,* 65.

P. 160 *"The first puts..."* Bernard Malamud, interview by Daniel Stern, in *Writers at Work,* 6th ser., 167.

P. 161 *"It's something I love..."* Raymond Carver, interview by Mona Simpson, "The Art of Fiction, LXXVI," *Paris Review,* no. 88 (summer 1983): 211.

P. 161 *"Some scenes I save..."* Ibid., 209–10.

P. 162 *"Get black on white..."* Frank O'Connor, in *A Writer's Chapbook,* 91.

P. 165 *"Typically, what I'll do . . ."* Richard Price, *Paris Review*, no. 138 (spring 1996): 141.

P. 166 *"Give yourself a chance . . ."* Stephen King, *On Writing*, 210.

P. 167 *"read it with the cold . . ."* Richard Bausch, *Letters to a Fiction Writer*, 29.

P. 170 *"If you write quickly . . ."* John Braine, *How to Write a Novel*, 23.

P. 174 *"If a man writes . . ."* Ernest Hemingway, *Death in the Afternoon* (New York: Scribner Classics, 1999), 50.

P. 175 *"It's what I do when I write . . ."* Georges Simenon, interviewed by Carvel Collins, in *Writers at Work*, 1st ser., 146.

P. 176 *"Not bad, but puffy . . ."* Stephen King, *On Writing*, 222.

P. 176 *"Evidently not seeing me . . ."* Peter Ackroyd, *Dickens* (New York: HarperCollins Torchbooks, 1992), 161, 163.

P. 177 *"My working rule . . ."* John Braine, *How to Write a Novel*, 103.

P. 177 *"You must learn to reread . . ."* Richard Bausch, *Letters to a Fiction Writer*, 28–29.

CHAPTER 8: FINISHING

P. 180 *"Your job in the second . . ."* Stephen King, *On Writing*, 201.

P. 181 *"Once the novel gets going . . ."* Chinua Achebe, interviewed by Jerome Brooks, in *The Writer's Chapbook*, 207.

P. 184 *"It is hard enough . . ."* Ernest Hemingway, in *Writers at Work*, 2nd ser., 229.

P. 184 *"The behavior of the persons in . . ."* W. Somerset Maugham, *A Writer's Notebook*, 291.

P. 186 *"If you've . . . written . . ."* Tom Wolfe, in *Writers at Work*, 9th ser., 245.

P. 186 *"Read the last chapter . . ."* Ibid., 245–246.

P. 186 *"When I really know what . . ."* Toni Morrison, in *Women Writers at Work*, 361–62.

P. 187 *"I am not sure every book . . ."* Patricia Highsmith, *Plotting and Writing Suspense Fiction*, 53.

P. 190 *"When he was working on a book . . ."* Katia Mann, *Unwritten Memories*, 140.

P. 190 *"The idea that what inspires you . . ."* John Irving, interview by Mel Gussow, *New York Times*, 28 April 1998, E1.

P. 192 *"Only when a piece of work . . ."* Paul Johnson, *The Pick of Paul Johnson*, 14.

P. 192 *"Story writing and an independently operating . . ."* Eudora Welty, "Learning to Write Fiction," tape recording, 1961 (Guilford, Conn.: Jeffrey Norton Publishers, Tape Library, #23065, 1961).

P. 192 *"If you know how to read . . ."* Toni Morrison, in *Women Writers at Work*, 348.

P. 193 *"In my experience of writing . . ."* Michael Crichton, in *The Writer's Chapbook*, 150.

P. 195 *"More likely, they'll think that some parts . . ."* Stephen King, *On Writing*, 216–17.

P. 196 *"If the part you love is not there . . ."* Ian Frazier, in *Inventing the Truth*, 179.

P. 196 *"The two years it generally takes . . ."* Philip Roth, interview by Jesse Kornbluth, *Conversations with Philip Roth*, 147.

P. 197 *"As soon as I finished . . ."* Henry Louis Gates Jr., in *Inventing the Truth*, 180.

P. 197 *"I put the manuscript . . ."* Truman Capote, in *Writers at Work*, 1st ser., 297.

P. 197 *"When I've finished . . ."* Philip Roth, interview by Sara Davidson, in *Conversations with Philip Roth*, 106.

P. 198 *"You know it's finished . . ."* James Baldwin, in *The Writer's Chapbook*, 139.

P. 198 *"No book, when it is finished . . ."* Patricia Highsmith, *Plotting and Writing Suspense Fiction*, 59.

P. 199 *"Here in the few minutes that remain . . ."* Virginia Woolf, *The Diaries of Virginia Woolf*, ed. Anne Oliver Bell, assisted by Andrew McNellie, vol. 4: 1931–1935 (New York, Harcourt Brace Jovanovich, 1982), 10.

PERMISSION CREDITS

INDEX

STEPHEN KOCH taught the craft of fiction to graduate students for twenty-one years in the writing division of the School of the Arts at Columbia University and to undergraduates for seven years in the Program in Creative Writing at Princeton University. Koch is the author of two enthusiastically acclaimed and widely translated novels, *Night Watch* and *The Bachelor's Bride,* and several nonfiction works, including *Stargazer: Andy Warhol's World* and *Double Lives: Stalin, Willi Münzenberg and the Seduction of the Intellectuals.* He lives with his wife and daughter in New York City.